D1194861

NORMAN HALL'S

STATE TROOPER
&
HIGHWAY PATROL
EXAM
PREPARATION BOOK

Also by Norman Hall

Norman Hall's Corrections Officer Exam Preparation Book
Norman Hall's Firefighter's Exam Preparation Book
Norman Hall's Police Exam Preparation Book
Norman Hall's Postal Exam Preparation Book

NORMAN HALL'S

STATE TROOPER
&
HIGHWAY PATROL

EXAM
PREPARATION BOOK

ADAMS MEDIA CORPORATION
Holbrook, Massachusetts

Copyright ©1999, Norman S. Hall. All rights reserved.
This book, or parts thereof, may not be reproduced in any form without permission
from the publisher; exceptions are made for brief excerpts used in published reviews.

Published by
Adams Media Corporation
260 Center Street, Holbrook, MA 02343

ISBN: 1-58062-077-9

Printed in Canada.

J I H G F E D C B

Hall, Norman.
      [State trooper & highway patrol exam preparation book]
      Norman Hall's state trooper & highway patrol exam preparation book/Norman Hall.
         p.   cm.
      ISBN 1-58062-077-9
      1. Police, State—Unites States—Examinations, questions, etc. 2. Traffic police—
United States—Examinations, questions, etc. 3. Employment tests—United States.
I. Title. II. Title: Norman Hall's state trooper and highway patrol exam preparation book.
III. Title: State trooper & highway patrol exam preparation book. IV. Title: State trooper
and highway patrol exam preparation book.
HV8143.H328   1998
363.2'076—dc21   98-46211
                                                                                          CIP

This publication is designed to provide accurate and authoritative information with regard to
the subject matter covered. It is sold with the understanding that the publisher is not engaged
in rendering legal, accounting, or other professional advice. If legal advice or other expert assistance is required, the services of a competent professional person should be sought.
            — From a *Declaration of Principles* jointly adopted by a Committee of
      the American Bar Association and a Committee of Publishers and Associations

The names used in this book (of suspects and victims) are fictional.
Any similarities to real people are unintentional.

Illustrations by Marnie Holt Swenson, Mache Works Art Studio

This book is available at quantity discounts for bulk purchases.
For information, call 1-800-872-5627 (in Massachusetts, 781-767-8100).

Visit our home page at http://www.adamsmedia.com

Contents

Preface

Over the years that I have been analyzing various civil service tests, I have observed first hand too many job applicants that approach the selection process with complacency and the lack of any test preparation. Then, afterwards, they seem perplexed by the degree of difficulty the exam posed or express concern over the surprising time constraints involved. The competition for such positions can be impressive, to say the least. The last thing any test applicants need at this point is to look retrospectively at the selection process and wish they had invested more time in the necessary studies. The fact that you have purchased this study guide with the intention of using it to assist you in your job endeavors precludes that event from happening. You now have it within your means to gain a distinct competitive advantage over others and become the candidate that is most likely to get hired.

At the completion of your studies, you will know what to expect on various aspects of the exam and the best way to handle difficult test questions, as well as how to avoid common mistakes or pitfalls, manage your time effectively, prepare for the physical fitness exam, and many other techniques too numerous to include here.

You can be certain that you will be able to approach the exam with confidence and a sense of ease. This publication even takes that confidence one step further with its *Guaranteed Test Results*. If you do not score 80% or better on your written exam, you can return this study guide to the publisher for a complete refund. No other publication offers such an assurance. (See details on the last page of this guide.)

I am serious about helping you in your endeavors to become a state trooper/highway patrol officer. I have a personal stake in your success and, as such, I will provide you with the most current, up-to-date material available. Before you begin your studies, I would like to wish you the best. Once you are hired by a state police department, the rewards and job satisfactions are great and the service you provide to the community is invaluable.

— **Norman S. Hall**

Chapter 1

Becoming a State Trooper/ Highway Patrol Officer

Nationwide there are close to 80,000 people employed by primary state police agencies; approximately three quarters are full-time sworn officers and the remainder work in various civilian support positions (e.g., Human Resource Division, Commercial Vehicle Inspection, Communications, etc.). State traffic officers are assigned to various geographic districts throughout the state according to the perceived needs of the motoring public. Typically, most positions center around counties containing the larger municipalities or heavily traveled state highway/interstate corridors. There are also a limited number of assignments relegated to rural areas of the state that do not have police protection services. All positions considered, the annual personnel turnover rate can be anywhere from 5 to 15 percent, which is relatively low in comparison to other occupations. This rate can be attributed to transfers, promotions, retirements, disabilities, deaths, and other unspecified personal reasons. Because of normal attrition and the implication of hiring additional officers to accommodate statewide community growth, a state police department must maintain an active register of qualified applicants to hire from as vacancies arise or new positions are created. The frequency of exams given to screen prospective applicants can vary. Usually, exams are given once a year; however, some departments examine two or three times annually, depending on their personnel needs. Public announcements are made several weeks in advance of the exam in the local media (newspapers, radio, and even television) specifying when and where people can apply for the test. Another means of keeping abreast of exam dates is to submit a job application form at the Department of Personnel for the State Patrol, or, as is the case for many states, the Department of Public Safety. Regardless of which agency is responsible within your state, a toll-free number is usually provided to accommodate job application requests. This option circumvents the possibility of overlooking a public test announcement. Some states also publish a monthly or quarterly newsletter that specifies the time and location of various law enforcement exams being given around the state. To obtain such publications, call your state Civil Service Commission and request to be placed on the mailing list for current updates. The service is free.

Before you invest further time and effort in your job search, it is extremely important to be aware that all applicants to state agencies must meet minimum employment requirements. Although there is some degree of variance between different states, it is imperative that you meet these guidelines. In order to qualify, you must:

- be a citizen of the United States.

- be at least twenty-one years of age (some departments have programs that accept applicants that are eighteen years of age). There also may be maximum age limits (usually thirty-five to forty) that apply prior to academy appointment.

- provide proof of high school graduation or satisfactory completion of the GED test. In some instances a minimum of thirty to sixty credit hours from an accredited college will be required as well.

- possess a valid unrestricted driver's license AND a driving record that is clear of any drug or alcohol-related driving offenses. An applicant will usually not be considered for employment if he or she has committed between three to five moving violations or has had driving privileges revoked within the last three years.

- be free of any felony convictions or a dishonorable discharge from the military. Misdemeanor convictions are evaluated on a case-by-case basis. As a general rule, aggravated or serious misdemeanors that involve hit and run, reckless driving, failure to stop and render aid, theft, possession of controlled substances, or crimes of violence or larceny are sufficient grounds for dismissal from the selection process.

- have normal color vision and better than 20/100 vision in both eyes, corrected to 20/25 (some departments require 20/20) in each eye. Night blindness is unacceptable.

- have normal hearing and no serious speech impediments.

- be of height and weight that is proportional and in compliance with departmental medical standards. (General guidelines will be provided in the medical evaluation section.)

- not use or traffic illegal drugs/controlled substances. Drug standards between various departments do vary, but for the most part are very stringent with regard to those convicted for the transportation and sale of ANY illegal or nonprescribed drug. Applicants that have a record of such convictions will automatically be disqualified. If, on the other hand, a person is convicted for drug possession, he or she must be drug free for a minimum of five years. This time frame can be extended to ten years depending on the drug(s) of choice involved. You must be able to pass a drug screening test as part of the medical evaluation. Additionally, your drug use history, if any, will be verified by a polygraph test.

- meet minimum medical standards prescribed by Civil Service (e.g., no history of epilepsy or serious diabetic complications, normal blood pressure without medication, etc.).

- meet your state's residency requirement, if any. Some states impose a residency requirement of at least one year before a candidate can become eligible to apply.

- be current with any and all debt obligations. A pattern of delinquent payments, account overdrafts, or filing for protection from creditors is grounds for dismissal from further employment consideration. Even if this is not a matter of great concern to you, be sure to provide a thorough profile of your credit history when requested. Misleading or incomplete information that is discovered during a background check will be extremely difficult to explain without appearing deceptive.

These are several other requirements that state police officer candidates should be aware of. You must:

- be willing to accept any statewide assignment as well as working rotating shifts, weekend, and holiday detail.

- maintain a professional appearance according to departmental standards.

- abstain from any behavior, while on or off duty, that can compromise or outright violate departmental guidelines.

- be willing and able to work in all weather conditions or extended hours when the situation requires.

- be willing to accept dangerous risks that are inherent with high-speed pursuits or the utilization of physical/lethal force where deemed necessary.

Other desirable accomplishments or abilities that would better qualify an applicant include:

- an associate degree or course work relating to law enforcement from an accredited college or university.

- good communication skills, both oral and written. Bilingual applicants are especially sought after by state police departments, particularly if the non-English language known is prevalently used within various district jurisdictions.

- some knowledge of first aid and emergency medical care.

- the ability to work under stress and maintain a collective sense of direction.

- the ablity to accept guidance/criticism from superiors and change accordingly to improve oneself professionally.

- enjoyment of working with the public.

THE SELECTION PROCESS

State police officers are essentially the embodiment of a public trust and, as such, carry a wide degree of responsibility. If one were to generalize about the kind of work a police officer does, one could say that the protection of life and property is the primary goal. However, it cannot be emphasized enough that this is, at best, a vague synopsis of a state police officer's job. There are a myriad of duties and responsibilities that serve to protect life and property.

These duties can include the enforcement of laws and ordinances, accident prevention, emergency roadside assistance, crime investigation, and court appearances. Community service functions can involve a degree of marriage counseling during a domestic dispute, acting as a quasi-lawyer with respect to protecting citizens' constitutional rights, and even acting as a psychologist in knowing how best to handle aggressive or mentally disturbed individuals.

The workload of a state police officer can be as diverse as it is challenging. As a consequence, it is easy to understand why departments are extremely thorough in screening job applicants. The steps that most departments follow in their selection process include the written exam, physical ability test, oral review board, polygraph exam, psychological, background, and medical evaluations.

There may be exceptions to either the order or contents of this screening process, but by and large this accurately reflects what is to be expected by an applicant. A brief description of each step involved is given here, with further elaboration given in sections throughout this book.

THE WRITTEN EXAM

The state police officer exam is a general aptitude test normally comprising from 75 to 150 multiple-choice questions. You are generally given 1 1/2 to 3 hours to complete the test. The test questions themselves will concern such areas as:

■ memory

■ reading comprehension

■ situational judgment and reasoning

■ directional orientation (map reading)

■ report writing

■ grammar, vocabulary, and spelling

■ basic mathematics

Although most questions relate to law enforcement/criminal justice, you are not expected to have the same knowledge as an experienced state police officer. Instead, your grasp of general concepts, logic, and reasoning are the main focus of the exam. A passing score consists of 70 percent or better; however, some departments require applicants to score in the top 20 to 25 percent to be eligible for employment.

Note: Veterans who served in Vietnam between August 5, 1964 and May 7, 1975, or have received the Armed Forces Expeditionary Medal or Marine Corps and Navy Expeditionary Medal for opposed action on foreign soil (e.g., Iran, Southeast Asia, Grenada, or Lebanon), Service Medal for Operation Desert Storm, and who have not been discharged longer than eight years by the actual date of the state police officer written exam, may qualify for preference points. A copy of your DD Form 214 will be required to substantiate the claim. For specifics, contact the office of personnel of the department you wish to apply to.

In some instances, when you are notified via mail as to the time and place of the written exam, sample test material will be enclosed. By all means study every page made available. There is an excellent chance that that very material, or a comparable facsimile, may be incorporated in the actual exam. For this very reason do not take any of this information for granted.

There should also be a map and/or set of directions provided on how to get to the examination site. Review these as well, allowing yourself plenty of time to get there. Arriving thirty minutes to one hour early is desirable. Traffic congestion or unforeseen road construction, particularly in metropolitan areas, have prevented a fair share of applicants from taking the exam. Once the exam has started, latecomers are not permitted to take the test. Rescheduled make-up exams are rarely given unless there are extenuating circumstances, and even then it may be submitted at a much later date. The bottom line is to not miss an exam in the first place due to poor planning.

Prior to being admitted to the exam room, you will need to furnish a current picture identification card, which can either be a driver's license or military ID card. Additionally, the validated test application form that was mailed to you earlier will need to be furnished as well. An applicant that lacks any of this documentation will not be permitted in the exam room. Do not bring briefcases, purses, note paper, calculators, spell checkers/dictionaries, or thesauruses with you to the exam. None of these items are permissible; only a couple of No. 2 pencils will be acceptable. All other materials needed for the exam will be provided by those administering the exam.

When the examiner gives any kind of instruction, pay close attention. The examiner will explain how to properly fill in personal information that will be used to identify your exam results. He or she will further explain how and when to proceed on the exam. Do not deviate in any manner from established test procedure. If you do, you may disqualify yourself altogether.

A real advantage to multiple-choice exams is that you know one of the choices has to be the correct selection. Even if the right answer is not immediately apparent, some choices can be eliminated on their own merit, thus further increasing your chances of selecting the correct answer. Another advantage to this form of exam is that, if the time remaining to complete the test becomes a crucial factor, you can still mark answers at random (i.e., guess) and still have a 25 percent chance (A, B, C, or D) of picking the correct choice. You are not penalized for incorrect choices unless otherwise stipulated by the examiner. Therefore, it behooves you not to leave any questions unanswered, if possible.

You will be provided an answer sheet that is usually separate from the test booklet, and a blank sheet of paper for mathematical calculations, notes, or general figuring. It is imperative not to make extraneous marks on an answer sheet. The machine that scores your exam can misconstrue such marks as an incorrect answer. An example of an answer blank is provided below to demonstrate how to mark an answer properly.

The following examples are answer blanks that have been improperly marked, leading to a poor test score.

If you change your mind about any answer, be certain to erase the original answer completely. If two answers for the same question are marked, it will be scored as incorrect. This holds true even if one of the selections was indeed correct. Invariably, a few applicants make the very costly mistake of marking answers that do not correspond to the question they are working on. A simple oversight like this can be devastating as far as test results are concerned. Check every ten questions or so to make sure you are marking an answer for the corresponding question at hand.

When you look over test questions, be sure to read them carefully and completely. It is easy to fall prey to reading the first or second choice and selecting one of them as the correct answer without bothering to examine the remaining options. Read the entire passage thoroughly and then mark your answer sheet accordingly. Pay close attention to conjunctions such as *and, but, or, when, if, because, though, whereas,* and *besides.* These key words can completely alter the meaning of a question. If you overlook one of these words, there is a good chance that you will select the wrong answer. It cannot be emphasized enough to read the entire passage closely before even thinking about the answer sheet.

Do not spend too much time on a question that you are unsure about. Either make an educated guess or skip that question and return to it when you have finished with the rest of the exam. As a time saver, you can cross out the options in the test booklet that you know are wrong. When you return to that question, you can quickly focus on the remaining selections. If you do elect to skip a question, be sure to skip the corresponding answer blank as well.

A note worth mentioning here is that, statistically speaking, your first choice as an answer to a question is usually correct. Answers that are changed are typically wrong. All too frequently, applicants will read too much into a question and obscure the proper choice. Mark the first answer that seems apparent and leave it as it is unless you can make a strong case for one of the remaining options.

At some point after the exam a scoring key is usually made available to check your answers. If you disagree on any particular answer given, there are forms made available to challenge given questions. The appeals process normally takes thirty to sixty days before a final score is rendered. Appeals aside, test results are mailed to applicants usually within thirty days. Applicants are ranked according to test results on employment registers kept by the agency's department of personnel. Those who scored highest will be given priority in subsequent screening.

THE PHYSICAL ABILITY TEST

Since a state police officer's job can place significant demands on his or her overall stamina, it is not hard to understand why an applicant must be physically fit. This portion of the exam may be administered in one of two different ways. There is a possibility that the physical activity of the test will be entirely bypassed during the preliminary screening process. However, at some point during the probationary period or academy training, one must be able to pass the minimum departmental physical standards. On the other hand, the physical ability test may be administered in tandem with the written exam as a prequalification. If the latter option holds true in your case, there will be specifics provided regarding what will be expected of you to pass in the information packet sent to you with your application. If the department you applied to offers you the chance to participate in physical agility simulation trials prior to the actual exam, by all means take advantage of the opportunity. That way, you can get a comprehensive feel for what to expect and perhaps do a little toning up in your weakest areas.

Essentially, various physical ability exercises are set up to test an applicant's flexibility, muscular strength and endurance, and aerobic conditioning. Exercises seen on past exams include:

- running an obstacle course involving short-distance sprints, weaving around traffic cones, ducking overhead obstructions, crawling through a drainage culvert, climbing stairs, jumping over railings, and walking a balance beam.

- sit-up, push-up, and pull-up repetitions.

- trunk flexion (determines flexibility and extent of reach).

- running a predetermined distance (e.g., $1/2$, 1, or $1^1/2$ miles) and climbing over some form of barriers such as guardrails, or a 6 to 8 foot wall or chain link fence.

- 165-pound dummy drag (simulated victim carry).

- Bench-pressing, curling, and squatting with various weights, using either barbells or variable-resistance weight-training equipment.

- hand grip strength (both left and right) as measured by a dynamometer.

- stair climbing (specifically designed to measure pulse rate).

Note: As a rule, most states have some degree of disparity when it comes to minimum fitness expectations between men and women. These differences, as minor as they may be, should be indicated on the physical fitness standard forms sent earlier.

Normally, applicants are rated on a pass/fail basis in accordance with a department's established minimum standards. Passing this stage of the screening process is mandatory; no exceptions are made. Recently, however, some departments are rating how well a candidate performs on the physical ability test in terms of percentage. Test score parameters can range from 100 percent for top performance to minimum acceptable standards of 70 percent. What's more, this score is combined with the written test score to determine an overall assessment. For this reason, it is imperative that you always put forward your best efforts. Simply passing this part of the test may not be enough to make you a competitive candidate.

Additional information detailing how to prepare for this part of the exam is in Chapter 10 of this study guide.

ORAL BOARD

Applicants with the highest test scores will be requested to appear before an applicant review board/oral board. This interview is normally conducted by a panel of three to five people who serve as staff officers or are involved in state police personnel management. Typically, interviews can last anywhere from thirty minutes to one hour. Immediately following the preliminary introduction, the initial direction of questions will pertain to the information you furnished regarding your personal history. Be assured that any and all things about your past, albeit either good or bad, become relevant at this stage. Conduct unbecoming of moral character or a documented record of reckless indiscretions will, in fact, receive intense scrutiny. Of course, there is nothing you can do to change the past, but it is imperative to give the board straightforward and truthful responses to issues raised. Copies of your birth certificate, high school/college transcripts and diplomas, Social Security identification, and DD-214 form for any military service will be requested to substantiate your qualifications as well. The rest of the interview will consist of questions that are intended to give panelists a means of gauging your personal characteristics, oral communication skills, and ability to respond decisively and effectively to given situations. Guidelines, as well as hypothetical test questions asked by the board, are provided in Chapter 11. After studying this section, you will feel better prepared and subsequently more relaxed during the interview. Well-thought-out answers to anticipated questions not only make you appear more confident, but give a favorable impression to those conducting the interview.

PSYCHOLOGICAL EVALUATION

Because a state police officer works independently most of the time, it is imperative that he or she be mentally fit to respond appropriately to any incident. The profile of a professional officer not only encompasses a thorough knowledge of police procedure, it also involves sound judgment.

When an officer is the first to respond to a crime scene, accident, or incident, his or her decisions and actions can dramatically affect the outcome. Often there is not enough time to second-guess an initial response. Decisions must be made quickly and in the best interests of those involved. This is particularly relevant when a weapon is involved. Sound judgment, good sense, and basic instinct are essential elements in a good officer. However, these can be undermined by prejudices or biases. If an officer is handicapped by either, it will be impossible for that officer to live up to the professional standards expected.

Psychological evaluations are conducted with the sole purpose of ferreting out such shortcomings. This kind of exam can come either in the form of a one-on-one interview with a qualified psychologist or psychiatrist or a written exam called a *personality test*. Either way, the applicant is asked questions that can effectively discern both the sincerity of the candidate and the likelihood of behavior unbecoming a professional police officer.

The best advice that can be given to applicants for such an exam is, again, to be absolutely honest with all your responses. It's unfortunate, but all too often candidates will provide the kind of answers they assume the department wants to hear. However, these tests (written or oral) are so well cross-referenced with regard to question format that patterns of inconsistency are more than likely to emerge, thus bringing into question the applicant's integrity. It cannot be emphasized enough to be truthful when proceeding through the selection process.

BACKGROUND INVESTIGATION/POLYGRAPH EXAM

As mentioned earlier, the information you provide on your job application form concerning personal history is subject to intense scrutiny. Typically, a detective or other qualified staff member is assigned to conduct a thorough investigation into your past. Such areas as your education, employment history, past residences, military career, driving record, personal references, and health status will be reviewed for validity and completeness. It is extremely important that you furnish accurate and complete information about your background. Information is kept confidential. Leaving portions of a personal history statement blank and/or providing information that doesn't reconcile with a background check is a mistake that has disqualified many candidates in the past. If a discrepancy is discovered, it will be difficult for you to continue in the screening process as a viable contender. Outside of the disqualifying offenses pointed out earlier, other minor indiscretions can often be overlooked if the offender has learned a lesson and matured to become a better citizen. Denying there was a problem or placing the blame on someone else is a sure way to discredit yourself.

Background checks are very thorough. The investigators assigned to your file may not only check academic records but talk to teachers or professors under whom you have studied. Past neighbors may be consulted as well. Every detail of your past is subject to examination. Additionally, departments will go one step further in the investigation and utilize a polygraph or "lie detector" test. A standard format of questions concerning an applicant's personal history is asked by a qualified technician. The results are interpreted and forwarded to personnel. In conjunction with what was learned in the background investigation, these results can ultimately determine whether an applicant is recommended for further employment consideration. If a problem shows up in this stage, unlike the other steps of the screening process, it may be difficult for an applicant to find out why he or she didn't receive a recommendation. This can be particularly frustrating to those who have made it this far in the screening process. Filing a formal appeal at this stage of the procedure will be of no avail. Once again, the best advice here is to be honest and forthright about your past and demonstrate a positive attitude toward any past mistakes. Remember, the police department recognizes the fact that no one is perfect. However, a person who shows sincerity and a high degree of integrity is more likely to receive a recommendation than is one who tends to have a sketchy or questionable background.

MEDICAL EVALUATION

Medical guidelines followed by departments can and do vary, as well as change over the years. What may be acceptable to one department may not be acceptable to another (e.g., height and weight requirements, or vision correction through either glasses or contact lenses). Thus, it is recommended that you pick up a medical standards form and medical history questionnaire from the department you intend to apply to. That way you will know exactly what is required by that department. Be truthful in filling out the medical questionnaire; this is one more element subject to being cross-checked during a background investigation. False information on these forms is bound to be discovered during the course of a thorough medical exam. If you have a borderline condition, such as diabetes, hernias, or the like, consult your regular physician to see what, if any, steps can be taken to improve or alleviate the problem altogether. If a candidate must take medication for a medical condition, it can be safely said that most, if not all, police departments will reject that person from further screening. The major concern is what may happen to an officer afflicted with an illness that requires regular medication if he or she is deprived of that medication in the line of duty. Will that officer become disabled as the illness manifests itself unchecked? This is a significant concern to both the department and the officer involved.

You should be made aware, too, that medical evaluations are required not only prior to appointment but periodically throughout one's career. This is particularly true as some agencies may require random tests to check for illegal substances. A clean bill of health is mandated both for the aspiring state police officer and the veteran officer.

The information provided below is only intended to give you general guidelines of what may be expected by the department in question. These guidelines are not by any means nationally accepted standards. Tremendous variation between state jurisdictions is the rule more often than the exception.

Visual Acuity Requirements

- uncorrected vision must be no worse than 20/100 in each eye and corrected to 20/20.

- no night blindness.

- normal color vision determined by achieving a minimum of 70 percent on an Isochromatic Plates Test.

Hearing Requirements

■ normal hearing for either ear shall not exceed 22 decibels at 1000, 2000, and 3000 Hz.

Cardiovascular Requirements

■ normal blood pressure (absent of controlling medication) shall not exceed 160/90.

■ chronic heart disease or protracted hypertension affecting abnormal blood pressure is unacceptable.

Miscellaneous Requirements

■ any systematic metabolic disease or disorder that can potentially inhibit an officer candidate's ability to perform the duties expected by the department is grounds for dismissal.

HEIGHT AND WEIGHT STANDARDS

The following chart gives the maximum allowable weight according to gender and age brackets.

FEMALE				MALE			
		Age				Age	
Height	22-29	30-39	40 & up	Height	21-29	30-39	40 & up
4'11"	132	135	139	5'3"	159	162	169
5'0"	135	138	141	5'4"	162	166	171
5'1"	138	142	145	5'5"	166	171	176
5'2"	141	145	148	5'6"	172	177	182
5'3"	146	149	153	5'7"	176	180	185
5'4"	150	153	156	5'8"	181	185	190
5'5"	153	156	159	5'9"	185	189	194
5'6"	158	162	166	5'10"	190	194	199
5'7"	163	166	169	5'11"	196	200	204
5'8"	166	170	173	6'0"	202	207	212
5'9"	171	174	177	6'1"	207	212	216
5'10"	176	179	183	6'2"	214	218	223
5'11"	180	184	187	6'3"	218	223	228
6'0"	184	188	192	6'4"	226	230	234
6'1"	189	193	197	6'5"	232	237	241
6'2"	194	197	200	6'6"	237	241	246
6'3"	198	202	206	6'7"	244	249	254
6'4"	202	206	210	6'8"	250	255	260

Note: In some instances, candidates who do not prequalify according to the height-weight limitations issued by the department may opt for a Hydro Static Weight Test. The test, which is normally administered by a licensed medical provider, can accurately guage an individual's body fat percentage. Men and women's body fat assessments cannot exceed 20 percent and 26 percent, respectively.

GENERAL JOB DESCRIPTION

Once a candidate successfully passes the various stages of the selection process, he or she must then be accepted (i.e., appointed) by the patrol commander. Only at that point will an applicant receive a conditional offer of employment. Some states prefer new hires to participate in an officer-cadet program which normally runs for one or two months. Cadets then receive a limited amount of on-the-job training prior to admission to academy training. This kind of program serves a twofold purpose: aspiring officers will get some first-hand experience with what they can expect on the job as a commissioned veteran; additionally, it allows supervisory staff to monitor and analyze a cadet's training progress. Those who meet departmental expectations will receive a favorable command rating, which is a prerequisite for academy admission. The overall intent of such procedures is to identify those candidates that are less than totally committed. As a consequence, academy enrollments usually experience lower attrition rates among cadets as opposed to other state programs that allow direct admissions into academy training immediately following appointment. In either case, officer-cadets will spend several months in academy training. Areas of study include civil rights and constitutional law; federal, state, and local laws; the criminal justice system; police ethics; patrol procedures; highway safety; traffic control; crisis intervention; first aid; self-defense; firearm training; and criminal investigation. In tandem, a cadet must go through rigorous physical training. Mastering the prescribed studies and meeting minimal physical standards are both required to successfully complete academy training. Following graduation, a newly commissioned patrol officer will work under the close supervision of either an experienced veteran or Field Training Officer (FTO). During a probationary period that normally lasts from six to eighteen months, every facet of the recruit's performance will be reviewed. It is important to note that aspiring officer candidates can be dismissed at any time during the probationary period at the discretion of the department. Therefore, conduct both on and off duty must be exemplary and display a continued willingness to achieve the highest standards. State Merit System Rules and Regulations do not cover such positions. Consequently, there is no legal avenue of appeal in the event of employment termination. If the officer candidate's performance measures up to departmental standards, he or she will then be entitled to the full benefits bestowed on veteran commissioned state police officers. Benefits usually include:

- comprehensive medical and dental plans.

- optional paid life insurance/supplemental insurance plans.

- liberal retirement programs and pension.

- uniform allowance.

- paid vacation and paid holidays.

- sick leave and military leave.

- continuing in-service training.

- promotional opportunities.

Average beginning salaries for state police recruits can range anywhere from $27,000 to $33,000, with semiannual raises over the first few years, raising that range from $40,000 to $46,000. State police sergeants, lieutenants, captains, and patrol chiefs can earn $42,000, $48,000, $52,000, and $75,000 per year, respectively. (Salary packages can vary tremendously between different state jurisdictions.) Layoffs within a state police department are relatively rare, and most cuts that have to be made because of budgetary constraints can be handled through early retirements and no new hiring. An important consideration here is that a state police department has a significant investment in your training to become a qualified officer. It is not about to sacrifice such positions unnecessarily, nor to deprive the community of an imperative service.

The working conditions encountered by state police officers can be diverse as well as challenging. A typical work week is forty hours; anything beyond is considered overtime, for which the officer is compensated time and one-half. An officer can be assigned one of three shifts (day, evening, or graveyard) and will be expected to work weekends and holidays. Most, if not all, departments offer shift differential pay as well. Activities during a shift can include directing traffic at the scene of an emergency, rendering first aid to an accident victim, patrolling various districts for the sake of crime prevention, enforcing traffic ordinances, apprehending criminal suspects, rendering roadside assistance to stranded motorists, providing executive security, helping quell public disturbances, or becoming involved in public relations such as conducting driver exams or implementing safety training/drug awareness and resistance education in the schools. The list of responsibilities is lengthy and varied, and a state police officer has to be able to respond to any of these kinds of demands at any time and in any kind of weather. The best summary of what exactly is required of a state police officer is seen in the Law Enforcement Code of Ethics advanced by the International Association of Chiefs of Police. The Code of Ethics is comprehensive in the respect that it addresses four very important fundamentals: duty description, standards of performance expected in the line of duty, standards to adhere to in your personal life, and an oath of commitment to follow these guidelines.

If an officer is willing to dedicate him- or herself to the principles described below and will strive for self-improvement through training programs and education, he or she will reap the personal benefits and serve to improve the community as a whole.

CODE OF ETHICS

As a Law Enforcement Officer, my fundamental duty is to serve mankind; to safeguard lives and property; to protect the innocent against deception, the weak against oppression or intimidation, and the peaceful against violence or disorder; and to respect the Constitutional rights of all men to liberty, equality, and justice.

I will keep my private life unsullied as an example to all; maintain courageous calm in the face of danger, scorn, or ridicule; develop self-restraint; and be constantly mindful of the welfare of others. Honest in thought and deed in both my personal and official life, I will be exemplary in obeying the laws of the land and the regulations of my department. Whatever I see or hear of a confidential nature or that is confided to me in my duties will remain confidential unless revelation is necessary in the performance of my duty.

I recognize the badge of my office as a symbol of public faith, and I accept it as a public trust to be held so long as I am true to the ethics of the police service. I will constantly strive to achieve these objectives and ideals, dedicating myself before God to my chosen profession . . . law enforcement.

PREPARATION FOR THE WRITTEN EXAM

As noted earlier, the written exam can be broken down into seven areas. Each of these topics will be discussed in subsequent chapters of this study guide, followed by sample test questions and answers. Test strategies and hints will be provided and elaborated on as they apply to each subject area. It is important to note that there can be significant variations in test content, judging by what has been seen on past exams around the country. Some tests place a stronger emphasis on one or more subject areas while having few questions, if any, relating to other topics. To prepare yourself adequately for such a test, all seven areas warrant equal consideration; then you will be prepared regardless of what you may encounter on your exam.

STUDY SUGGESTIONS

The state police officer examination is not the kind of exam on which you can hope for a high test score after just cramming the night before. Good study habits can have a significant impact on how well you do on the exam. If you follow these few simple guidelines, you can approach the exam more relaxed and confident, two essential ingredients for top performance on any exam.

Regular study times should be established and tailored to your comfort. Each person's schedule is different. Some people prefer to study for one or two hours at a time and then take a break, while others prefer several hours of straight study. Regardless of how you study, it is important that you do it regularly; do not rely on a marathon. You will remember the subject matter more easily and comprehend it better if you establish regular study habits.

Where you study is important, too. Eliminate any distractions that can disrupt your studies. The television, telephone, and children can hinder quality study time. It is suggested you set aside one room in your home as a study place and use it to isolate yourself from distractions. If you elect to use a bedroom as a study area, avoid lying in bed while you read. Otherwise, you may find yourself more inclined to sleep than to learn. It is important to have a good desk, a comfortable chair, and adequate lighting; anything less can hamper studying. If studying in your home is not feasible, go to your local library or some other place that offers an environment conducive to study.

Again, be sure to get plenty of rest. It is counterproductive and will slow learning if you try to study when you are overly tired. It is also important not to skip meals. Your level of concentration during the exam can suffer if you lack proper nutrition. Coffee and other stimulants are not recommended.

Chapter 2

Memory Recall

One of the most important skills a state police officer uses in the line of duty is memory recall. Officers who remember specific physical descriptions of people or vehicles wanted in connection with criminal activity stand a much better chance of apprehending suspects than those who have only a partial recollection of the facts. Another prime example of the importance of memory involves directives issued by a superior. It is imperative that such directives be followed quickly, accurately, and completely without having to be repeated. Valuable time can be lost and an emergency call may be handled less effectively if directives are second-guessed, forgotten, or jumbled. Additionally, it may be necessary for a state police officer to memorize the geographical layout of jurisdictional boundaries and know the quickest route to any given location. Other tasks may include memorization of the various codes and procedures on police radio networks, remembering people in your area of patrol that have the propensity to commit various crimes, and the like.

This memory section has been placed at the beginning of this study guide because memory normally is the first subject encountered on the actual exam. Test examiners prefer to arrange an exam in this manner so that the rest of the exam can be given without any further interruptions. Typically, a memory exam booklet, film, video, key, or some other form of diagram is passed out to test applicants. Applicants are allowed limited time to memorize as much of the diagram as possible, then the material is collected. The question-and-answer sheet for this section may be handled separately, but is likely to be an integral part of the main exam. In any case, the key or diagram will not be available for reference during the test. All your answers must be arrived at by memory alone.

From what has been encountered on past exams, memory recall sections follow one of three different formats. The first approach may involve studying a picture or sketch of an emergency or crime scene. Virtually any detail is subject to questioning. A second approach may entail studying a portfolio of various criminals, complete with composite sketches or pictures, physical descriptions, personal data, and details pertaining to the crime involved. The third involves descriptive passages. A written passage is given that pertains to an incident involving a crime or provides information regarding law enforcement policy. Questions are based on what the reading specifically said. This closely parallels reading comprehension questions that will be seen at a later point in this study guide. However, memory recall questions ask only about specifics of what was stated in the reading and do not involve making any kind of inferences.

Whichever format is seen on your exam, you will be given anywhere from five to fifteen minutes to study the key or passage provided. The memory test may appear simple at first, but may require you to memorize between fifty and seventy-five items quickly. Unless you are gifted with a photographic memory, memorizing such volumes of material in such a short time may seem impossible. Don't despair, because this study guide offers a system that will substantially help those with marginal memory skills as well as improve the skills of those who are fairly proficient. The technique employed is called *imagery and association*. Any memory task can be simplified by using this system. It requires you to form images in your mind relevant to the item to be memorized. Each of these images is then linked together in a specific order by means of association. It may sound complicated, but learning to stretch the boundaries of your imagination can be enjoyable.

A. NAMES

Street names may be among the items that need to be committed to memory for the exam. Use the following street names as examples:

Jorganson Street
Phillips Avenue
Tremont
Tricia
Edgewater Boulevard
Bloomington

Most people would approach this exercise by rote memorization, or in other words, repetition of thought until recall can be accomplished. This is a boring way of doing things, wouldn't you say?

Believe it or not, by using the imagery and association techniques, you can actually have a little fun doing memory exercises. Now, look at those same street names again and see what key word derivatives have been used and what images we can associate with them.

For example:

Jorganson Street — Jogger
Phillips Street — Phillips screwdriver
Tremont — Tree
Tricia — Tricycle
Edgewater — Edge
Bloomington — Blossoms

Carry the process one step further and place those key word derivatives in a bizarre context, story, or situation. Using this process, we have developed the following story.

A **JOGGER** with his pockets completely stuffed with **PHILLIPS SCREWDRIVERS** wasn't paying attention and ran into a giant **TREE**. After dusting himself off, he jumped on a child's **TRI-CYCLE** and pedaled it to the **EDGE** of a pool filled with flower **BLOSSOMS**.

Sounds ridiculous, doesn't it? However, because of its strong images, you will not easily forget this kind of story.

Another advantage of the imagery technique is that you can remember items in their respective order by simply reviewing where they fit in relation to the other items in the story.

Look at each of the street names below and develop a story using imagery. There are no right or wrong key word derivatives. What is important is that the images conjure up a clear picture in your mind and then interlink.

Work on each of these columns separately:

Bedford Ave.	Apple Dr.	Anderson Blvd.	Bayberry Rd.
Wellington	Constantine Way	Cannon Ave.	Hickory Ridge
Walker St.	Bristol	Foxtail Run	Ebony Ln.
Penny Ln.	Echo Ave.	Arsenal Way	Ester Ct.
Ridgemont Dr.	Darrington	Jacobson St.	Steinbald Ln.
Bowmont	Smalley St.	Prince Williams	Georgia St.

Once you have finished this exercise, cover the street names and see if you can remember all twenty-four items. If your four stories are bizarre enough, you certainly can have this entire list committed to memory in a short time.

B. NUMBERS

Numbers are another problem in memory recall. For most people, numbers are difficult to memorize because they are intangible. To rectify this problem, numbers can be transposed into letters so that words can be formed and associated accordingly. Here is the format for transposition (remember this format as if it were your Social Security number because on the exam you will draw from it regularly):

All other letters can be incorporated into words without any significance.

For instance, let's say you are given the number 10603328157. Memorizing this number so well that you can recall it after any length of time would be very difficult. However, by using this memory system, you could use the number to spell out a variety of memorable things. Here is your chance to use your creativity!

After you have had the chance to figure out what words can code such a number, one particular problem should become apparent; the more numbers you try to cram into one word, the harder it is to find a compatible word in the English vocabulary. To simplify matters, there are two alternative ways to form words. The first method is to take two numbers at a time, form a word, and associate it with the next word. Dealing with the same number (10603328157) **DOG** could be derived from the number 10, **RUG** from 60, **PIPE** from 33, **CAT** from 28, **BONE** from 15, and **S** from 7. There are many ways you could imagine and link these words. One possibility would be a **DOG** lying on a **RUG** and smoking a **PIPE** while a **CAT** prances by carrying a **BONE** shaped like an **S**. This is just one way to memorize this long number. Other words and stories could work just as well.

The second alternative, which offers greater flexibility, is using words of any length but making only the first two significant letters of the word applicable to your story. For example, the word **DIG/GING** could represent 10 in the number 10603328157.

RAV/EN = RUG/BY = REV/OLVER = 60
POP/ULATION = PUP/PY = PEP/PER = 33
CAT/ERPILLAR = CAT/TLE = COT/TON = 28
BIN/OCCULAR = BEAN/S = DIN/NER = 15

By doing this, you have a larger number of words at your disposal to put into stories. With a little originality, it can be fun to see what you can imagine for any number given.

Below are exercises to help you apply this system. The first group of numbers is meant to be used as a transposition exercise. See how many different words you can use to represent each number. The second series is for practice with transposition and story fabrication. This technique may seem difficult at first, but with practice it will enhance your memory capabilities tenfold.

I.	44	63	86	40
	53	97	93	32
	61	10	48	26
	13	3	60	91
	12	57	35	99
	8	52	27	16
	41	11	21	68

II.	1754732115810	63211347890
	6980421569497	145344175328
	14732994710	917403218977
	8321355572119	638146119900
	488779509453	433351896487
	1530197865321	765320146991

C. PICTURES/SKETCHES

When you are presented with a picture or sketch on your exam, try to mentally walk your way through the diagram. Pay particular attention to details. For example, if there are any people, determine their relative position with respect to other landmarks in the scene. Are they initiating some kind of criminal event, being victimized, or just standing by idly serving as potential witnesses to what (if anything) is taking place? Look for location references such as street names, numbered addresses, and store signs or logos. If any vehicles are present, what are the license numbers and general descriptions (e.g., two-door, four-door, sedan, van, truck, etc.)? If an emergency is apparent, what exactly is involved? Is a weapon present? If so, how is the perpetrator dressed and what are his/her physical characteristics (e.g., approximate height and weight, color, and length of hair, etc.)? Are there any time references such as clocks or calendars? Is it day or night? Can the weather be accounted for? Being aware of such things and answering these kinds of questions will definitely sharpen your skills of observation. Now you will need to systematically develop lasting mental images of what was observed and link these into a memorable story. Look at the example sketch on the following page and determine a way that all the details shown can be committed to memory. Time will not be a factor in this particular exercise.

Note: Remember, you are limited only by your imagination. There really is no one particular story that is correct. It is the intent here to demonstrate the mechanics of imagery and association and not to convey any absolutes. Chances are, you will develop a story better tailored to your own interpretative abilities than anyone else can develop for you. For further insight into this concept, one potential story line is provided immediately following this exercise.

Near a mile post marker that resembles an oversized ban/anna (15) stands a speed limit sign that's nervously wrin/ging (65) its hands. The apparent edginess was due to the fact that two motorcyclists passing by were blatantly ignoring the stranded motorist to the side of the road. Even the license plate number of the broken down vehicle, NFI-944 (Needs Fixing Immediately—lem/on m/obile—944) didn't catch their attention. What was really peculiar, though, was that both motorcycles had huge Peanut Butter Cookies for wheels. It was obvious the motorcyclist closest to the concrete median was fr/antically s/peeding (PBC-367) in the passing lane while his or her companion was having a dif/ficult t/ime (PBC-138) just keeping up. This apparent rush was an attempt to overtake an extremely large Crate With Wheels filled with a heapin/g p/ile (CWW-353) of Bacon, Lettuce and Tomato (Brown & Lacy Trucking) sandwiches before it passed beneath a rainbow (pedestrian overpass) arching over the highway. As most stories have it, every rainbow has a pot (Pottersville) of gold at its end. However, in this case the pot is brimming full of don/uts (15). These same special donuts, when tossed into an electric dryer (Dryerston), miraculously turn into vast amounts of pop/corn (33). Of course, none of it spills onto the highway because every bit of it is rapidly (Rapids City) consumed by an extremely hungry st/ork (78). The well-fed, if not bloated, stork then perches itself atop a baby stroller being pushed by a woman crossing over the rainbow. Compelled by story-time tradition, the stork lifts the child wrapped in a blanket out of the stroller, but unfortunately, misdelivers it in the back of a pickup truck headed south for the winter. The lone driver of the pickup was so startled by the new addition in the back, he swerved toward the concrete median Causing Considerable Damage to its rus/ting f/rame (CCD-673).

Note: As you can see by example, acronyms were effectively applied in several places throughout the story. Their use is not only convenient, but it can save precious time when threading a story together.

You can see how a story can become outlandishly crazy. Perhaps it could be said that the crazier the story, the easier it becomes to memorize. More importantly, be sure all concocted images are properly linked together. Otherwise, you will be left with a collage of cute fabrications that can become somewhat meaningless when viewed independently of the main story. You should have a pretty fair idea by now of how to use this memory system to your advantage. Examine the next sketch for five minutes. After the five minutes has elapsed, proceed to the questions on the next page and fill in the answers without looking at the diagram again. Check your answers with those provided at the end of the exercise to determine the effectiveness of your storytelling memorization skills. If you get through only part of your story development before time expires, don't despair. You will find that the more you use this system, the easier it will become to apply it to any memorization task.

SAMPLE SKETCH 1

Study the sketch below for five minutes. *DO NOT* exceed the time allowed; if you do, you will forfeit the true sense of how an exam is actually conducted. When time is up, turn to the questions given without making further reference to the sketch. In the actual exam, the test examiner will collect the sketches when the time for studying is up, and then you will be directed to answer the related questions in your test booklet or supplement. You will not be allowed to review the sketch in the course of answering the applicable questions.

SAMPLE QUESTIONS, SKETCH 1

1. What is the approximate time of day shown in the sketch?
   A. 9:30 A.M.
   B. 3:00 P.M.
   C. 5:30 P.M.
   D. 12:00 noon

2. Franklin's Appliance Co. is located at
   A. 1812 Evandale Ave.
   B. 1675 Evandale Ave.
   C. 1650 Finn St.
   D. None of the above

3. What is the license-plate number of the fuel truck entering the intersection?
   A. LIW-686
   B. ZMA-502
   C. WIL-687
   D. None of the above

4. The Postal Service mail collection box is closest to what address?
   A. 1660 Highway 140
   B. 1650 Finn St.
   C. 1675 Johnson St.
   D. 1660 Johnson St.

5. What is the name of the town depicted in the sketch?
   A. Granite Falls
   B. Franklin City
   C. Falcon Heights
   D. Crestonville

6. The State Patrol unit traveling east on Johnson St. had which of the following numerical designations on its top?
   A. 502
   B. 531
   C. 35
   D. 65

7. According to the sketch, what individual(s) or vehicle is committing an obvious traffic infraction?
   A. The fuel truck going the wrong direction on a one-way street
   B. The bicyclist pedaling down the wrong lane on Highway 140
   C. The two people jay walking in front of Creston's Hardware Store
   D. The pickup truck speeding on Johnson St.

8. What is the posted speed limit for Johnson St.?
   A. 15 MPH
   B. 20 MPH
   C. 25 MPH
   D. 55 MPH

9. In which direction and how far would one have to travel to reach Falcon Hts. from the town shown?
    A. South 27 miles
    B. East 37 miles
    C. West 17 miles
    D. North 17 miles

10. What was the license plate number of the vehicle getting refueled at Skelley's Petro?
    A. ALH 113
    B. AWH 113
    C. AMZ 502
    D. It was not discernable in the sketch

11. The posted population figure for the town in question was which of the following?
    A. 376
    B. 3,076
    C. 3,672
    D. No such reference was given in the sketch

12. The Living Water Chapel fronted which street?
    A. Finn St.
    B. Highway 140
    C. Johnson St.
    D. Evandale Ave.

13. How many people were shown to be standing out front of Creston's Hardware Store?
    A. 1
    B. 2
    C. 3
    D. 4

14. The solitary yield sign shown in the sketch was located at which street intersection?
    A. Evandale Ave. and Highway 140
    B. Johnson St. and Highway 140
    C. Finn St. and Evandale Ave.
    D. None of the above

15. All of the following statements about the sketch are true except
    A. The vehicle with license plate number ALH 113 was shown heading east on Johnson St.
    B. There was a fire hydrant located adjacent to Franklin's Appliance Co.
    C. The vehicle with license plate number WIL 687 was shown heading north on Evandale Ave.
    D. All of the above statements are true.

ANSWER SHEET FOR SAMPLE SKETCH 1

1. (A) (B) (C) (D)　　　6. (A) (B) (C) (D)　　　11. (A) (B) (C) (D)

2. (A) (B) (C) (D)　　　7. (A) (B) (C) (D)　　　12. (A) (B) (C) (D)

3. (A) (B) (C) (D)　　　8. (A) (B) (C) (D)　　　13. (A) (B) (C) (D)

4. (A) (B) (C) (D)　　　9. (A) (B) (C) (D)　　　14. (A) (B) (C) (D)

5. (A) (B) (C) (D)　　　10. (A) (B) (C) (D)　　　15. (A) (B) (C) (D)

Answers can be found on page 48.

As mentioned earlier in the discussion of memory recall, another format seen on exams utilizes sketches of various criminals accompanied with physical descriptions and other information pertinent to the issuance of a warrant. Since there are a lot of numbers to remember, this is where the number transposition system can be very useful. Study the next three sketches and associated personal data for ten minutes. Do not exceed the time allowed; if you do, you will forfeit the true sense of how an exam is actually conducted. When time is up, turn to the questions provided without making any further references to the composites just studied.

Note: Study each of the suspects for only three minutes each. That will leave an extra minute for quick review.

SAMPLE COMPOSITE SKETCH/FILE 1

Suspect 1

Name:	Bryan Scott Rollman
Alias:	Phillip Rogers
Date of Birth:	August 10, 1958
(DOB):	(Hint: look at this as 08-10-58)
Height:	6'0"
Weight:	185 pounds
Hair:	Black
Eyes:	Brown
Sex:	Male
Race:	Caucasian
Scars or Marks:	Small circular birthmark on left forearm
Social Security No.:	810-52-6711

Wants and Warrants:	Wanted for attempted murder and unlawful possession of a firearm.
Criminal Record:	First-degree assault and criminal trespass
Case number:	18-573

Suspect 2

Name:	Suzanne Kay Jordan
Alias:	None
Date of Birth:	January 13, 1970
Height:	4'11"
Weight:	150 pounds
Hair:	Blonde
Eyes:	Hazel
Sex:	Female
Race:	Caucasian
Scars or Marks:	None
Social Security No.:	572-50-3431
Wants and Warrants:	Wanted for conspiring to manufacture and distribute a controlled substance.
Criminal Record:	Possession of methamphetamine and heroin.

National Crime Information Center (NCIC) File Number: 16-043

Suspect 3

Name:	Charles Alan Frindell
Alias:	Tony Alan Reed
Date of Birth:	July 13, 1969
Height:	6'3"
Weight:	215 pounds
Hair:	Brown
Eyes:	Brown
Sex:	Male
Race:	African American
Scars or Marks:	None
Social Security No.:	792-54-3711
Wants and Warrants:	Wanted for first-degree kidnapping and first-degree sexual assault. Considered armed and dangerous.
Criminal Record:	Second-degree sexual assault and parole violation.
NCIC File Number:	12-782

SAMPLE QUESTIONS, COMPOSITE SKETCH/FILE 1

1. Which of the three suspects on file did not utilize an alias in the commission of his or her crimes?
   A. Charles Alan Frindell
   B. Bryan Scott Rollman
   C. Suzanne Kay Jordan
   D. Tony Alan Reed

2 Which of the three suspects did not have an NCIC file number assigned to their record?
   A. Phillip Rogers
   B. Suzanne Kay Jordan
   C. Charles Alan Frindell
   D. All three suspects had NCIC file number assignments.

3. According to the file, Tony Alan Reed's respective hair and eye color is which of the following?
   A. Blonde and blue
   B. Brown and hazel
   C. Black and green
   D. Brown and brown

4. Which suspect was assigned NCIC file number 16-043?
   A. Bryan Scott Rollman
   B. Suzanne Kay Jordan
   C. Phillip Rogers
   D. None of the above

5. What kind of distinguishing scars or marks does Suspect 1 have?
   A. Circular scar on right wrist
   B. Small circular birthmark on left forearm
   C. S-shaped scar on the right thigh
   D None are known

6. The picture shown to the right is a sketch of which suspect?
   A. Bryan Scott Frindell
   B. Tony Alan Reed
   C. Charles Alan Frindell
   D. Phillip Rogers

7. Who is described as armed and dangerous?
   A. Suspects 1 and 2
   B. Only Suspect 3
   C. Only Suspect 1
   D. Suspects 1 and 3

8. What is Suzanne Kay Jordan's record for prior convictions?
   A. Conspiracy to manufacture and distribute a controlled substance
   B. First-degree assault and criminal trespass
   C. Parole violation
   D. Possession of methamphetamine and heroin

9. Which date given below represents Bryan Scott Rollman's DOB?
   A. 08-10-58
   B. 10-18-67
   C. 01-13-58
   D. 07-13-67

10. According to NCIC file number 12-782, the suspect described possessed which of the following Social Security numbers?
    A. 729-50-3431
    B. 572-54-6711
    C. 792-54-3711
    D. 810-52-6431

11. Which date given below represents Charles Alan Frindell's DOB?
    A. 01-13-69
    B. 07-10-58
    C. 07-13-69
    D. 08-01-58

12. Which of the three suspects is described as being Caucasian and weighing 150 pounds?
    A. Phillip Rogers
    B. Suzanne Kay Jordan
    C. Tony Alan Reed
    D. Charles Alan Frindell

13. What is on Bryan Scott Rollman's record for prior convictions?
    A. First-degree sexual assault
    B. Possession of controlled substances
    C. Second-degree kidnapping and criminal trespass
    D. First-degree assault and criminal trespass

14. Which of the three suspects given is an African American?
    A. Tony Alan Reed
    B. Suzanne Kay Jordan
    C. Phillip Rogers
    D. All three suspects were Caucasian

15. According to case number 18-573, the suspect in question weighs how much?
    A. 185 pounds
    B. 155 pounds
    C. 150 pounds
    D. No such case number was given

16. Which choice below inaccurately describes Suspect 2?
    A. Height: 4'11"
    B. Alias: Sarah Kay Jordan
    C. Sex: Female
    D. Hair: Blonde

17. According to the files provided, Social Security number 572-50-3431 belongs to whom?
    A. Suspect 1
    B. Suspect 2
    C. Suspect 3
    D. None of the suspects given

18. The suspect shown in the sketch to the right is wanted for which of the following crimes?
    A. First-degree assault and criminal trespass
    B. First-degree kidnapping and second-degree sexual assault
    C. Possession of controlled substance
    D. Unlawful possession of firearm and attempted murder

19. Which choice below accurately describes Suspect 3?
    A. Sex: Male
    B. Eyes: Brown
    C. Hair: Brown
    D. All of the above are accurate descriptions

20. Which of the suspects shown below is wanted for conspiring to manufacture and distribute a controlled substance?

A.

B.

C.

    D. Wants and warrants of this type did not apply to any of the suspects given.

ANSWER SHEET FOR SAMPLE COMPOSITE SKETCH/FILE 1

1. Ⓐ Ⓑ Ⓒ Ⓓ
2. Ⓐ Ⓑ Ⓒ Ⓓ
3. Ⓐ Ⓑ Ⓒ Ⓓ
4. Ⓐ Ⓑ Ⓒ Ⓓ
5. Ⓐ Ⓑ Ⓒ Ⓓ
6. Ⓐ Ⓑ Ⓒ Ⓓ
7. Ⓐ Ⓑ Ⓒ Ⓓ

8. Ⓐ Ⓑ Ⓒ Ⓓ
9. Ⓐ Ⓑ Ⓒ Ⓓ
10. Ⓐ Ⓑ Ⓒ Ⓓ
11. Ⓐ Ⓑ Ⓒ Ⓓ
12. Ⓐ Ⓑ Ⓒ Ⓓ
13. Ⓐ Ⓑ Ⓒ Ⓓ
14. Ⓐ Ⓑ Ⓒ Ⓓ

15. Ⓐ Ⓑ Ⓒ Ⓓ
16. Ⓐ Ⓑ Ⓒ Ⓓ
17. Ⓐ Ⓑ Ⓒ Ⓓ
18. Ⓐ Ⓑ Ⓒ Ⓓ
19. Ⓐ Ⓑ Ⓒ Ⓓ
20. Ⓐ Ⓑ Ⓒ Ⓓ

Answers can be found on page 48.

If you are like most people, you may have felt a little rushed completing this last exercise. Since the informational format (name of suspect, date of birth (DOB), height, weight, etc.) is standard on wants and warrants, a fair amount of test time can be saved by becoming thoroughly familiar with the format. Thus, your number transposition and associated stories will not have to include that information. Awareness of your stories' chronological order will enable you to correctly interpret what information is pertinent to the question at hand. You may even wish to remember this informational format in a different order and plug in the facts as they are given. However, don't vacillate between different format orders because doing so can lead to some confusion.

Once you are comfortable with a certain conformation of the facts, commit them to your long-term memory. You will find this technique to be particularly time-saving when you run across such test questions.

Study the three sketches and associated personal data below for ten minutes. Do not exceed the time allowed; if you do, you will forfeit the true sense of how an exam is actually conducted. When time is up, turn to the questions provided without making any further reference to the composites just studied.

SAMPLE COMPOSITE SKETCH/FILE 2

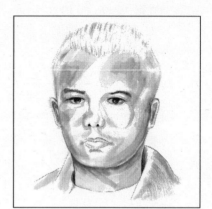

Suspect 1

Name:	Mike Hutchins
Alias:	Dean L. Kraft
DOB:	February 16, 1974
Height:	5'10"
Weight:	175 pounds
Hair:	Blonde
Eyes:	Brown
Sex:	Male
Race:	Caucasian
Scars or Marks:	None
Social Security Nos.:	113-51-7359, 437-22-9019, 681-25-0321
Wants and Warrants:	Wanted for unlawful possession of false identification documents and first-degree extortion.
Criminal Record:	Possession with intent to distribute counterfeit Social Security cards
NCIC File Number:	11-57

Suspect 2

Name: David P. Burk

Alias: Paul B. David

DOB: November 2, 1962

Height: 6'2"

Weight: 195 pounds

Hair: Silver grey

Eyes: Blue

Sex: Male

Race: Native American

Scars or Marks: L-shaped scar on left cheek

Social Security No.: 839-10-2000

Wants and Warrants: Wanted for burglary and attempted murder

Criminal record: No priors

Suspect 3

Name: Maxine Kimball

Alias: Patricia Howard;
Veronica Irwin

DOB: March 18, 1971

Height: 5'3"

Weight: 140 pounds

Hair: Brown

Eyes: Hazel

Sex: Female

Race: Asian American

Scars or Marks: None

Social Security No.: 378-15-1205

Wants and Warrants: Wanted for second-degree murder and interstate flight.

Criminal Record: First-degree assault, forgery, and unlawful possession of a firearm

NCIC File Number: 15-36

Considered armed and dangerous.

SAMPLE QUESTIONS COMPOSITE SKETCH/FILE 2

1. According to the information provided, which of the suspects utilized multiple aliases in the commission of his or her crimes?
   A. Suspect 1
   B. Suspect 2
   C. Suspect 3
   D. None of the above

2. Which of the suspects given did not have any prior convictions?
   A. David P. Burk
   B. Dean L. Kraft
   C. Veronica Irwin
   D. Mike Hutchins

3. Which of the sketches below identify the individual wanted for first-degree extortion and unlawful possession of false identification documents?

A.   B.   C.

   D. Wants and warrants of this type did not apply to any of the suspects given.

4. Which of the sketches below identify the individual wanted for attempted murder and burglary?

A.   B.   C.

 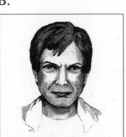 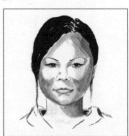

   D. Wants and warrants of this type did not apply to any of the suspects given.

5. Which of the three suspects is an Asian American?
   A. Suspect 1
   B. Suspect 2
   C. Suspect 3
   D. Suspects 1 and 3

6. Which of the three suspects weighed 195 pounds?
   A. Veronica Irwin
   B. Dean L. Kraft
   C. Mike Hutchins
   D. Paul B. David

7. What is the color of Maxine Kimball's hair according to the records provided?
   A. Blonde
   B. Black
   C. Gray
   D. Brown

8. Which suspect was assigned NCIC file number 15-63?
   A. Suspect 1
   B. Suspect 2
   C. Suspect 3
   D. None of the above

9. Who is described as armed and dangerous?
   A. Patricia Howard
   B. Paul B. David
   C. Dean L. Kraft
   D. None of the above suspects

10. What kind of distinguishing scars or marks did Suspect 2 have?
    A. C-shaped scar on right cheek
    B. L-shaped scar on left cheek
    C. L-shaped scar beneath left ear
    D. Suspect 2 did not have any scars or marks noted on record.

11. Which date below represents Dean L. Kraft's date of birth?
    A. 11-16-74
    B. 3-16-74
    C. 2-16-74
    D. 3-18-74

12. Which of the three suspects used multiple Social Security numbers presumably for fraudulent reasons?
    A. Maxine Kimball
    B. Paul B. David
    C. Mike Hutchins
    D. None of the above suspects

13. With regard to the previous question, which of the following Social Security numbers was not among those on record as having been used for illicit purposes?
    A. 681-25-0321
    B. 311-57-1019
    C. 437-22-9019
    D. 113-51-7359

14. Social Security number 839-10-2000 identifies whom?
    A. David P. Burk
    B. Patricia Howard
    C. Veronica Irwin
    D. Mike Hutchins

15. All of the following information about Suspect 2 is accurate with the exception of which of the following?
    A. Alias: David B. Burk
    B. Height: 6'2"
    C. Race: Native American
    D. Hair: Silver gray

16. The suspect that weighs 165 pounds has what kind of criminal conviction in his or her case file?
    A. Possession with intent to distribute counterfeit Social Security cards
    B. This particular individual did not have any prior convictions
    C. Forgery and second-degree assault
    D. None of the suspects studied weighed 165 pounds

17. According to the NCIC file number 11-57, which of the following statements is true?
    A. The individual in question is a male Native American.
    B. Height and weight descriptions for the suspect are 5'10" and 175 pounds, respectively.
    C. Wants and warrants for this particular suspect exclusively centered around the charge of first-degree extortion.
    D. All of the above statements are accurate descriptions of the suspect in question.

18. The suspect identified by Social Security number 378-15-1205 was born when?
    A. 2-5-62
    B. 11-3-70
    C. 3-18-71
    D. 4-15-69

19. Who is wanted for second-degree murder and interstate flight?
    A. Suspect 1
    B. Suspects 1 and 3
    C. Suspect 2
    D. Suspect 3

20. According to the files provided, Suspect 3 had a criminal record that included all of the following except:
    A. Unlawful possession of a firearm
    B. First-degree murder
    C. First-degree assault
    D. Forgery

ANSWER SHEET FOR SAMPLE COMPOSITE SKETCH/FILE 2

1. (A) (B) (C) (D)   8. (A) (B) (C) (D)   15. (A) (B) (C) (D)
2. (A) (B) (C) (D)   9. (A) (B) (C) (D)   16. (A) (B) (C) (D)
3. (A) (B) (C) (D)   10. (A) (B) (C) (D)   17. (A) (B) (C) (D)
4. (A) (B) (C) (D)   11. (A) (B) (C) (D)   18. (A) (B) (C) (D)
5. (A) (B) (C) (D)   12. (A) (B) (C) (D)   19. (A) (B) (C) (D)
6. (A) (B) (C) (D)   13. (A) (B) (C) (D)   20. (A) (B) (C) (D)
7. (A) (B) (C) (D)   14. (A) (B) (C) (D)

Answers can be found on page 48.

D. DESCRIPTIVE PASSAGES

The third form of memory exercises seen on past exams involves descriptive passages. Such passages are designed to test an applicant's ability to remember literal details from a reading. Normally, you will be given a reading that pertains to either a crime or emergency scene or some kind of technical or procedural issues. This kind of test differs from reading comprehension exams in that you are not required to make deductions; rather, you are to memorize the facts only as they appear in the passage. Trivial items become just as important as main concepts.

The best advice here is to become a part of the article instead of just reading it. If the reading details how a crime scene or other emergency unfolds, think of it as if you were witnessing the events as they occur. It can be helpful to incorporate some bizarre or funny aspects into the story to facilitate better memory of the passage.

Regardless of the passage's length and content, you will be given only a specified amount of time to read. When your time is up for studying the article, the test examiner will collect the readings and then direct you to answer related questions in your test booklet or supplement. You will not be allowed to review what was read while answering the questions provided.

SAMPLE DESCRIPTIVE PASSAGE 1

Study the passage given below for ten minutes. When your time is up, answer the questions that follow without further reference to the passage.

Chuck McGregor, Teresa Goodwill, and Mr. and Mrs. Vince Matley had just attended a monthly Economic Development Council meeting at the Sheridan Hotel. Normally, these meetings start at 7:30 P.M. and last only a couple of hours, but on this evening, important issues had to be addressed that protracted the meeting an extra twenty minutes. En route to their parked cars, the group was confronted by two juveniles and one adult, the latter of whom brandished a nickel-plated .45-caliber pistol. They were told to relinquish wallets, purses, jewelry, and anything else of value or risk being shot. As the victims of the robbery were complying with the perpetrators' demands, a parking attendant witnessed the crime and immediately dialed 911. The call was made at exactly 9:55 P.M. Officer Melvin Jenkins, Shield Number 740, was on bicycle patrol in the downtown precinct one block southwest of the incident when dispatched to investigate. It was only a matter of a couple of minutes before Officer Jenkins arrived at the parking lot; however, one of the juveniles quickly spotted the officer's approach and the trio immediately dispersed. One juvenile ran south down an adjacent alley and the other pair jumped into a 1977 two-door Monte Carlo, license plate number LNT 503. It was too dark for Officer Jenkins to provide any physical descriptions of the suspects. The information he had concerning the getaway vehicle was immediately radioed to CenCom for further follow up.

Officer Jenkins obtained good physical descriptions of the suspects from the victims. Ms. Goodwill was particularly adept at remembering details. The first juvenile was a white male, approximately 17 years of age, 6 feet, 140 pounds, black, curly, shoulder-length hair, and brown eyes. He was dressed in lightly faded blue jeans with the left knee worn through, white tennis shoes, and a dark blue T-shirt that revealed an axe-like tattoo on his right bicep. The second juvenile was a white male, approximately 15 years of age, 5'6", 130 pounds, brown hair, hazel eyes, wearing dark-colored pants, black loafers, white T-shirt, and a Toronto Blue Jays baseball cap. The third suspect was a white male, approximately 30 years of age, 6'2", 190 pounds, blonde hair cut extremely short, brown eyes. This suspect was wearing acid-wash denim jeans and jacket. He had a deep smallpox scar on his left temple.

These physical descriptions and the fact that the trio was considered armed and dangerous were radioed into CenCom.

Officer Jenkins obtained the names of the victims, their respective addresses, and a list of the personal effects that were stolen. The following information was included in Officer Jenkins' stolen property summary:

Teresa Goodwill

— lynx-trimmed dress jacket valued at $750

— silver jewelry valued at $75

— $150 in cash and two credit cards

Chuck McGregor

— wallet containing $85

Mr. Vince Matley

— wallet containing $125

— gold Rolex watch valued at $1850

— gold wedding band

Mrs. Vince Matley

— diamond ring valued at $1300

Officer Jenkins submitted a completed report detailing the robbery to Sergeant Bruce Day, Shield Number 432. Sergeant Day signed the report and assigned report number 1561 to the record.

SAMPLE QUESTIONS ON DESCRIPTIVE PASSAGE 1

1. Where was the location of the meeting referred to in the reading?
   A. Sheriton Motel
   B. Holiday Inn
   C. Sheridan Hotel
   D. Ramada

2. What was Officer Day's shield number?
   A. 1516
   B. 503
   C. 470
   D. 432

3. What time did the meeting referred to in the reading actually come to a close?
   A. 9:50 P.M.
   B. 9:30 P.M.
   C. 9:55 P.M.
   D. 10:05 P.M.

4. Who alerted the authorities to the fact that a robbery was in progress?
   A. Chuck McGregor
   B. The parking attendant
   C. Melvin Jenkins
   D. Teresa Goodwill

5. What was the height and weight of the oldest suspect?
   A. 6'5", 130 pounds
   B. 6'2", 190 pounds
   C. 5'6", 140 pounds
   D. 6', 140 pounds

6. What was the license plate number of the getaway vehicle?
   A. BVT 740
   B. NBT 911
   C. LNT 503
   D. ECD 103

7. How often did the members of the Economic Development Council meet?
   A. Daily
   B. Weekly
   C. Monthly
   D. Annually

8. Which of the four victims lost a wallet and $85 cash as a result of the robbery?
   A. Chuck McGregor
   B. Teresa Goodwill
   C. Mrs. Vince Matley
   D. Bruce Day

9. What time was it when the authorities were first notified that a robbery was taking place?
    A. 9:55 A.M.
    B. 9:52 P.M.
    C. 9:52 A.M.
    D. 9:55 P.M.

10. All of the following descriptions fit the second suspect except:
    A. 5'6"
    B. Approximately 17 years of age
    C. Wore a Toronto Blue Jays baseball cap
    D. White male

11. Who was described as being particularly adept at remembering details?
    A. Officer Bruce Day
    B. Vince Matley
    C. Teresa Goodwill
    D. No one in the reading was given that distinction.

12. The oldest of the three suspects was described as having:
    A. Blonde, curly, shoulder-length hair
    B. Brown hair
    C. Blonde hair, cut extremely short
    D. Black, curly hair

13. What was the year and make of the vehicle used by the suspects?
    A. 1975 two-door Monte Carlo
    B. 1977 two-door Grand Prix
    C. 1975 four-door Pontiac
    D. 1977 two-door Monte Carlo

14. Which of the four victims of the robbery had a gold Rolex watch stolen?
    A. Mr. Vince Matley
    B. Mrs. Vince Matley
    C. Chuck McGregor
    D. Teresa Goodwill

15. What kind of weapon was used by the suspects in the course of the robbery?
    A. Switchblade knife
    B. Silver-plated .44-caliber pistol
    C. 12-gauge shotgun
    D. Nickel-plated .45-caliber pistol

16. When Officer Jenkins was told by CenCom to investigate the robbery, where was he in relation to the crime scene?
    A. One block northeast
    B. One block southwest
    C. Two blocks south
    D. One block west

17. Which of the suspects was described as wearing faded blue jeans with the right knee worn through?
    A. The first juvenile suspect
    B. The second juvenile suspect
    C. The third suspect
    D. None of the suspects fit that description.

18. The superior officer that accepted Officer Jenkins report was a:
    A. Captain
    B. Sergeant
    C. Lieutenant
    D. Chief

19. What was Officer Jenkins' shield number?
    A. 503
    B. 740
    C. 977
    D. 130

20. Which of the numbers given below was assigned to Officer Jenkins' robbery report?
    A. 432
    B. 1651
    C. 1561
    D. 1551

ANSWER SHEET FOR SAMPLE DESCRIPTIVE PASSAGE 1

1. (A) (B) (C) (D)   8. (A) (B) (C) (D)   15. (A) (B) (C) (D)

2. (A) (B) (C) (D)   9. (A) (B) (C) (D)   16. (A) (B) (C) (D)

3. (A) (B) (C) (D)   10. (A) (B) (C) (D)   17. (A) (B) (C) (D)

4. (A) (B) (C) (D)   11. (A) (B) (C) (D)   18. (A) (B) (C) (D)

5. (A) (B) (C) (D)   12. (A) (B) (C) (D)   19. (A) (B) (C) (D)

6. (A) (B) (C) (D)   13. (A) (B) (C) (D)   20. (A) (B) (C) (D)

7. (A) (B) (C) (D)   14. (A) (B) (C) (D)

Answers can be found on page 48.

SAMPLE DESCRIPTIVE PASSAGE 2

Study the passage provided below for five minutes. When your time is up, answer the sample questions that follow without further reference the passage.

State Trooper Allison B. Jenner, badge number 169, a six-year veteran with Post 17 of the Oregon State Patrol, was on routine duty on Interstate 5 just north of Roseburg. She had the evening shift assignment for the Labor Day weekend. At 2015 hours (i.e., 8:15 P.M.) as she was traveling north, she observed a light blue 1990 Ford F-250 pickup truck bearing South Carolina license plates off to the side of the road, hood raised, and steam billowing from an apparently overheated engine. Trooper Jenner pulled up behind the stranded motorists and, as a matter of standard policy, did a quick radio check of her location as well as verifying that the license plate number, KJT 452, was clear of any existing wants or warrants. However, in the brief moments it took to get this information, Trooper Jenner noticed that the driver and passenger seemed kind of fidgety. The driver kept staring in his rear-view mirror and the passenger made quick glances out the back window trying to appear nondescript. Both men remained in their vehicle. The vehicle license check came clean; nevertheless, Trooper Jenner got out of her troop car and approached the driver side of the vehicle with extra caution. What really caught her attention at this point was the passenger leaning forward and apparently trying to place something beneath the truck's seat. Beyond the initial pleasantries and empathizing with their situation, Trooper Jenner asked the driver for his driver's license and vehicle registration. The driver, Clayton S. Seymour, complied accordingly, but as he was reaching over to the glove compartment to retrieve his registration, Trooper Jenner noticed what appeared to be either a .38-caliber or 9-millimeter round lying on the passenger-side floor. Trooper Jenner, at that point, told both of the vehicle occupants to keep their hands in plain view and to exit the vehicle. Both individuals were then instructed to place both hands on the truck hood so as to allow for a pat-down search. Trooper Jenner did not find anything suspicious on Mr. Seymour. However, the passenger, identified by his North Carolina driver's license as Kevin H. Tisdale, had a concealed, but empty, shoulder holster. Trooper Jenner asked Mr. Tisdale if he had a concealed weapon permit but she did not receive an answer. A cursory search beneath his side of the truck seat yielded several items: a 9-millimeter Browning hi-powered semi-automatic pistol (matched caliber for the round seen earlier); a small paper sack containing what appeared to be approximately half a kilogram of a white crystalline powder; and three various-sized hypodermic syringes. Both individuals were arrested for suspicion of trafficking narcotics (RCO 01.85.956) and Mr. Tisdale was additionally charged with unlawful possession of a concealed firearm (RCO 92.73.721). Sheriff Kyle M. Jenkins, badge number 183, took custodial responsibility of transporting the pair to Douglas County Detention for booking and intake. Trooper Jenner filed a completed arrest report, number 14874, on the incident with post command desk officer Charles Williams, badge number 167, upon completion of her shift at 2330 hours (i.e., 11:30 P.M.).

SAMPLE QUESTIONS, DESCRIPTIVE PASSAGE 2

1. According to the reading, what state jurisdiction did this particular incident take place in?
   A. Ohio
   B. North Carolina
   C. South Carolina
   D. Oregon

2. What was the license-plate number of the stranded vehicle involved?
   A. TKJ 425
   B. KJT 452
   C. TJK 524
   D. KTJ 454

3. The state trooper named in the reading had served with the State Patrol for how long?
   A. Six years
   B. Four years
   C. Two years
   D. Less than one year and still on probation

4. With regard to the previous question, what was the State Trooper's post assignment?
   A. 16
   B. 169
   C. 17
   D. 179

5. The name of the officer that took custodial responsibility of the individuals arrested was which of the following:
   A. Tisdale
   B. Jenkins
   C. Jenner
   D. Seymour

6. Which of the following selections is an accurate description of the vehicle used by those arrested?
   A. White on blue two-toned 1990 Custom Deluxe Chevrolet pickup truck
   B. Light blue 1989 F-350 Ford pickup truck with a crew cab
   C. Dark blue two-door 1992 Pontiac Firebird
   D. Light blue 1990 F-250 Ford pickup truck

7. All of the following items were discovered in the suspects' vehicle during a cursory search conducted by the arresting officer with the exception of which of the following?
   A. .38-caliber ammunition
   B. Hypodermic syringes
   C. Hi-powered Browning semi-automatic pistol
   D. 9-millimeter ammunition

8 Both the driver and passenger of the suspect vehicle were charged with which of the following infractions according to the Revised Code of Oregon (RCO) Statutes?
   A. RCO 01.85.956 and RCO 92.73.721   C. RCO 10.85.956 and RCO 92.37.721
   B. RCO 92.73.721   D. RCO 01.85.956

9. The arresting officer filed a completed arrest report at the end of her shift to whom?
    A. Sheriff Allison Jenner
    B. Trooper Sergeant Clayton S. Seymour
    C. District Commander Charles Williams
    D. None of the above

10. The arrested suspects were taken into custody and escorted to what particular destination for booking and intake?
    A. Lane County Superior Court
    B. Roseburg Adult Detention
    C. Douglas County Detention
    D. Douglas County District Court

11. What were the names of the driver and passenger arrested?
    A. Charles S. Williams and Clayton S. Seymour, respectively
    B. Clayton S. Seymour and Kevin H. Tisdale, respectively
    C. Kevin H. Tisdale and Kyle M. Jenkins, respectively
    D. Kyle M. Jenkins and Clayton S. Seymour, respectively

12. Which of the following selections was noted in the reading as the time that the trooper initially observed the suspects' vehicle?
    A. 2330 hours
    B. 2015 hours
    C. 0815 hours
    D. 0230 hours

13. What was the approximate locational reference made in the reading of where the suspects' vehicle broke down?
    A. On Interstate 5 just north of Roseburg
    B. On Highway 169 just south of Eugene
    C. On Interstate 5 just north of Portland
    D. A locational reference was not provided within the context of the reported incident.

14. What was Officer Jenner's badge number?
    A. 167
    B. 169
    C. 185
    D. 5

15. What was the number assigned to the arrest report for future case file reference?
    A. 73721
    B. 18721
    C. 14874
    D. 15721

ANSWER SHEET FOR SAMPLE DESCRIPTIVE PASSAGE 2

1. (A) (B) (C) (D)   6. (A) (B) (C) (D)   11. (A) (B) (C) (D)

2. (A) (B) (C) (D)   7. (A) (B) (C) (D)   12. (A) (B) (C) (D)

3. (A) (B) (C) (D)   8. (A) (B) (C) (D)   13. (A) (B) (C) (D)

4. (A) (B) (C) (D)   9. (A) (B) (C) (D)   14. (A) (B) (C) (D)

5. (A) (B) (C) (D)   10. (A) (B) (C) (D)   15. (A) (B) (C) (D)

Answers can be found on page 48.

ANSWERS FOR MEMORY RECALL SAMPLE QUESTIONS

SAMPLE SKETCH 1

1. B	4. D	7. B	10. C	13. B
2. D	5. A	8. B	11. C	14. C
3. C	6. C	9. D	12. A	15. A

SAMPLE COMPOSITE SKETCH FILE 1

1. C	5. B	9. A	13. D	17. B
2. A	6. D	10. C	14. A	18. D
3. D	7. B	11. C	15. A	19. D
4. B	8. D	12. B	16. B	20. B

SAMPLE COMPOSITE SKETCH FILE 2

1. C	5. C	9. A	13. B	17. B
2. A	6. D	10. B	14. A	18. C
3. C	7. D	11. C	15. A	19. D
4. B	8. D	12. C	16. D	20. B

SAMPLE DESCRIPTIVE PASSAGE 1

1. C	5. B	9. D	13. D	17. D
2. D	6. C	10. B	14. A	18. B
3. A	7. C	11. C	15. D	19. B
4. B	8. A	12. C	16. B	20. C

SAMPLE DESCRIPTIVE PASSAGE 2

1. D	4. C	7. A	10. C	13. A
2. B	5. B	8. D	11. B	14. B
3. A	6. D	9. D	12. B	15. C

Your score for each of the exercises would be as follows:

For the 15-question exercises:	For the 20-question exercises:
141–15 correct — EXCELLENT	18–20 correct — EXCELLENT
12–13 correct — GOOD	16–17 correct — GOOD
10–11 correct — FAIR	14–15 correct — FAIR
Less than 10 correct — POOR	Less than 14 correct — POOR

Chapter 3

Reading Comprehension

The amount of written information provided to State Police Academy cadets, as mentioned in the introduction, is nothing short of impressive. An applicant with marginal reading skills will, in all likelihood, not successfully graduate from the academy, much less get through the initial phases of screening. However, the learning does not terminate upon successful completion of academy training. State officers, continually throughout their careers, will have to understand and interpret new policies and/or procedures, note changes in State and Federal statutes that have implicit ramifications on enforcement, or may elect to pursue the necessary studies for promotional advancement within the department. Therefore, it is vitally important that applicants be competent with regard to reading comprehension skills.

It has long been held by psychologists that, aside from overt differences attributed to a person's inherited abilities, most reading skills are largely determined by the kind of education received during the elementary school years. Whether that education was characterized by an ABC letter recognition format or phonics system, or some combination thereof, is irrelevant. What is important are the kind of reading habits acquired that may, in fact, hinder reading comprehension. It was once a widely accepted belief that if students attempted to subvocalize (i.e., move their lips or other parts of the mouth without actually speaking) while they were reading, it would diminish the speed at which they could progress through the reading itself, diminishing overall comprehension. Some teachers even went to the extent of passing out candy in class to prevent students from engaging in the practice. Ironically, various studies of the subject undertaken by research psychologists have unequivocally disproved the claim. Students who did subvocalize while reading were shown to actually have a better understanding of most material studied. This was particularly true when difficult or technical information was involved.

Another practice embraced by some educators was to instruct students not to read the text verbatim. Instead, several words were to be looked at as a unit, and then the units taken collectively would provide sufficient insight into the article's content; the concept was that time was saved while reading comprehension was improved. Again, studies done by educational psychologists have refuted the concept. Reading comprehension is undeniably improved only when each word is read.

As unbelievable as it may seem, some educators even went so far as to say that if students do not fully understand the material presented, it is better for them to continue on instead of rereading the text. The line of reasoning here is that if students do not learn what is read the first time, repetitive reading will only prove to be unproductive and a waste of time. As you can well imagine, many studies have disproved this concept. In fact, rereading may be a necessity when the material being studied is complicated or abstract. Articles should be reread as many times as necessary to get the full meaning of the text before continuing.

Perhaps the most debated educational approach to reading involves the technique referred to as scanning or skim-reading. The belief is that key words can be discerned within the text, and taken as a whole, an individual can quickly comprehend the basic meaning of the article read. This very concept has given rise to the speed-reading industry. Speed-reading experts claim that reading at 250 to 300 words per minute is too slow when it is possible to skim at a rate of three to six times that speed. However, what they fail to mention is that comprehension is sacrificed for the sake of speed. This raises the question: What is gained if a fair share of information is not fully understood, or retained?

The other major shortcoming of skim-reading practices is that key words may be taken out of context and when viewed cumulatively may cause the reader to misconstrue the underlying meaning of the article. Verbs and prepositions that link nouns can dramatically alter the tenor of the material being studied. If verbs and prepositions are not given attention as key words, a passage may be read as meaning one thing when skimmed, when, in fact, it actually means something entirely different. You can be assured that college students studying for the L.S.A.T., V.A.T., M.C.A.T., or other professional exams do not skim their readings. Subject matter expected to be covered on these exams is closely scrutinized without regard to speed. There is no acceptable substitute for full and accurate reading comprehension.

To better hone your reading skills, practice reading as much material as possible, taking care to avoid the problems just discussed. You will find it easier to do this if the articles you read are on topics of interest. Nothing will discourage reading more than a dull or boring article. Reading of any kind is beneficial: newspapers, magazines, and fiction and nonfiction books are a few possible sources.

As you read an article, try to discern the underlying meaning of the reading. What is the author trying to say? Are there ideas or other forms of information that support any conclusions? If so, which are the most important? In this respect, certain concepts can be prioritized. You will find that if you follow such an inquiry into all your reading, your comprehension and reading efficiency will improve immensely.

Another way to enhance reading efficiency is to develop a better vocabulary. Quite often, words encountered in your readings may be unfamiliar to you. Don't skip over such words. Use a dictionary to discover the meanings of unfamiliar words, then make a mental note of them. Some people find it easier to write each word on a small card as a reminder. As a challenge, try incorporating that particular word into your everyday language. A continuance of this practice is a viable way of building a strong vocabulary.

If a dictionary is not handy when you encounter an unfamiliar word, it is still possible to discern the meaning of the word. Start by looking at the word to see how it is used within the sentence. This should give you some clue as to its general meaning. For example:

The restaurant patron was extremely **vexed** when the waiter accidentally spilled coffee on his lap.

Obviously, the customer would not be happy under such circumstances, so we know the word *vexed* implies a degree of dissatisfaction.

Another method that can be used to further understand or define an unfamiliar term uses basic word derivations or etymology. Word derivations can provide a partial, if not complete, meaning for a term. For example, take a look at the word *injudicious*. The first two letters, *in-*, are a prefix that means "not" or "lack of." The root of the word, *judiei*, means "judgment." The last portion of the word, *-ous*, is the suffix, and means "characterized by." Therefore, *injudicious* may be interpreted as a characterization of someone who lacks judgment.

The following etymology table has been provided for your convenience. This, in conjunction with viewing unfamiliar terms in context, will lend the best possible insight without the assistance of a dictionary.

Common Prefixes

Prefix	Meaning	Example
a-	not or without	atypical — not typical
ab-	away from	abnormal — deviating from normal
ac-	to or toward	accredit — to attribute to
ad-	to or toward	adduce — to bring forward as evidence
ag-	to or toward	aggravate — to make more severe
at-	to or toward	attain — to reach to

an-	not or without	anarchy — a society with no government
ante-	before or preceding	antenatal — referencing prior to birth
anti-	against or counter	antisocial — against being social
auto-	self or same	automatic — self-acting
bene-	good or well	benevolence — an act of kindness or goodwill
bi-	two or twice	bisect — to divide into two parts
circum-	around	circumscribe — draw a line around or encircle
com-	together or with	combine — join
con-	together or with	conciliate — united or drawn together
contra-	against or opposite	contradict — opposed or against what someone else says
de-	removal from	decongestant — relieves or removes congestion
dec-	ten	decade — a ten-year period
demi-	half	demigod — partly divine and partly human
dis-	apart, negation, or reversal	dishonest — a lack or negation of honesty
dys-	diseased, bad, difficult, faulty	dyslexia — impairment of reading ability
e-, ex-	from or out of	evoke — draw forth or bring out
extra-	beyond	extraordinary — outside or beyond the usual order
hemi-	half	hemisphere — half of the globe
hyper-	excessive or over	hyperactive — excessively active
hypo-	beneath or under	hypodermic — something introduced under the skin
im-	not	impersonal — not personal
in-	not	inaccessible — not accessible
ir-	not	irrational — not having reason or understanding
inter-	among or between	interdepartmental — between departments
intra-	inside or within	intradepartmental — within a department
kilo-	thousand	kiloton — one thousand tons
mal-	bad or ill	malcontent — dissatisfied
mis-	wrong	misinterpret — to interpret wrongly
mono-	one or single	monochromatic — having only one color
non-	not	nonresident — person who does not live in a particular place
ob-	against or opposed	object — declared opposition or disapproval
omni-	all	omnivore — an animal that eats all foods, either plant or animal
per-	through or thoroughly	perennial — continuing or lasting through the years
poly-	many or much	polychromy — an artistic combination of different colors
post-	after or later	postglacial — after the glacial period
pre-	before or supporting	previous — going before in time or order
pro-	before or supporting	proalliance — supportive of an alliance
re-	again, former state or position	reiterate — do or say repeatedly

retro-	backward or return	retrogressive — moving backwards
self-	individual or personal	self-defense — act of defending oneself
semi-	half or part	semifinal — halfway final
sub-	below or under	submarine — reference to something underwater
super-	above or over	superficial — not penetrating the surface
tele-	distance	telegraph — an instrument used for communicating at a distance
trans-	across, over or through	transparent — lets light shine through
ultra-	beyond or excessive	ultraconservative — beyond ordinary conservatism
un-	not	unaccountable — not accountable or responsible

Common Suffixes

Suffix	Meaning	Example
-able, -ible	capacity of being	readable — able to be read, eligible — qualified to be chosen
-ac	like or pertaining to	maniac — like a mad person
-age	function or state of	mileage — distance in miles
-ally	in a manner that relates to	pastorally — in a manner that relates to rural life
-ance	act or fact of	cognizance — knowledge through perception or reason
-ary	doing or pertaining to	subsidiary — serving to assist or supplement
-ant	person or thing	tyrant — a ruler who is unjustly severe
-ar	of the nature or pertaining to	nuclear — pertaining to the nucleus
-ation	action	excavation — act or process of excavating
-cede, -ceed	to go or come	intercede — to go or come between; succeed — to follow
-cide	destroy or kill	homicide — the killing of a person by another
-cy	quality	decency — the state of being decent
-dy	condition or character	shoddy — pretentious condition or something poorly made
-ence, -ery	act or fact of doing or pertaining to	despondence — loss of hope
-er	one who does	lawyer — one who practices law
-ful	abounding or full of	fretful — tending to fret or be irritable
-ic	like or pertaining to	artistic — having a talent in art
-ify	to make	magnify — to make large
-ious	full of	laborious — full of labor or requiring a lot of work
-ise	to make	devise — to create from existing ideas
-ish	like	childish — like a child
-ism	system or belief	capitalism — an economic system that revolves around private ownership
-ist	person or thing	idealist — a person who has ideals
-ize	to make	idolize — to make an idol of
-less	without	penniless — without a penny

-ology	the study of	archaeology — the study of historical cultures using arti-facts of past activities
-ly	in a manner	shapely — well-formed
-ment	the act of	achievement — the act of achieving
-ness	state of or quality	pettiness — the state of being petty or small-minded
-or	person who acts	legislator — person who enacts legislation
-ory	place	dormitory — building that provides living quarters
-ship	condition or character	censorship — overseeing or excluding items that may be objectionable to those concerned
-tude	state of or result	solitude — state of being alone or apart from society
-ty	condition or character	levity — lightness in character
-y	quality or result	hefty — moderately heavy or weighty

Common Roots

Root	Meaning	Example
acou	hearing	acoustical — pertaining to sound
acro	furthest or highest point	acrophobia — fear of heights
acu	needle	acupuncture — puncturing of body tissue for relief of pain
aero	air or gas	aeronautics — study of the operation of aircraft
alt	high	altitude — a position or region at height
ambi	both	ambidextrous — capable of using both hands equally well
anter	in front	anterior — toward the front
anthrop	human being	anthropology — science of mankind
aqua, aqui	water	aquatic — living in water
audio	hearing	audiology — science of hearing
auto	self	autocratic — ruled by a monarch with absolute rule
avi	bird, flight	aviary — large cage for confining birds
bio	life	biography — written history of a person's life
bona	good	bonafide — in good faith
capit	head	capital — involving the forfeiture of the head or life (as in capital punishment)
carb	carbon	carboniferous — containing or producing carbon or coal
carcin	cancer	carcinogen — substance that initiates cancer
carn	flesh	carnivorous — flesh-eating
cent	a hundred	centennial — pertaining to 100 years
centro, centri	center	centrifugal — movement away from the center
cepha	head	hydrocephalus — condition caused by excess fluid in the head
chron	time	synchronize — to happen at the same time
citri	fruit	citric acid — sour tasting juice from fruits
corpor, corp	body	corporate — combined into one body

crypt	covered or hidden	cryptology — an art of uncovering a hidden or coded message
culp	fault	culprit — criminal
cyclo	circular	cyclone — a storm with strong circular winds
demo	people	democracy — government ruled by the people
doc	teach	doctrine — instruction or teaching
dox	opinion	paradox — self contradictory statement that has plausibility
duo	two	duologue — conversation involving two people
dyna	power	dynamometer — device for measuring power
eco	environment	ecosystem — community of organisms interacting with the environment
embry	early	embryonic — pertaining to an embryo or the beginning of life
equi	equal	equilibrium — balance
ethn	race, group	ethnology — study of human races or groups
exter	outside of	external — on the outside
flor	flower	florist — dealer in flowers
foli	leafy	defoliate — to strip a plant of its leaves
geo	earth	geophysics — the physics of the earth
geri	old age	geriatrics — division of medicine pertaining to old age
graphy	write	autograph — a person's own signature
gyro	spiral motion	gyroscope — rotating wheel that can spin on various planes
horti	garden	horticulture — science of cultivating plants
hydro	water	hydroplane — form of boat that glides over water
hygi	health	hygiene — practice of preservation of health
hygro	wet	hygrometer — instrument used to measure moisture in the atmosphere
hypno	sleep	hypnology — science that treats sleep
ideo	idea	ideology — study of ideas
iso	equal	isotonic — having equal tones or tension
jur	swear	jury — body of persons sworn to tell the truth
lac, lacto	milk	lacteal — resembling milk
lamin	divided	laminate — bond together layers
lingui	tongue	linguistics — study of languages
litho	stone	lithography — art of putting design on stone with a greasy material to produce printed impressions
loco, locus	place	locomotion — act or power of moving from place to place
macro	large	macrocosm — the great world; the universe
man	hand	manual — made or operated by hand
medi	middle	mediocre — average or middle quality
mega	large	megalopolis — urban area comprising several large adjoining cities

mero, meri	part or fraction of	meroblastic — partial or incomplete cleavage
micro	small or petty	microscopic — so small as to be invisible without the aid of a microscope
mini	small	miniature — an image or representation of something on a smaller scale
moto	motion	motive — what moves someone to action
multi	many	multimillionaire — person with several million dollars
navi	ship	navigation — to direct course for a vessel on the sea or in the air
neo	new	neonatal — pertaining to the newborn
noct, nocti	night	nocturnal — occurring in the night
oct, octo, octa	eight	octagonal — having eight sides
olig, oligo	scant or few	oligarchy — a government which is controlled by a few people
oo	egg	oology — a branch of ornithology dealing with bird eggs
opto	vision or eye	optometry — profession of testing vision and examining eyes for disease
ortho	straight	orthodontics — dentistry dealing with correcting the teeth
pent, penta	five	pentagon — having five sides
phob	panic or fear	arachnophobia — fear of spiders
phon	sound	phonograph — instrument for reproducing sound
pod	foot	podiatry — the study and treatment of foot disorders
pseudo	false	pseudonym — fictitious name
psych	mental	psychiatry — science of treatment mental disorders
pyro	fire	pyrotechnics — art of making or using fireworks
quad	four	quadruped — animal having four feet
quint	five	quintuple — having five parts
sect	part or divide	bisect — divide into two equal parts
spiri	coiled	spirochete — spiral shaped bacteria
stasi	to stand still	hemostatic — serving to stop hemorrhage
techni	skill	technician — skilled person in a particular field
terri	to frighten	terrible — capable of exciting terror
tetra	four	tetrahedron — a shape with four faces
therm	heat	thermostat — device that automatically controls desired temperatures
toxi	poison	toxicology — science concerning the effects, antidotes, and detection of poisonous substances
uni	single	unilateral — involving one person, class, or nation
urb	city	suburb — outlying part of a city
uro	urine	urology — science of studying the urinary tract and its diseases

verb	word	proverb — a name, person, or thing that has become a byword
veri	truthful	verify — to prove to be truthful
vit	life	vitality — liveliness
vitri	glass or glass-like	vitreous — resembling glass
vivi	alive	viviparous — giving birth to living young
vol	wish	volunteer — to enter into or offer oneself freely
zo, zoi, zoo	animal	zoology — science of studying animal life

Vocabulary at one time constituted a major part of the State Police exam. Now, however, it is fairly common to see vocabulary test questions constitute only five to ten percent of the entire exam. Additionally, however, some words not commonly used are incorporated into reading comprehension questions. Without some understanding of what those terms mean, your comprehension of the article can be diminished.

Most reading comprehension test questions encountered on past exams are concerned with three things. First, what is the basic underlying theme of the passage, or what would be a suitable title or heading that summarizes the article? In most cases, this is an inferential question. In other words, you have to assimilate all the information given and select the one of four possible options that best encompasses the meaning of the article. There will not be a sentence taken directly out of the article to serve as a potential option. These questions require more judgment on your part.

Secondly, some questions may concern literal reading comprehension. In other words, questions about certain details, ideas, or facts will be asked. If the answer is not immediately apparent, it can be determined by simply going back to the applicable part of the reading and picking out the correct answer directly.

The last type of question may concern interpretation. After studying the information in an article, a comparable or hypothetical situation may be posed, and it will be left to you to interpret how what you have read applies to it.

It is ironic, but you may find it easier to read the questions before reading the passage presented. This is somewhat of a backward approach to reading comprehension questions, but it will alert you to what is considered important, and hence what to look for in the article, thus saving time.

Sample questions complete with answers and supporting explanations follow. The questions presented are not copies of past exams, but they do represent a good overview of what to expect on the actual exam.

SAMPLE QUESTIONS FOR READING COMPREHENSION

Passage 1

All crimes, regardless of their nature, leave some degree of evidence behind. How an officer goes about gathering physical evidence can make the difference between offering evidence that is material and relevant in a trial versus that which is bound to be thrown out under cross examination.

Preservation of the crime scene is the number one priority before and during the actual investigation. The number of investigators or specialists surveying the crime scene should be kept to an absolute minimum. Unauthorized persons should be removed from the premises until the investigation is complete. Bystanders can inadvertently step on or otherwise destroy or remove valuable evidence. In fact, some people have been known to obstruct justice willfully by destroying evidence in the hope of protecting a friend or relative. For obvious reasons, efforts should also be made to protect evidence from the elements, such as wind, sun, rain, or snow.

Not only is minimizing the potential for evidence contamination very important, but so is the way an officer proceeds with the search for and collection of evidence. The mechanics of the search itself, if conducted in a careful and orderly manner, can preclude duplication (i.e., covering the same area twice) in the investigation. This search and collection needs to be carried out within a reasonable time because certain kinds of evidence are perishable (principally organic compounds such as blood and semen) and begin to deteriorate quickly. In addition to the time element, temperatures higher than 95° Fahrenheit or below freezing can also have a detrimental effect on such evidence.

In the course of the actual search itself, officers should be on the lookout for any evidence prior to actually entering the crime scene. Normally, searches are begun by scanning the floor and walls, finally proceeding to the ceiling. When marking and securing evidence, investigators should be extremely careful not to destroy any of it. Dropping a delicate article or accidentally marking or scratching items are two examples of how evidence can be damaged. All evidence, once located, should be cataloged (recorded), listing a description and relative location where found in the crime scene. This compiling of records essentially provides the chain of evidence prosecutors can use at trial to secure a conviction.

Answer questions 1–5 on the basis of Passage 1.

1. What would be an appropriate title for this passage?

    A. How best to secure criminal convictions through evidence handling

    B. What an officer should not do during the investigation of a crime scene

    C. The intricacies of evidence gathering

    D. Procedural guidelines and cautions for crime scene investigations

2. What two words would be considered suitable adjectives in summarizing the content of this article?

    A. Prudent and compulsory

    B. Intelligent and inquisitive

    C. Circumspect and expeditious

    D. Attentive and compliant

3. Officer Pat Gregory was quick to respond to a warehouse burglary after receiving an anonymous tip. The burglars were not on the premises when Officer Gregory arrived. However, in their haste to flee they had left a crowbar on the warehouse floor. The warehouse door had obviously been jimmied to allow entry. Officer Gregory, in confirming that belief, picked up the crowbar and carefully placed the prying edge against the impression marks made on the door. The crowbar was placed in its original position on the warehouse floor after Officer Gregory had confirmed his suspicions. Assuming someone other than Officer Gregory was responsible for the burglary investigation, Officer Gregory's actions were

    A. Right, because the evidence, even though it had been moved, was replaced in its original position.

    B. Wrong, because he may have left an extra scratch or even traces of paint from the crowbar in the impression on the door.

    C. Right, because his confirmation will save another investigator valuable time.

    D. Wrong, because he should have wrapped the crowbar handle in either plastic or a paper towel prior to picking it up.

4. Which type of evidence given below is most prone to deterioration with time and temperature extremes?

    A. Blood stains

    B. Fired casings and bullets

    C. Hairs and fibers

    D. Dirt and soil particles

5. Which of the following is not considered an underlying objective for investigators in sealing off a crime scene?

    A. To prevent willful obstruction of justice by persons close to the investigation

    B. To prevent persons outside of the investigative unit from inadvertently destroying evidence

    C. To illustrate to the public that police know what they are doing

    D. To preserve the crime scene as is

Passage 2

In 1969, the Supreme Court made a landmark decision in overturning a lower California Appeals Court and California Supreme Court ruling. The case in question involved Ted Chimel, who was arrested for the burglary of a local coin shop. Incidental to his arrest, authorities thoroughly searched his residence against his wishes. Officers were successful in locating evidence that implicated Mr. Chimel in the coin shop robbery. That evidence was used in the trial to convict Mr. Chimel. Both the California Appeals Court and the California Supreme Court upheld the decision. It was, however, reversed by the Supreme Court, which held that Mr. Chimel's Fourth and Fourteenth Amendment rights were violated when the search (incident to the arrest and without a warrant) went beyond that area of his person or the area within his reach from which he might have obtained a weapon. Consequently, today how and what is searched is rigidly defined. Incident to arrest, an officer is only allowed to search the person and area within proximate reach for a potential weapon. Searches cannot be expanded further unless there is a warrant issued by a magistrate specifying exactly what can be searched, or the arrested person gives permission, or an officer has reasonable belief that another person's life may be in danger. The word *reasonable* is and has been subjected to various interpretations in the courts. The most dependable way of conducting a search without the "color of authority" potentially affecting the outcome of a trial is with a written warrant from an impartial magistrate.

Answer questions 6–10 on the basis of Passage 2.

6. What would be an appropriate title for this passage?

    A. *Chimel v. California* (1969)

    B. Search and seizure guidelines as established by the Supreme Court

    C. The consequences of an unreasonable search

    D. The disadvantages of not utilizing a warrant

7. The word *incident* (to arrest) as it is applied in the reading most nearly means:

    A. As a preliminary

    B. Dependent on

    C. In the course of

    D. Preparatory

8. (*Note:* When selecting your answer, consider only the original case decision.)
   Police Officer Tom McClintock pulled over a motorist for a minor speeding infraction. As Officer McClintock was issuing a citation, he noticed the pungent smell of marijuana. He placed the driver under arrest. A quick check of the suspect's shirt pockets revealed three marijuana joints. Nothing else was in plain view. However, upon examining the trunk, he found two kilos of cocaine. Officer McClintock acted:

   A. Properly and within the full limits of warrantless search of the vehicle.

   B. Properly by searching the suspect as well as the entire vehicle.

   C. Improperly because, according to the *Chimel v. California* decision, the "area within the suspect's immediate control" would preclude the search of the trunk without a warrant.

   D. Improperly because, according to the *Chimel v. California* decision, he should have obtained permission from the suspect to search the passenger seats.

9. Which of the following factors could ultimately determine the legality of a warrantless search in the court's view?

   A. The position of the arresting officers in relation to the arrestee

   B. The degree of physical restraint placed on the arrestee

   C. The relative degree of ease or difficulty of the arrestee reaching a given area

   D. All of the above

10. According to the reading, which of the following statements is the most accurate?

   A. Mr. Chimel's Fourteenth Amendment rights were violated in the landmark case of *Chimel v. California.*

   B. Warrants give a broad definition as to what area can be searched during criminal investigations.

   C. Warrants, in effect, remove the prospect of a court's consideration of whether "color of authority" may have in any way biased the case.

   D. The California Supreme Court overturned Mr. Chimel's conviction on the basis that his civil rights were neglected.

Passage 3

Robbery, by definition, is not a crime against property; rather, it is considered a crime against a person. If someone illegally takes the property of another by means of force or the threat of force, the law prescribes that a robbery has been committed. On the other hand, if property of some value is stolen from a person directly and the aspect of force is absent in the crime, the incident is then considered larceny. Whether it is petty or grand larceny is dependent upon the value of the property stolen.

This definition by itself may seem fairly straightforward. However, several factors need to be taken into consideration when determining if, indeed, a robbery did take place or if, instead, the crime was larceny. If intimidation such as libel, extortion, or blackmail precludes the use of force and is used to obtain property from another person, this is not considered robbery. Additionally, if an individual is unaware that property is being stolen from his or her person because he or she is either inattentive or unconscious, the action constitutes larceny, not robbery.

Finally, the use of force must be preliminary in the commission of the theft for it to be considered a robbery. If force takes place after the perpetrator has committed the crime, it cannot be considered a robbery. Both the timing and circumstances of a theft can make a crucial difference in how that crime will be charged according to common law.

Answer questions 11–15 on the basis of Passage 3.

11. Bill Smith had a few too many drinks one evening at a local tavern. Instead of attempting to drive home, he decided to go to the city park and "sleep it off" on a park bench. As Mr. Smith was sleeping, two juveniles rifled through his coat and pants pockets for his wallet. The two came away disappointed because their "take" was only $5. According to the passage, which of the statements given below is the most accurate?

    A. The theft would be considered robbery because, if Mr. Smith had been awake, the juveniles were prepared to use force to obtain the wallet.

    B. The theft is purely considered petty larceny because force was absent.

    C. The theft would be considered robbery since $5 cash was taken.

    D. The theft would not be considered robbery because neither juvenile was in unlawful possession of a weapon.

12. Jack Arnold was riding the bus, as was his daily routine in commuting to work. This particular Monday morning, however, a larger than usual crowd took the bus downtown. Jack elected to stand in the aisle to provide a seat for a mother and her infant. A few stops later, there was standing room only. This was, in Tom Bessinger's mind, the perfect opportunity to pick someone's pocket. Tom was a real pro at lifting wallets and not getting caught. The stop-and-go action of the bus allowed Mr. Bessinger to "accidentally" bump into his victim (in this case Mr. Arnold) and create the minor distraction needed to pick the wallet. Consequently, it was only when Mr. Arnold went to lunch that he discovered his wallet was missing. In this case, it can be said that Tom Bessinger committed:

    A. Robbery, because his bumping into the victim constitutes force.

    B. Larceny, because the victim was totally unaware of the theft.

    C. Robbery, because cash and credit cards were taken from the person of another.

    D. No crime was committed, because Mr. Arnold didn't report the incident to the authorities.

13. Linda Minn was riding the subway to the Fourteenth Street station at 11:30 P.M. At this hour the subway was practically empty of passengers. Rob White, a heroin addict, was on the same subway train and sensed opportunity when he saw Ms. Minn's purse lying on the seat beside her. As the train began to pull into the Fourteenth Street station, Mr. White nonchalantly walked over to Ms. Minn and grabbed her purse from the seat. Ms. Minn immediately began to yell for help. By the time anyone came to her assistance, Mr. White had fled the Fourteenth Street station. In this case, Mr. White could be charged with:

    A. Robbery, because the victim was fully aware of the theft.

    B. Robbery, because Ms. Minn was in a state of panic from the incident.

    C. Larceny, because Ms. Minn gave little resistance to the theft.

    D. Larceny, because even though Ms. Minn may have screamed, Mr. White did not use force to acquire the purse.

14. Having spent most of his life in the Bronx, Ben Harris was no stranger to violence. One evening, after visiting a corner grocery store, Mr. Harris was confronted by two juveniles who demanded his wallet. Rather than risk the potential of one of the offenders producing a weapon, Mr. Harris complied with their demands. A minute later, however, Mr. Harris decided he had all he was going to take. He pursued the two offenders and a fistfight quickly ensued. Mr. Harris was beaten badly and required immediate medical attention. In this case, what should the two juveniles be charged with?

   A. Larceny, because the aspect of force was not a precondition to Mr. Harris handing over his wallet

   B. Robbery, because the two juveniles had an altercation with Mr. Harris in connection with the theft of the wallet

   C. Larceny, because the two offenders were juveniles

   D. Robbery, because Mr. Harris thought that one or both of the juveniles may have been armed

15. All of the following were mentioned in the reading as forms of intimidation that preclude the use of force *except*:

   A. Extortion

   B. Bribery

   C. Libel

   D. Blackmail

Passage 4

According to Webster's dictionary, *duress* is defined as:

> *(1) compulsion by threat or force; coercion. (2) constraint or coercion of a degree sufficient to void any legal agreement entered into or any act performed under its influence. (3) forcible restraint, especially imprisonment.*

In other words, duress implies that an individual is not acting on his or her own free will. Specifically, under duress, someone may act wrongfully without criminal intent. However, whoever dictates the wrongful behavior of another by duress is responsible for the criminal intent.

Therefore, someone who commits a crime under a threat against his or her person will not be held accountable for the criminal act (murder being the exception). In the courts' view of the matter, the conduct of the person actually committing the crime is justifiable under such circumstances. However, once the threat ceases to exist, any further acts contributing to the commission of a crime can no longer be justifiable. The courts further point out that the threat perceived by anyone forced into conducting criminal activity must be in the present, not the future. The prospect of the threat of force being carried out at some future time if the individual in question doesn't cooperate is not reason enough for criminal behavior to continue. Any criminal act under such circumstances is committed with intent and is, therefore, subject to prosecution.

Answer questions 16–20 on the basis of Passage 4.

16. What would be an appropriate title for this passage?

   A. The complete definition of *duress* according to Webster's

   B. Duress, the perfect defense

   C. The definition and legal parameters of duress

   D. Duress, a synonym for criminal immunity

17. A person can commit most forms of criminal activity under duress without being guilty, except for:

    A. Robbery

    B. Burglary

    C. Libel

    D. Murder

18. Mary Adams, an assistant manager for a clothing retailer, was about to lock up the business for the evening when she was approached by two men. One of the men proceeded to tell Ms. Adams that they knew where she lived and, if she didn't go back into the store and empty the vault that contained the day's receipts of cash and checks, they would be at her house within the week to "finish" her and her family. Assuming that Ms. Adams complied with their demands while the two perpetrators remained outside the store, it would be considered that:

    A. Ms. Adams was indeed acting under duress and would be exempt from prosecution for theft

    B. Ms. Adams would not be viewed by the courts as acting under duress

    C. Ms. Adams was acting under duress because of the threat made to finish her and her family

    D. None of the above

19. Frank "Little Joe" Lorenzo was determined to join a local gang composed of his peers. After completing various rites, Mr. Lorenzo learned that his ultimate acceptance into the organization entailed his committing arson against a residence of the leader's choosing. Mr. Lorenzo was about to back out for moral reasons when one of the gang's members pulled out a gun and handed him a Molotov cocktail. Mr. Lorenzo was told in no uncertain terms that if he didn't follow through he was going to be shot. Mr. Lorenzo begrudgingly did commit the act and was ultimately inducted into the gang. Strangely enough, Mr. Lorenzo somewhat enjoyed burning the house. Under the circumstances, which of the following statements below would be considered true?

    A. Mr. Lorenzo would be guilty of arson because he enjoyed doing it.

    B. Mr. Lorenzo would be guilty of arson because he was the one who actually threw the Molotov cocktail.

    C. Mr. Lorenzo would not be considered guilty of arson because he is morally against a crime of that nature.

    D. Mr. Lorenzo would not be considered guilty of arson because he was coerced at gunpoint.

20. Mike Johnson was armed with a shotgun when he walked into Cascade Savings and Loan. Mr. Johnson walked directly up to Phil Stevens, a customer waiting in line to make a bank transaction, and ordered him to assist in the impending robbery. Mr. Stevens was handed several sacks and told to go teller to teller and empty each till. Mr. Stevens complied under the threat of being shot. Mr. Johnson began to have second thoughts about his actions and hastily left the premises. Mr. Stevens saw Johnson retreat out of the building, but he went ahead with what he was told to do. In this case, Mr. Stevens:

    A. Could be charged with robbery, because duress ceased to apply when Johnson left the building.

    B. Could not be charged with robbery, because he was under duress to comply with Johnson's demands.

    C. Could be charged with robbery, because regardless of the circumstances, Mr. Stevens should not have aided Mr. Johnson in the commission of a robbery.

    D. Could not be charged with robbery, because Mr. Stevens was an innocent bystander randomly selected to assist in a crime.

ANSWER SHEET FOR READING COMPREHENSION SAMPLE QUESTIONS

1. (A) (B) (C) (D)   8. (A) (B) (C) (D)   15. (A) (B) (C) (D)
2. (A) (B) (C) (D)   9. (A) (B) (C) (D)   16. (A) (B) (C) (D)
3. (A) (B) (C) (D)   10. (A) (B) (C) (D)   17. (A) (B) (C) (D)
4. (A) (B) (C) (D)   11. (A) (B) (C) (D)   18. (A) (B) (C) (D)
5. (A) (B) (C) (D)   12. (A) (B) (C) (D)   19. (A) (B) (C) (D)
6. (A) (B) (C) (D)   13. (A) (B) (C) (D)   20. (A) (B) (C) (D)
7. (A) (B) (C) (D)   14. (A) (B) (C) (D)

Answers can be found on page 71.

VOCABULARY

The next twenty-five questions will test your vocabulary. Study how the word in the question is used in the context of the sentence. In many cases, the meaning of unfamiliar terms can be discerned. If this method still leaves doubt, attempt to break the word down using the etymology tables provided earlier. Between these two methods, most words seen in entry-level State Police officer exams can be determined.

1. Establishing the point at which to arrest someone is an important factor in determining the *admissibility* of evidence. *Admissibility* most nearly means:

    A. Condition

    B. Likelihood of being allowed

    C. Necessity

    D. Interpretation

2. The prospect of imminent danger to either the public or law enforcement personnel constitutes *exigent* circumstances. *Exigent* most nearly means:

    A. Broad and far-reaching

    B. Extenuating

    C. Requiring immediate action

    D. Unfortunate

3. A *cursory* search of the area was made prior to leaving. *Cursory* most nearly means:

    A. Extensive

    B. Thorough

    C. Superficial

    D. Detailed

4. Lawfully impounded inventory should not be used as a *pretext* to search for evidence. *Pretext* most nearly means:

    A. Precondition

    B. Means

    C. Rule

    D. Excuse

5. The Exclusionary Rule was adopted for the purpose of upholding the *integrity* of the courts. *Integrity* most nearly means:

    A. Moral character

    B. Superiority

    C. Fairness

    D. Improbable

6. The report said that the accused was convinced that the danger of serious harm was *imminent*. *Imminent* most nearly means:

    A. Justifiable

    B. Impending

    C. Remote

    D. Irrelevant

7. The landmark case would serve as a *precedent* for future court rulings. *Precedent* most nearly means:

    A. Source of confusion

    B. Majority view

    C. Visible reminder

    D. None of the above

8. The State of New York could not try Gary Willhouse for kidnapping because it did not have *jurisdiction*. *Jurisdiction* most nearly means:

    A. Justification

    B. Authority

    C. Enough power

    D. Probable cause

9. The theft of professional services and public utilities is still considered theft of property, albeit *intangible* property, whether taken by deception or by failure to pay for such services. *Intangible* most nearly means:

    A. Insignificant

    B. Invaluable

    C. Not corporeal

    D. White collar

10. The evidence was ruled *immaterial* to the case at hand. *Immaterial* most nearly means:

    A. Not pertinent

    B. Admissible

    C. Substantive

    D. Relevant

11. The fact that Mr. Wilson had been convicted twice for trafficking in narcotics lessened his *credibility* as a star witness. *Credibility* most nearly means:

    A. Trustworthiness

    B. Anxiety

    C. Incredulity

    D. Demure

12. Violence was so common in one neighborhood that residents soon became *indifferent* to the occurrences. *Indifferent* most nearly means:

    A. Attentive

    B. Apathetic

    C. Intolerant

    D. Indignant

13. Cheryl was quite *overt* in her sexual advances toward an undercover officer. *Overt* most nearly means:

    A. Shy

    B. Blunt

    C. Conspicuous

    D. Slow

14. There can be fairly substantial *disparities* in what police officers earn depending on where they live and serve. *Disparities* most nearly means:

    A. Penalties

    B. Similarities

    C. Compensations

    D. Differences

15. Detective Peterson was hoping his actions would not be *misconstrued* as aggressive. *Misconstrued* most nearly means:

    A. Misinterpreted

    B. Judged

    C. Criticized

    D. Analyzed

16. Officer Mitchell demonstrated flagrant *incompetence* by not mirandizing the suspect at the time of the arrest. *Incompetence* most nearly means:

    A. Inability

    B. Inhibition

    C. Incongruity

    D. Disregard

17. It is *imperative* that someone be told at the time of his or her arrest what specifically it is that he or she is being arrested for. *Imperative* most nearly means:

    A. Unimportant

    B. Immaterial

    C. Compulsory

    D. Considerate

18. Officer Miller experienced some degree of *trepidation* every time he had to unholster his handgun in the line of duty. *Trepidation* most nearly means:

    A. Having power

    B. Hesitation

    C. Quandary

    D. Trembling

19. The buildings in the downtown core were pretty *dilapidated. Dilapidated* most nearly means:

    A. Modern

    B. Tall

    C. Neglected

    D. New

20. The purpose of investigative detention is to resolve an *ambiguous* circumstance. *Ambiguous* most nearly means:

    A. Infallible

    B. Uncertain

    C. Argumentative

    D. Interesting

21. Officers are instructed not to act *condescendingly* toward citizens in the line of duty. *Condescending* most nearly means:

    A. Discourteous

    B. Harsh

    C. Unprofessional

    D. Patronizing

22. Unconscious intoxicated persons should be transported to a nearby medical facility by an ambulance instead of a patrol car to alleviate potential civil *liability. Liability* most nearly means:

    A. Responsibility

    B. Exemption

    C. Scrutiny

    D. Considerations

23. The phone calls were intended to *intimidate* the witness. *Intimidate* most nearly means:

    A. Comfort

    B. Ostracize

    C. Frighten

    D. Relieve

24. Building containment for the two officers was nearly impossible because there were too many means of *egress* for the suspect. *Egress* most nearly means:

    A. Entrance

    B. Exits

    C. Approach

    D. Attack

25. The purpose of traffic control is twofold: to *expedite* traffic and to eliminate potential traffic conflicts. *Expedite* most nearly means:

    A. Deter

    B. Speed the progress of

    C. Prevent congestion

    D. Monitor

ANSWER SHEET FOR VOCABULARY SAMPLE QUESTIONS

1. Ⓐ Ⓑ Ⓒ Ⓓ
2. Ⓐ Ⓑ Ⓒ Ⓓ
3. Ⓐ Ⓑ Ⓒ Ⓓ
4. Ⓐ Ⓑ Ⓒ Ⓓ
5. Ⓐ Ⓑ Ⓒ Ⓓ
6. Ⓐ Ⓑ Ⓒ Ⓓ
7. Ⓐ Ⓑ Ⓒ Ⓓ
8. Ⓐ Ⓑ Ⓒ Ⓓ
9. Ⓐ Ⓑ Ⓒ Ⓓ

10. Ⓐ Ⓑ Ⓒ Ⓓ
11. Ⓐ Ⓑ Ⓒ Ⓓ
12. Ⓐ Ⓑ Ⓒ Ⓓ
13. Ⓐ Ⓑ Ⓒ Ⓓ
14. Ⓐ Ⓑ Ⓒ Ⓓ
15. Ⓐ Ⓑ Ⓒ Ⓓ
16. Ⓐ Ⓑ Ⓒ Ⓓ
17. Ⓐ Ⓑ Ⓒ Ⓓ
18. Ⓐ Ⓑ Ⓒ Ⓓ

19. Ⓐ Ⓑ Ⓒ Ⓓ
20. Ⓐ Ⓑ Ⓒ Ⓓ
21. Ⓐ Ⓑ Ⓒ Ⓓ
22. Ⓐ Ⓑ Ⓒ Ⓓ
23. Ⓐ Ⓑ Ⓒ Ⓓ
24. Ⓐ Ⓑ Ⓒ Ⓓ
25. Ⓐ Ⓑ Ⓒ Ⓓ

Answers can be found on page 72.

ANSWERS TO READING COMPREHENSION QUESTIONS

1. *D.* Only D best describes the scope of the article. Selections A and C are, at best, ambiguous in defining the content of the reading. Selection B was, in fact, mentioned in the passage, but it only addresses what an officer is not to do rather than providing a more complete overview of what is involved in evidence collection, as the passage does.

2. *C.* Circumspect and expeditious are the correct selections. The article points out that an officer has to look around a crime scene carefully and then be expeditious or prompt in gathering the evidence found in order to avoid potential contamination.

3. *B.* Selection B is correct because the officer may have inadvertently damaged crucial evidence or even created false leads for investigators if, in fact, the crowbar on the floor was not the tool used to gain entry. Selection A may seem correct, but Officer Gregory, no matter how good his intentions may have been, actually moved the evidence from its original position. Selection C is not a viable concern for Officer Gregory. Selection D further exemplifies the potential for contaminating crucial evidence (i.e., misplacement of physical evidence).

4. *A.* Selection A is the correct answer because the article mentioned that organic compounds are more prone to deterioration with time and temperature extremes and cites blood as an example. Hair is considered organic in nature as well, but it does not have the same kind of enzymatic or bacterial breakdown as blood. The remaining selections are inorganic and not subject to the same kind of degradation from the elements.

5. *C.* Only C is considered as being false. The rest of the alternatives provided are, in fact, underlying objectives for authorities to rope off a given crime scene.

6. *B.* Selection A was indeed discussed, but it fails to include the entire content of the article. Selections C and D touch only on specifics and do not properly summarize the passage's underlying meaning.

7. *B.* Selection B is the correct interpretation of the word *incident* as used in the reading.

8. *C.* Statements A and B are patently false according to the *Chimel v. California* decision. Selection D is false also because the passenger seats are considered to be within the immediate reach of the suspect and, therefore, Officer McClintock is indeed within his rights to search that area without a warrant.

9. *D.* Selections A, B, and C are all factors that define areas within an arrestee's reach and from which a weapon may be obtained. After the *Chimel v. California* decision, courts take three factors into consideration when determining what a reasonable search without a warrant may entail.

10. *C.* Selection A is correct, but the question asks for the most accurate statement of the four given. This selection would have been more complete had it specified that his Fourth Amendment rights were violated as well. Selection B is incorrect because warrants are very specific with regard to what can be searched. They are not broad in definition. Selection D is incorrect because it was the Supreme Court of the United States, not the California Supreme Court, that reversed a lower court's decision in Chimel's case.

11. *B.* Selection A is incorrect because the intent of the juveniles, in the event the victim woke up, was never established in the passage. The reader can only speculate as to the outcome. Selection C is incorrect because the dollar value of property taken from a person is not the determining factor in deciding whether the crime is robbery or larceny. Selection D is incorrect for two reasons, the first being that this issue wasn't mentioned in the passage, and the second that the threat of force can be accomplished without the physical presence of a weapon.

12. *B.* Selection A is incorrect because Tom Bessinger's method of operation is not considered force or the threat of force, particularly when the victim is unaware of the theft in the first place. Selection C is wrong because the reading didn't stipulate if there were cash or credit cards involved. Additionally, the taking of cash or credit cards from the person of another is, by itself, not a definition of robbery according to the passage. Selection D is incorrect because a crime did take place; it just wasn't discovered or reported immediately.

13. *D.* Neither statement A nor statement B constitutes grounds for Mr. White to be charged with robbery. Selection C is incorrect because Ms. Minn offered no resistance to Mr. White during the theft.

14. *A.* Selection A is correct. Despite what Mr. Harris may have perceived as being a threat (as suggested in C), the fact is that the pair did not use force or the threat of force to obtain his wallet. They merely demanded he hand it over without the predication of dire consequences if he did not comply. Choice B is incorrect because the altercation took place after the theft. The altercation itself was not a precondition to the juveniles obtaining the wallet. Choice C is wrong because the age of the offenders has no bearing on whether a theft is considered a larceny or a robbery.

15. *B.* Only bribery was not mentioned in the reading.

16. *C.* Selection A was mentioned in the reading, but it fails to describe the contents of the entire passage. Selections B and D were neither mentioned nor implied in this reading.

17. *D.* Murder was pointed out in the passage as being the one exception. In a court's view, it is necessary to take one's own life before that of another.

18. *B.* Statements A and C both assume that Ms. Adams, a future defendant in a court of law, could use duress as a defense against the charge of theft. While it was true that the two men did make a threat against her to coerce her cooperation in the theft, it was done so in future terms. In other words, they would be back at a later time to execute the threat against her. The courts would view that she also had ample time to have contacted and involved the authorities to stop such a plot. She also might have been able to call the police from inside the store while the two men were waiting outside.

19. *D.* Choice A is incorrect because Mr. Lorenzo's change of feelings regarding the arson is not the issue that determines whether or not he is guilty. The fact that he was coerced under gunpoint to commit the crime is the crucial point. Choice B is true in that Mr. Lorenzo did indeed throw the Molotov cocktail, but the important point is that intent was absent because he was forced to commit the act. Choice C is incorrect for the same reason given for A.

20. *A.* Statement B is true up to the point Mr. Johnson leaves the premises. At that point, the defense of "under duress" would no longer apply. Choice C is incorrect because Mr. Stevens was under the threat of death to comply, circumstances understandable in a court of law for Mr. Stevens to participate in a robbery without demonstrating intent. However, circumstances changed at the point Mr. Johnson left the Savings and Loan. Selection D is true as far as what actually happened to Phil Stevens, but it does not necessarily preclude his liability for assisting Mr. Johnson.

ANSWERS TO VOCABULARY SAMPLE QUESTIONS

Note: The answers have been provided for the vocabulary section without explanation. If further reference is needed, consult a dictionary.

1. *B*	4. *D*	7. *D*	10. *A*	13. *C*	16. *A*	19. *C*	22. *A*	25. *B*
2. *C*	5. *A*	8. *B*	11. *A*	14. *D*	17. *C*	20. *B*	23. *C*	
3. *C*	6. *B*	9. *C*	12. *B*	15. *A*	18. *D*	21. *D*	24. *B*	

Your score for each exercise would be as follows:

Reading comprehension exercises:
    18–20 correct—EXCELLENT
    16–17 correct—GOOD
    13–15 correct—FAIR
    Less than 13 correct—POOR

Vocabulary exercises:
    23–25 correct—EXCELLENT
    21–22 correct—GOOD
    19–20 correct—FAIR
    Less than 19 correct—POOR

Chapter 4

Situational Judgment and Reasoning

Of all the sections in this study guide, this one covers the bulk of questions seen on most exams. The types of questions involving judgment and reasoning are varied, but include such topics as:

- interdepartmental protocol

- public relations

- appropriate use of equipment and related safety practices

- how to best handle emergency situations

- chart and table interpretation

- sentence-order logistics

- composite sketch cross comparisons

All questions draw upon your ability to think and reason.

The first type of question involves general police procedure and policy. These questions do not necessitate complete familiarity with police procedures. Rather, enough information is provided within the question to answer it solely on the basis of common sense. Keep in mind that the problem in the question must be identified first. How to best solve that problem within the scope of the alternatives provided in the quickest and safest manner should be apparent.

Questions of this nature can be fairly difficult to study for. Common sense or power of reasoning is not something that can be learned from a study guide. The best advice that can be offered is to read each question carefully and completely. Often words such as *always, except, not, least* and *first* can entirely change the meaning of the question. Any answers that seem to be illegal or contradictory or pose a threat to the public or police personnel are probably incorrect. Options that appear self-serving or contrary to the goal of the police to serve and protect are probably wrong as well. Look at the example given below and determine the correct answer.

> Police officers are told that consent searches can be conducted in lieu of a warrant provided that the person who granted the search has the authority to do so. The courts also hold that permission must be knowingly, voluntarily, and intelligently given to legitimize such searches. Which of the consent searches given below would be considered the most questionable in view of these prerequisites?

A. A parent giving police officers the consent to search the guest bathroom used by their teenage son

B. A landlord permitting police to search a common storage area shared by tenants and himself

C. An hysterical wife who permits police to search her husband's sports car

D. All of the above constitute legitimate consent searches

If you chose C, you are correct. A parent, landlord, and wife are all parties who have joint access to or control of the property in question. However, the wife's state of mind may preclude a competent waiver of rights.

A second type of question seen on exams involves the use of tables or charts that contain specific information. On the basis of what is given, correlations or relationships may need to be extrapolated, or the figures they contain may need to be understood and recognized for their significance. Look at the sample give below.

Lieutenant Blackmore was revising crime reports compiled for the month of September in Sector Thirteen. Incident report details are as follows:

Date	Day	Crime Involved	Time Occurred	Street Location
9/1	Wednesday	Burglary	1:17 A.M	2200 block of 1st Avenue
9/2	Thursday	Burglary	10:39 P.M.	100 block of 3rd Avenue
9/6	Monday	Malicious Mischief	2:15 A.M.	3300 block of 16th Avenue
9/10	Friday	Larceny	3:30 P.M.	1600 block of 3rd Street
9/10	Friday	Rape	9:36 P.M.	300 block of 16th Avenue
9/15	Wednesday	Burglary	3:45 A.M.	1500 block of 1st Avenue
9/18	Saturday	Malicious Mischief	5:00 P.M.	1200 block of 3rd Avenue
9/22	Wednesday	Burglary	2:20 A.M.	3800 block of 1st Avenue
9/23	Thursday	Domestic Dispute	5:15 P.M	2300 block of 16th Avenue
9/25	Saturday	Malicious Mischief	12:29 A.M.	1400 block of 1st Street
9/26	Sunday	Malicious Mischief	5:45 P.M.	1700 block of 3rd Avenue
9/26	Sunday	Malicious Mischief	7:50 A.M.	1900 block of 3rd Avenue
9/27	Monday	Burglary	10:20 P.M.	3300 block of 16th Avenue
9/28	Tuesday	Burglary	1:52 P.M.	500 block of 1st Street

Shift schedules are as follows:

Tour I   8:00 A.M. – 4:00 P.M.

Tour II   4:00 P.M. – Midnight

Tour III Midnight – 8:00 A.M.

If Lieutenant Blackmore wanted to assign extra patrols in an effort to reduce the incidence of burglary and malicious mischief, which of the following actions would most likely achieve that goal?

A. Assign a Tour II patrol unit to 1st Avenue on Wednesdays and a Tour II patrol unit to 3rd Avenue during the weekends

B. Assign a Tour III patrol unit to 1st Avenue on Wednesdays and a Tour II patrol unit to 3rd Avenue during the weekends

C. Assign a Tour II patrol unit to 3rd Street on Thursdays and a Tour II patrol unit to 3rd Street on Fridays

D. Assign a Tour I patrol unit to 1st Avenue on Wednesdays and a Tour III patrol unit to 3rd Avenue during the weekends

If you selected B, you were correct. According to the chart, burglaries occur most frequently early Wednesday mornings on 1st Avenue during the third tour shift (1:17 A.M., 3:45 A.M., and 2:20 A.M.). The other burglaries can be considered isolated incidents that demonstrate no discernable patterns. Malicious mischief incidents, on the other hand, occur most frequently on weekend evenings on 3rd Avenue during the second tour shift (Saturday 5:00 P.M. and Sunday 5:45 P.M.). Again, the remainder of cases could be considered isolated incidents, and for the purpose of the question, they can be ignored. Trends are what are important. If appropriate correlations are made, emphasis patrols will stand a better chance of being an effective deterrent.

Another form of judgment and reasoning question often seen is sentence-order logistics. Sentence-order logistics simply involves four or five separate sentences that, when combined properly, describe an incident found in a police report. You will need to rearrange randomly ordered sentences into their proper chronological order. Look at the example given below and try to determine the correct sequence of events.

Detective Connelly was assigned to investigate the homicide of Don Merriweather, the owner of a small downtown pawn shop. Detective Connelly's incident report contained the following five sentences:

1. Mr. Merriweather died at 6:30 P.M. at Methodist General Hospital as a result of the attack.
2. Mr. Merriweather resisted the assailant's demands and was consequently shot twice in the chest.
3. Under the threat of being shot, Mr. Merriweather was told to open the safe.
4. The assailant, currently unknown, forced entry through the back door.
5. The unknown perpetrator attempted but could not gain access to the back room vault.

The easiest strategy is to determine what took place first and last. In this case, the perpetrator had to break into the store first to set off the chain of events that occurred. The result, of course, is Mr. Merriweather's death. By looking at the choices of sentence arrangement below, the correct answer can be arrived at fairly easily through the process of elimination.

A.	3	4	1	2	5
B.	2	3	4	5	1
C.	4	1	5	3	2
D.	4	5	3	2	1

If you selected the combination of Sentences 4, 5, 3, 2, 1 you were correct. Only D lists the fourth sentence as the beginning of the incident and Sentence 1 as the end. Since one of the answers must be correct, it can be confidently assumed that D is the correct answer. The other three sentences are insignificant for the most part. The key here, however, is that you must be sure of what took place in the beginning and at the end. Misinterpreting one or both of these will in all likelihood cause you to pick the wrong answer.

Unfortunately, not all questions will be as easy as this example. Some questions will have two or more answers that properly account for the beginning and end of a hypothetical incident. Those choices are the ones that deserve further scrutiny. Read the story as prescribed by each of these choices and see if they follow a logical sequence. Chances are, one of the stories will seem somewhat out of place and should therefore be eliminated from further considerations. Look at the second example provided below and try to apply this technique.

Officer Martin was writing an incident report regarding a suicide attempt. His report contained the following five sentences.

1. Ms. Hargrove dialed 911 and explained that her boss, Mr. Abernathy, was on a fourth story ledge threatening to jump.

2. Mr. Abernathy had obvious reservations about jumping by the way he was clinging to the ledge.

3. Mr. Abernathy was arrested for attempted suicide and sent to Eastern State Hospital for psychological evaluation.

4. Mr. Abernathy told his secretary, Ms. Hargrove, she would be well taken care of after his death.

5. I persuaded Mr. Abernathy not to jump.

A.	3	4	2	1	5
B.	4	5	2	1	3
C.	4	1	2	5	3
D.	4	2	5	1	3

It should have been fairly evident that Sentence 4 took place first and Sentence 3 last. That, by itself, eliminates A. However, the three remaining choices list Sentences 4 and 3 as first and last, respectively. So, go to B, read the sentences in that order, and see if that story makes sense. In this case, Sentence 5 seems clearly out of context following the fact that Mr. Abernathy had just told his secretary she was going to be well cared for after his death. At that point, how could his secretary understand his true motives until he was actually out on the window ledge? Also, that "I" persuaded Mr. Abernathy not to jump statement is made by Officer Martin. This story seems to be disjointed, so it can be eliminated as a viable choice. Choice C seems very plausible as the correct answer, but it would be premature to come to that conclusion without giving D its due consideration. Here again, Sentence 2 following Sentence 4 seems somewhat out of order. The same holds true for Sentence 5 following Sentence 2. The real clincher is Sentence 1 following Sentence 5. How can Mr. Abernathy be persuaded not to jump by Officer Martin when Ms. Hargrove hasn't even summoned the police yet? Therefore, D can be eliminated, and it can be assumed that C has to be the correct answer. This type of question is really not very difficult if you reason them out in this manner. Just keep a good perspective on what the story is about, and don't rush your conclusions.

The other form of judgment and reasoning questions you may encounter on the exam is composite-sketch cross comparison. You will be given a sketch of a suspect, accompanied by sketches of four other people. You are to select the one out of the four sketches given that is actually the suspect attempting to disguise him or herself. It is important to note here that it is generally assumed that the suspect in question has not undergone any surgical procedures to change physical appearance. Working on that premise, ears, eyes, nose, mouth, cheekbone structure, chin, scars, and facial lines will not vary. However, the suspect may grow a beard or moustache, change hair styles, or wear eyeglasses or various assortments of clothing in an attempt to conceal his or her true identity.

As you compare these sketches, try to overlook these features and concentrate only on those aspects that cannot easily be changed. Usually, one or two of the composite sketches provided are quite apparently not sketches of the suspect. However, the remaining two sketches can have very subtle yet discernable differences that challenge a test taker's judgment skills. It can't be emphasized enough to focus on only those characteristics that cannot be changed.

One last hint here: As you work through these kinds of questions, cross out those sketches or choices that you have concluded cannot be the suspect. This will eliminate the potential for any confusion or backtracking and will ultimately narrow the field down to the correct choice.

When you work your way through the exercises provided in this section of the study guide, use your best judgment to discern the right answers. The correct answers, complete with explanations, are provided at the end of the exercises.

SAMPLE QUESTIONS ON SITUATIONAL JUDGMENT AND REASONING

1. The National Advisory Commission on Criminal Justice Standards and Goals states that every police agency should immediately establish programs that encourage members of the public to take an active role in preventing crime, provide information leading to the arrest and conviction of criminal offenders, facilitate the identification and recovery of stolen property, and increase liaison with private industry in security efforts. What does the above statement imply?

    A. Citizen involvement is imperative in crime prevention.

    B. Citizens better educated about the law should take criminal matters into their own hands.

    C. Crime should be the major concern of the criminal justice system and only a secondary consideration for the community.

    D. Planning, education, and training of the citizenry in crime prevention will lessen the overall workload for the criminal justice system.

2. What is the most compelling reason State Patrol officers must be brief, yet accurate, in relaying information over a police radio network?

    A. To appear professional to others who may be listening.

    B. Because air time is expensive and therefore it saves the department considerable expense.

    C. Protracted messages may be misinterpreted or misconstrued.

    D. Since many departments use the same radio network, officers should not tie up the line with long messages.

3. Troopers are told not to appear at places within their patrol jurisdiction at regular intervals. What is the best reason for this policy?

    A. A Trooper can more thoroughly patrol his or her beat.

    B. Staggered inspection times give the public the impression that Troopers are constantly on patrol.

    C. A regular routine inspires complacency.

    D. Established patterns of patrol make it easier for the criminal element to go about its business without the threat of getting caught.

4. During a routine patrol, Trooper Matthews comes across a downed power line in the middle of a busy roadway. No arcing or burning is apparent. What is the appropriate way for Trooper Matthews to handle such a situation?

    A. Secure the area immediately and call the electric utility repair department.

    B. Pick up the wire and move it to the side of the road where it would no longer pose a hazard to traffic.

    C. Attempt to move the wire to the side of the road with a stick or other such object to avoid direct contact.

    D. File a report on the matter and then resume patrol.

5. While you are off duty and attending a Sunday luncheon, a woman learns you are a State Patrol officer. She then explains that a traffic citation she received earlier in the week was totally unjustified. What should you do?

    A. Tell her that tickets are never issued unless they are totally warranted.

    B. Explain that since you were not there at the time of the issuance, it would be difficult to say one way or the other.

    C. Tell her that you will investigate the matter as soon as you begin your shift.

    D. Tell her you will fix the ticket since she comes across as an honest individual.

6. Most witnesses to traffic incidents or some form of criminal activity are ineffective observers. Unlike a police officer, they lack the developed skill to remember in detail the people who break the law or the events involved. Which of the statements provided below would accurately summarize the contents of this passage?

    A. Police officers have recall abilities that are over and above those of the public they serve.

    B. As a general rule, witnesses to crime have lower mental capabilities.

    C. Violations of the law are not always recognized by people. Consequently, details of a crime are usually sketchy.

    D. Most people are not truly cognizant of their surroundings.

7. If it is known that over 80 percent of the people are right-handed, it can be reasonably assumed that an officer's safest approach to a suspect wielding a gun in a nighttime situation would be:

    A. Stay low and go to the suspect's right.

    B. Stay low and go to the left.

    C. Stay low and go to the right.

    D. Approach the suspect in a direct line.

8. State Patrol Officers Rick Gaston and Harvey Duper pull over a car for a minor traffic infraction. The driver of the vehicle shoots Officer Duper in the shoulder and drives away. Which of the following immediate actions by Officer Gaston would be appropriate?

    A. Give immediate chase to the suspect vehicle.

    B. Exchange gunfire so long as the suspect has not driven further than one block away.

    C. Attend to his partner's injuries and radio for immediate medical assistance, then relay a description of the suspect and vehicle, including the direction in which it was last seen heading.

    D. Drive his partner to the closest emergency facility for medical assistance.

9. Trooper Milton Hastings is currently investigating a minor traffic accident. A young woman runs up to him and claims that a stranger is in the basement of her home. What would be the best way for Officer Hastings to handle this situation?

    A. Continue with the accident investigation and assume, since the young woman could not offer any proof, the story was probably fabricated.

    B. Drop the accident investigation and immediately go to the young woman's home.

    C. Continue with the accident investigation after radioing for another unit to respond.

    D. Tell the young woman that he will go to her residence immediately after completing the reports necessary for the accident at hand.

10. State Patrol Officer Frank Milligan was in pursuit of someone who had just committed a felony. Vehicle speeds were in excess of 85 miles per hour when the suspect veered off a frontage road and headed for a residential area, maintaining a high speed. At this point, Officer Milligan's best action would be which of the following?

    A. Slow down to a reasonable speed and radio dispatch where the vehicle was last seen heading.

    B. Break off pursuit and attempt to locate the suspect again in another area.

    C. Attempt to stop the suspect vehicle with whatever means necessary because of the risk posed to the public.

    D. This is reason enough for the officer to utilize his firearm.

11. Trooper Brice Miller is working DWI patrol in the Westminster district when he pulls over a suspected drunk driver. Upon requesting identification, he learns that the driver is an off-duty police officer from a neighboring district. What would be the best way for Trooper Miller to handle this situation?

    A. Put the off-duty officer through the same kind of field sobriety test given to others; if suspicions are confirmed by the test results, book the officer for DWI as he would anyone else.

    B. Take his keys away and escort him home.

    C. Tell the driver to go directly home and not make a report of the matter.

    D. Contact his supervisor and request instructions on what action should be taken.

12. If a police department wanted to project a more positive image to the public, which of the following would be the most effective means to accomplish this goal?

    A. Treat persons suspected of committing felonies with a little less force and more dignity.

    B. Demonstrate equal enforcement of the criminal code as established by the state with respect to all persons charged.

    C. Address select community groups and meetings and explain the department's intentions.

    D. Police officers should be professional, courteous, and helpful when conducting routine traffic enforcement.

13. Late one Friday evening, State Patrol Officer Kent comes across a man who is unconscious in an alley. Further scrutiny reveals that the subject has an empty syringe clenched in his hand. Officer Kent attempts to wake the man but is unable to do so. Which of the actions given below would be the most appropriate for Officer Kent to undertake next?

    A. Arrest the man for possession of illegal drug paraphernalia.

    B. Ignore the situation and let the man wake up of his own accord.

    C. Take the man into protective custody and transport him to a regional detoxification treatment facility.

    D. Call for an ambulance immediately to transport the subject to a medical facility.

14. An off-duty Trooper attending a neighborhood social function is approached by one of the neighbors and told that obscene phone calls have been a real problem recently. What is the best advice the officer could give to this person?

    A. Call the phone company and notify officials there first. Phone numbers and telephone listings can be changed.

    B. Try to outdo the caller in terms of vulgarities and obscenities.

    C. Encourage the caller to call back in the hopes of tracing the offender.

    D. Give no advice whatsoever because he is off duty and such a discussion would detract from the festivities.

15. Which of the cases listed below would probably be considered the most difficult for law enforcement officials to investigate?

    A. Auto theft

    B. Malicious mischief

    C. Child abuse/neglect

    D. Securities fraud

16. Trooper Clinton is assigned traffic control at a construction site where street signs have recently been changed. Officer Clinton observes a motorist commit an infraction. What should Officer Clinton do?

    A. Ignore the incident because of the recent changes.

    B. Pull over the offender and issue a warning.

    C. Pull over the offender and issue a citation.

    D. Take note of the license plate, and if the same motorist commits the infraction again, then issue a citation.

17. Fingerprints are important in evidence collection. Latent prints are described as the indistinct impressions left by the perspiration or oily secretions that are exuded from the fingers onto those objects that are touched directly. Which of the following conditions would have a detrimental effect on the quality of a latent print?

    A. Hot and humid weather

    B. Warm and dry weather

    C. Cold and dry weather

    D. Weather has no bearing on the quality of latent prints

18. Some states issue driver's licenses that incorporate a lenticular security feature on the part of the license that includes the operator's signature and birth date. This feature is simply a series of raised bumps on the card's laminate. What is the most probable reason for doing this?

    A. It serves as identification for blind persons.

    B. It hinders potential alterations.

    C. It can still provide the information even after years of wear.

    D. It helps to prevent a driver's license from inadvertently being lost.

19. You are assigned traffic control at a particular intersection for a parade. An ambulance with its emergency lights and sirens going needs to cross the intersection. What should you do?

    A. Redirect the ambulance to circumvent the parade route.

    B. Temporarily stop the parade and allow the ambulance to proceed through the intersection.

    C. Call your immediate supervisor for direction or permission to stop the parade.

    D. Direct the ambulance driver to proceed to a point at least one block in front of the parade procession and then attempt the crossing.

20. State Patrol Officer Leslie Black decided to have lunch in one of the restaurants on her beat. After she finished eating, the restaurant owner refused to accept any money for the meal, explaining he wished to show his appreciation for her presence in the neighborhood. Under the circumstances, what should Officer Black do?

    A. Offer her humblest appreciation and make certain witnesses are not present.

    B. Insist that she be allowed to pay for the meal or threaten to arrest the restaurant owner on bribery charges.

    C. Leave enough money to cover the meal and then notify her supervisor regarding the matter.

    D. Patronize the establishment more often to show her appreciation.

Answer questions 21 and 22 on the basis of the pie chart presented below.

1997 FISCAL BUDGET APPROPRIATIONS FOR JOHNSON COUNTY DEPARTMENT OF PUBLIC SAFETY ARE AS FOLLOWS:

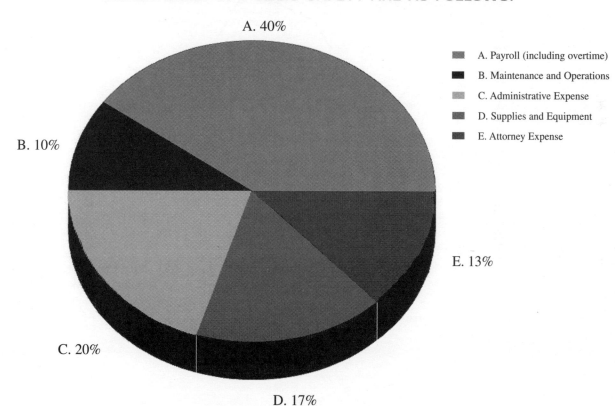

A. 40%

B. 10%

C. 20%

D. 17%

E. 13%

A. Payroll (including overtime)
B. Maintenance and Operations
C. Administrative Expense
D. Supplies and Equipment
E. Attorney Expense

21. Which of the following statements would be considered true with respect to Johnson County's budgetary appropriations?

    A. Both D and E represent the largest outlay of expense.

    B. Both A and B represent the largest outlay of expense.

    C. Supplies and Equipment represent the smallest of financial outlays.

    D. Both Administrative Expense and Payroll represent the largest outlay of expense.

22. All of the following statements are false except:

    A. Attorney expenses for the department is the third largest outlay, according to the chart provided.

    B. Supplies and Equipment in combination with Administrative expense constitute a larger percentage of the overall budget as opposed to Payroll.

    C. Administrative expense is second only to Payroll in terms of the overall budget.

    D. Maintenance and Operations comprises one quarter of the entire budget.

The line graph below represents a report compilation for a State Patrol district over a five-year period. Answer questions 23–25 based on the following data.

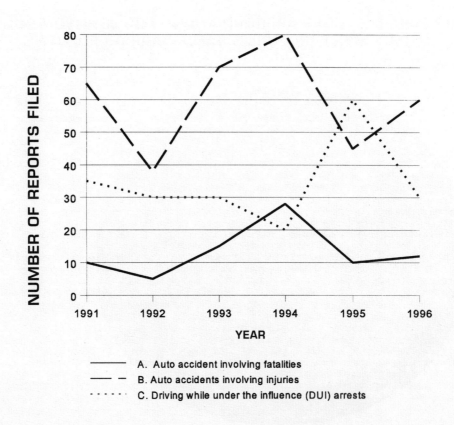

    A. Auto accident involving fatalities
    B. Auto accidents involving injuries
    C. Driving while under the influence (DUI) arrests

23. Which year clearly demonstrated that drunk driving emphasis patrols yielded tangible benefits with regard to public safety?

    A. 1992

    B. 1994

    C. 1995

    D. 1996

24. Public safety-wise, which year was conclusively the worst?

    A. 1996

    B. 1994

    C. 1993

    D. 1992

25. Assuming that population figures within the State Patrol District remained roughly the same over the five-year study, what year in particular most likely reflected either better than normal road conditions or the prospect that motorists exercised more caution while driving?

    A. 1992

    B. 1993

    C. 1995

    D. 1996

Below is a bar graph that represents statewide issuances of speeding citations by the State Patrol during a given 24-hour period. Answer questions 26–28 on the basis of the following data.

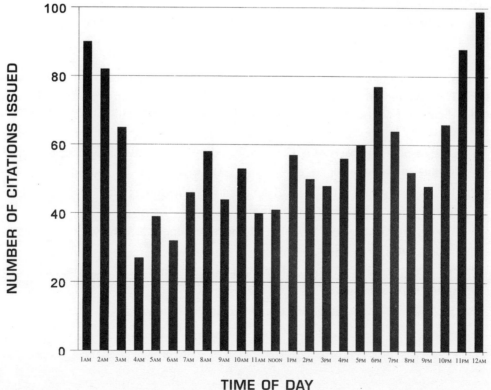

Shift rotation for the State Patrol is as follows:

Tour I   6:00 A.M. – 2:00 P.M.

Tour II   2:00 P.M. – 10:00 P.M.

Tour III   10:00 P.M. – 6:00 A.M.

26. According to the statistics provided, which of the following assumptions has merit?

    A. There are about twice as many speeding citations issued in the early afternoon hours as opposed to late morning hours.

    B. Perhaps for visibility reasons, motorists are much more cautious about speeding at night.

    C. "Rush hour" for the day would unequivocally be from noon to 1:00 P.M.

    D. Motorists tend to drive somewhat more conservatively during the late morning hours as opposed to late evening hours.

27. The lowest incidence of speeding occurred during which State Patrol shift rotation?

    A. Tour I

    B. Tour II

    C. Tour III

    D. A determination cannot be made from the data provided

28. Select the statement below that least accurately represents the information provided in the study.

    A. Tours I and II issued roughly the same number of speeding citations during their first hour of duty.

    B. Among the three shifts, Tour III issued the largest proportion of speeding tickets.

    C. There were significant increases in speeding incidents at about the half-way mark into each of the three shifts.

    D. The 10:00 P.M. – 6:00 A.M. shift, without question, demonstrated the widest variance with respect to speeding ticket issuances.

29. The following sentences are notes taken from an officer's activity log detailing a notice of infraction given to a motorcyclist earlier in the week. The sentences are not arranged in any particular order. Select the alternative that represents the facts as they would appear chronologically in the official activity log.

    1. At 1117 hours, I observed a motorcyclist going 15 mph over the acceptable speed limit for a designated school area.

    2. He was very adamant that he had not been speeding through the school area and seemed hesitant in offering his license as requested.

    3. I was assigned to patrol the Hale Elementary School area between the hours of 1100 and 1245, Monday through Wednesday.

    4. I gave him a citation for exceeding the speed limit in front of a school and a written warning for the expired license.

    5. His driver's license had been expired for almost a month.

A.	1	3	2	4	5
B.	3	1	5	2	4
C.	3	1	2	4	5
D.	3	1	2	5	4

30. Trooper Conners wrote an incident report regarding a DWI (Driving While under the Influence) traffic offense. The following five sentences were taken out of the text of that report in no particular order.

1. The owner of the vehicle, Mr. Keith Denner of 1419 9th Street, was wanted for failure to appear for an earlier charge of reckless driving.

2. Mr. Denner assured me it was medicine prescribed to him that caused some drowsiness.

3. Mr. Denner's blood-alcohol level registered 0.19%.

4. At 1:37 A.M., I noticed the driver of a 1990 Jeep Cherokee swerving erratically between the lines on Warren Avenue.

5. He agreed to take the breathalyzer test.

Which of the following alternatives represents the correct chronological order of events?

A.	4	1	2	3	5
B.	4	2	1	5	3
C.	4	1	2	5	3
D.	4	3	2	1	5

31. State Patrol Officer Hank Johnson had filed a missing person report earlier in the week. Each of the sentences provided below has been taken directly out of that report. The sentences are not arranged in any particular order. Select the alternative that represents the facts as they would appear chronologically in the report.

1. The party was hosted by the McNeil family, who live at 290 NW Brookdale Boulevard.

2. A vehicle of that general description had been reported stolen the same evening.

3. At 0800 hours, Mrs. Beth Hallestad called to report that her 13-year-old daughter, Tracy, and her best friend had not returned home from a party held the previous night.

4. Mrs. Hallestad provided a complete physical description.

5. Mr. McNeil recalled seeing the two leave in a late model Toyota pickup at approximately 11:15 P.M.

A.	4	3	1	5	2
B.	1	3	4	5	2
C.	3	4	5	2	1
D.	3	4	1	5	2

32. Trooper Harper wrote an accident report regarding a forgery. The following five sentences were taken out of the text of that report in no particular order.

1. Ms. Larson had asked Mrs. Hennessy, the store checkout clerk, if she could postdate her check by one week.

2. Harold Craswell, the store manager, detained Ms. Larson.

3. I placed Ms. Larson under arrest for check forgery at 7:45 P.M.

4. Cindy Larson picked out four dresses totaling $492 in value.

5. Mrs. Hennessy said the telecheck security system determined that the check was being written on a closed account.

Which of the following alternatives represents the correct chronological order of events?

A.	4	1	5	2	3
B.	4	2	1	5	3
C.	2	4	3	5	1
D.	1	4	5	2	3

Read the following laws and classifications listed below. Answer questions 33–40 on the basis of these statutes.

18.12 – Auto Larceny

A. An individual is guilty if he/she appropriates the use of a motor vehicle without consent of the owner; or

B. Accepts transportation in a vehicle known to be stolen; or

C. Demonstrates the intent to permanently deprive, encumber, liquidate, pledge, or otherwise transfer any interest in said vehicle to parties other than the rightful owner.

19.74 – Blackmail

A. An individual is guilty if he/she (public officials excluded) utilizes a threat, be it verbal or written, to acquire property not rightfully due him/her.

19.79 – Misappropriation of Misdelivered or Lost Property

A. An individual is guilty if he/she comes into the possession of misdelivered or lost property of another, bearing some form of identification of the rightful recipient or owner and fails to take reasonable measures in returning said property.

20.13 – Receiving or Concealing Stolen Property in the First Degree

A. An individual is guilty if he/she knows the property to be stolen and willfully receives or conceals said property with the intent to either deprive the rightful owner of its use or use it for his/her personal gain. Value of stolen property must be in excess of $1500.

20.31 – Receiving or Concealing Stolen Property in the Second Degree

A. An individual is guilty if he/she knows the property to be stolen and willfully receives or conceals said property with the intent to either deprive the rightful owner of its use or use it for his/her personal gain. Value of stolen property must be in excess of $250 but not to exceed $1500; or

B. Receiving or concealing a stolen firearm; or

C. Receiving or concealing a stolen credit card.

20.48 – Receiving or Concealing Stolen Property in the Third Degree

A. An individual is guilty if he/she knows the property to be stolen and willfully receives or conceals said property with the intent to either deprive the rightful owner of its use or use it for his/her personal gain. Value of stolen property must not exceed $250.

51.73 – Larceny in the First Degree

A. An individual is guilty if he/she has the intent to permanently deprive another of property or services and either uses said property for his/her own personal gain or disposes of it for other compensation. Value of property or services, not including a motor vehicle, must be in excess of $1500; or

B. Any property taken from the person of another.

51.83 – Larceny in the Second Degree

    A. An individual is guilty if he/she has the intent to permanently deprive another of property or services and either uses said property for his/her own personal gain or disposes of it for other compensation. Value of property or services, not including a motor vehicle, must be in excess of $250, but not exceed $1500; or

    B. Credit card theft.

51.91 – Larceny in the Third Degree

    A. An individual is guilty if he/she has the intent to permanently deprive another of property or services and either uses said property for his or her own personal gain or disposes of it for other compensation. Value of property or services, not including a motor vehicle, must not exceed $250.

33. Jennifer Hearst had an expensive addiction to cocaine that she could not afford to maintain on wages alone. As a store clerk at an upscale clothier, Ms. Hearst would periodically falsify merchandise return slips and then keep the amount of money that was to be supposedly refunded. Store security became wise to the scheme after an internal audit revealed some major discrepancies on her department accounts. Pursuant to her arrest, it was determined that she had stolen approximately $1250 from her employer to support her drug habit. According to the statutes provided, what would Ms. Hearst be guilty of?

    A. 19.79-A

    B. 20.31-A

    C. 51.83-A

    D. None of the above because premeditation was absent

34. Larry Kline, a two-time convicted felon for forgery, was serving the remainder of his ten-month sentence at a minimum security halfway house. By coincidence, another Kline family lived just down the street and, on one particular day, the mail service inadvertently delivered some of their mail to where he lived. Larry recognized one of the envelopes as an opportunity too good to be true. Enclosed was a MasterCard bearing his same last name. Activation of the card was a relatively simple matter for Larry under the circumstances. However, before he had a chance to charge the card to its $1500 limit, Ben Daily, another convict serving time at the halfway house, learned of his scheme and threatened to turn him in unless he received $250 in badly needed cash. On the presumption that both perpetrators were caught after the fact, Larry Kline could be prosecuted under which of the following statutes?

    A. 19.79-A

    B. 51.83-B and 19.79-A

    C. 20.31-C

    D. 20.13-A and 19.74-A

35. Referring to the previous question, under what statute(s) could Ben Daily be prosecuted?

    A. 19.79-A

    B. 19.74-A and 51.83-B

    C. 19.74-A and 20.31-C

    D. 51.83-B

36. Max Wells, a fairly proficient "shade tree mechanic," told his best friend, Albert Knolls, that hot-wiring virtually any vehicle was a relatively simple proposition. Knolls quickly pointed out an unattended late model two-door Buick with the windows rolled down that was parked close by. He challenged Mark to prove the claim or face certain humiliation from not only him but other mutual friends that would inevitably learn what had happened. Within five minutes Mark had the car started, and the both of them decided to take the vehicle for a joyride as a matter of celebration. Unbeknown to either was the fact that several neighbors witnessed the crime and promptly notified the authorities of their descriptions and make and model of the stolen automobile. Consequently, the pair was quickly apprehended by the State Patrol and placed under arrest. According to the statutes provided, what could Albert Knolls be prosecuted for?

   A. 51.73-A

   B. 20.13-A and 51.73-A

   C. 18.12-B

   D. None of the above because Mr. Knolls was not directly responsible for misappropriating the vehicle in question

37. Referring to the previous question, under what statute(s) could Mr. Wells be prosecuted?

   A. 18.12-B

   B. 19.79-A

   C. 18.12-A

   D. 51.73-B

38. Jay Wallingford had always wanted a Rolex watch. However, in light of his current earnings from a service industry job and financial obligations in supporting a wife and two kids, it was simply out of realistic reach. That was, until he accidentally came across an illicit street vendor by the name of "Fast Eddie." Eddie had just what he was looking for, but instead of the expected $2300 price tag, this particular Rolex was on "special" for $500. The watch was an authentic serial-numbered Rolex, but Eddie confided that the real reason for its substantial discount was the fact that it was "hot" (i.e., stolen recently). Assuming that Mr. Wallingford did purchase the watch, and through certain events that followed, the transaction became known to the authorities, under what statute could he be prosecuted?

   A. 19.79-A

   B. 20.31-A

   C. 20.13-A

   D. None of the above because he was victimized as well

39. Howard Bartlett, an ex-employee of a local cable TV company, hooked himself up to the local cable services without having the authorization to do so or notifying the company. Two months later, a cable repair technician discovers the illegal hookup and promptly disconnects the service. It was determined that Mr. Bartlett had not paid for two months of services, valued at $45. According to the statutes provided, Mr. Bartlett would be guilty under which statute?

   A. 51.91-A

   B. 20.48-A

   C. 19.79-A

   D. None of the above, since he used to work for the company in question

40. John Worthington, a county building inspector, tells Mr. Sherman that his office building is not quite in compliance with county building codes. However, for $1000, which would be far below the cost of upgrading the building to current standards, Mr. Worthington would "overlook" the infraction. According to the statutes provided, what would Mr. Worthington be guilty of?

    A. 19.74-A

    B. 19.79-A

    C. 20.31-B

    D. None of the above statutes.

Questions 41 through 45 involve composite-sketch cross-comparison. Look at the original sketch of the subject above and then try to discern which of the four other sketches provided is the same individual attempting to disguise his or her appearance. Unless otherwise stated, assume the individual in question has not undergone any surgery.

41.

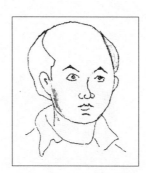

A.

B.

C.

D.

42.

A.

B.

C.

D.

43.

A.  B. 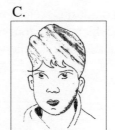 C. 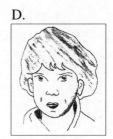 D.

44.

A.  B.  C.  D.

45.

A.  B.  C. D.

ANSWER SHEET FOR SAMPLE QUESTIONS ON SITUATIONAL JUDGMENT AND REASONING

1. Ⓐ Ⓑ Ⓒ Ⓓ
2. Ⓐ Ⓑ Ⓒ Ⓓ
3. Ⓐ Ⓑ Ⓒ Ⓓ
4. Ⓐ Ⓑ Ⓒ Ⓓ
5. Ⓐ Ⓑ Ⓒ Ⓓ
6. Ⓐ Ⓑ Ⓒ Ⓓ
7. Ⓐ Ⓑ Ⓒ Ⓓ
8. Ⓐ Ⓑ Ⓒ Ⓓ
9. Ⓐ Ⓑ Ⓒ Ⓓ
10. Ⓐ Ⓑ Ⓒ Ⓓ
11. Ⓐ Ⓑ Ⓒ Ⓓ
12. Ⓐ Ⓑ Ⓒ Ⓓ
13. Ⓐ Ⓑ Ⓒ Ⓓ
14. Ⓐ Ⓑ Ⓒ Ⓓ
15. Ⓐ Ⓑ Ⓒ Ⓓ

16. Ⓐ Ⓑ Ⓒ Ⓓ
17. Ⓐ Ⓑ Ⓒ Ⓓ
18. Ⓐ Ⓑ Ⓒ Ⓓ
19. Ⓐ Ⓑ Ⓒ Ⓓ
20. Ⓐ Ⓑ Ⓒ Ⓓ
21. Ⓐ Ⓑ Ⓒ Ⓓ
22. Ⓐ Ⓑ Ⓒ Ⓓ
23. Ⓐ Ⓑ Ⓒ Ⓓ
24. Ⓐ Ⓑ Ⓒ Ⓓ
25. Ⓐ Ⓑ Ⓒ Ⓓ
26. Ⓐ Ⓑ Ⓒ Ⓓ
27. Ⓐ Ⓑ Ⓒ Ⓓ
28. Ⓐ Ⓑ Ⓒ Ⓓ
29. Ⓐ Ⓑ Ⓒ Ⓓ
30. Ⓐ Ⓑ Ⓒ Ⓓ

31. Ⓐ Ⓑ Ⓒ Ⓓ
32. Ⓐ Ⓑ Ⓒ Ⓓ
33. Ⓐ Ⓑ Ⓒ Ⓓ
34. Ⓐ Ⓑ Ⓒ Ⓓ
35. Ⓐ Ⓑ Ⓒ Ⓓ
36. Ⓐ Ⓑ Ⓒ Ⓓ
37. Ⓐ Ⓑ Ⓒ Ⓓ
38. Ⓐ Ⓑ Ⓒ Ⓓ
39. Ⓐ Ⓑ Ⓒ Ⓓ
40. Ⓐ Ⓑ Ⓒ Ⓓ
41. Ⓐ Ⓑ Ⓒ Ⓓ
42. Ⓐ Ⓑ Ⓒ Ⓓ
43. Ⓐ Ⓑ Ⓒ Ⓓ
44. Ⓐ Ⓑ Ⓒ Ⓓ
45. Ⓐ Ⓑ Ⓒ Ⓓ

Answers can be found on page 93.

ANSWERS TO SAMPLE QUESTIONS ON SITUATIONAL JUDGMENT AND REASONING

1. *A.* Only A best sums up the statement's implications. Choice B is false on its own merit. Choice C is incorrect because crime should be a primary concern for the community, not just for the criminal justice system. Selection D was neither said nor implied.

2. *D.* Police radio networks are essentially party lines. When various agencies subscribe to the same transmission procedures, often officers cut one another off the air or make it difficult for an officer to even get on the air if messages are not kept to an effective minimum.

3. *D.* Letting criminals know precisely when a patrol car is scheduled for a given area basically defeats the purpose of patrolling a beat. Selection C may be true to some extent. The remaining selections are false on their own merit.

4. *A.* All downed power lines, cables, etc. should be treated as though they are "hot." The absence of arcing or burning does not necessarily indicate that the line is de-energized. Selections B and C can both result in the officer being electrocuted. Selection D is incorrect even though a report of the incident is filed. If the officer leaves the area to continue patrol, the situation remains a potential threat to the public. The area should be secured until utility repair crews arrive and take control of the matter.

5. *B.* This statement represents a truthful middle-of-the-road reply which neither further exacerbates this person's irritation over getting the ticket nor implies that you will do anything to rectify it. The other choices provided would be wrong for these very reasons.

6. *D.* Selection C may be partially true, but D best encompasses what was meant by the passage. Most people see but do not actually observe or consciously register the actions and movements of people or objects, events, and surrounding circumstances.

7. *C.* Both A and B are basically one and the same and can be eliminated on those grounds. Selection C would be considered correct since most people will shoot high and to the right. Responding in this manner will lessen the possibility of being shot. Selection D is wrong because it would render the officer an easy target for the suspect.

8. *C.* Selection A could potentially endanger Officer Duper because medical assistance is not rendered on the scene. Bleeding must be stopped. Selection B would unnecessarily place the public at risk of being struck by a stray bullet or ricochet. Selection D may seem appropriate; however, the best immediate action taken by Officer Gaston is to use the radio to summon medical help and then request backup to pursue the suspect.

9. *C.* Again, radioing for another unit to respond would make the best sense. If the young lady had mentioned that a family member was still in the house, it would be prudent for Officer Hastings to become involved even after another unit is radioed to investigate. Potentially life-threatening situations always take precedence over minor traffic accidents. Under the circumstances, though, Choice C would be the best. Choices A and D are simply ridiculous.

10. *A.* If State Patrol Officer Milligan does what is described in either C or D, he places public safety at unnecessary risk. This is especially true for a high-speed chase in a residential area. Officer Milligan should slow down and use the radio to coordinate a search and should get assistance from other officers in stopping the suspect. Teamwork is important in such a situation. Selection B works contrary to that notion.

11. *D.* Although A may seem appropriate, D is actually correct. Circumstances dictate that a supervisory-level decision should be made about how to handle such a situation. Ignoring the incident, as suggested in B, would be incorrect. Selection C is incorrect because it potentially places both the public and the driver himself at unnecessary risk.

12. *D.* More often than not, citizens come into contact with the police over a traffic incident. The other selections given in this question may or may not promote the desired effect. However,

the manner in which a police officer handles a traffic incident leaves a lasting impression on those involved.

13. *D.* Taking into account the fact that the man could not be awakened, and the presence of the empty syringe, which may be indicative of illicit drug use, it should be assumed by Officer Kent that a life-threatening condition prevails. Selection D is the only choice that offers immediate medical care. Detoxification centers offer programs that can be responsible for people recovering from their dependence on alcohol or drugs but are not emergency medical care facilities.

14. *A.* This selection represents the best advice that could be given. Selections B and C would, in all likelihood, exacerbate the problem. Selection D is wrong because, regardless of the fact that the officer is off duty, it is the officer's duty to serve and protect the public. Ethics do not change at the end of the shift.

15. *C.* Child abuse and neglect are the greater cause of concern. Both of these crimes normally occur within the privacy of a home. Law enforcement intervention into family life can generate deep feelings of resentment and distrust. What constitutes acceptable corporal punishment for children versus that which is considered excessive, as well as abusive, force can be a relative grey area also. The other crimes are of a more tangible nature that can more easily be addressed by law enforcement personnel.

16. *B.* The best course of action would be just to issue a warning. Remember, the change of traffic signs had occurred only recently. Motorists can be complacent when commuting over the same route every day. The warning for a first-time offender would be more appropriate than a citation. This will, at least, bring the change to motorists' attention without unnecessarily penalizing them. Selection A is wrong because, if the infractions were to continue, a traffic accident or injury could result.

17. *C.* Selection C will tend to close skin pores, thereby leaving a minimal amount of residue on anything touched. During warmer weather people tend to perspire more and, consequently, more readily identifiable prints will be left on most surfaces.

18. *B.* When a driver's license is lenticulated, it renders it difficult, if not impossible, to alter any information without the alterations being obvious. The other selections are either ridiculous or simply not true.

19. *B.* It can be safely assumed that someone is in need of immediate medical attention. The preservation of someone's life takes precedence over all other circumstances. Selections A, C, and D complicate the matter by unnecessarily detaining the ambulance and wasting critical time.

20. *C.* Police officers should not accept gratuities for any reason. Not only may an innocent gesture be construed as illegal, but it may place the officer in a potentially compromising position that could prejudice his or her actions. Selection C would be the best alternative because the supervisor could contact the owner directly and explain the implications.

21. *D.* Selection D (i.e., C and A according to the chart provided) account for the two largest shares (20% + 40%) of the total budget as opposed to either selection A (17% + 13%) or selection B (40% + 10%). Selection C is incorrect because Maintenance and Operations (10%) represent the smallest financial outlay.

22. *C.* Administrative expense is the second largest outlay in the department's budget. Attorney expense, on the other hand, is the fourth, not third, greater expense shown by the chart. Selection B is false because Administrative expense combined with Supplies and Equipment (20% + 17%) does not exceed that portion of the budget dedicated to payroll (40%). Selection D is false as well, because Maintenance and Operations comprises 10% or one tenth of the budget, not one quarter or 25%.

23. *C.*   DUI arrests nearly doubled in 1995 while auto accidents involving fatalities dropped by more than 50% from the year before. A similar correlation exists for auto accidents involving injuries. The inverse relationship of A and B and C in 1995 is rather profound.

24. *B.*   Auto accidents involving fatalities as well as injuries reached a pinnacle during 1994. No other year in the study fared as poorly with respect to the public safety issue.

25. *A.*   In comparison to the other years in the study, 1992 was a banner year for public safety. Better road conditions and/or driving with extra caution are two such factors that would have a beneficial effect on motorist safety.

26. *D.*   Selection D is, in fact, true when the number of citations issued is compared. A is incorrect because the two time frames examined are comparable to each other. B is false because, judging by the data presented, it is clear that the exact opposite is true. Speeding incidents were distinctly up during the later evening hours. That apparently carried over into the early morning hours as well. The usual application of the phrase "rush hour" typically refers to traffic volume. However, in this study, it has relevance to the hour of day that the most speeding citations were issued. Eleven P.M. to midnight fits that definition, instead of noon to 1:00 P.M.

27. *A.*   Tour I was responsible for issuing only 389 total citations. Tour II and Tour III were responsible for 471 and 522 citations, respectively.

28. *C.*   The key word in this statement is "significant." While it is true that Tours II and III followed that pattern, the same cannot be said for Tour I. Ticket issuances averaged close to fifty throughout the entire shift.

29. *B.*   It can be reasonably assumed that a description of the assignment would first be mentioned in the activity log as a point of reference and the end result of this activity was that the motorcyclist received the citation. These facts would preclude A and C. Between B and D, it would have to be decided which came first, Sentence 2 or Sentence 5. Obviously, Sentence 2 would have to happen before the officer could determine that the license had expired. Therefore, B is the correct choice.

30. *C.*   Statement 4 is obviously the beginning of Officer Conners' report. Unfortunately, all four choices given suggest that as well. However, Statement 3, being the conclusionary statement to the report, must be preceded by the fact that Mr. Denner agrees to have the breathalyzer test in the first place (Statement 5). Therefore, Selections A and D can be eliminated on that basis. Selection B is incorrect because Statement 1 should precede Statement 2. It can be assumed that Officer Conners ran the plates first to learn who the owner of the vehicle was and to determine if there were any wants and warrants. Once the subject was pulled over, the license and registration confirmed that Mr. Denner was the operator/driver of the vehicle. It is at this point that Mr. Denner offers the excuse made in the report.

31. *D.*   Sentence 3 is obviously the event that initiated the filing of the missing persons report. This fact alone precludes A and B. Between C and D, it will have to be determined whether Sentence 5 occurred before Sentence 1 or vice versa. Since Officer Johnson must learn where the party was before he can interview Mr. McNeil, the host, D would therefore be selected as the correct choice.

32. *A.*   Selection D could have been a correct choice if Mrs. Hennessy were a regular clerk delegated to assist customers with questions. However, since she is a checkout clerk, it can be presupposed that Ms. Larson had picked out the articles of clothing first and then, at the time of being checked out, inquired about postdating her check as a means of payment. It can be safely assumed that Statements 4 and 3 are the first and last events to happen, thereby eliminating C. By scrutinizing the second and third numbers of A and B, you can safely assume that A is the correct choice. It would not make sense that, as B implies, Ms. Larson

asked about postdating a check after the store manager detained her.

33.   *C.*   Although selections B and C may appear similar, the latter is an accurate assessment of Ms. Hearst's actions. Falsification of documents with the intent to deprive her employer of the cash proceeds is different than actually possessing stolen property with the intent to liquidate for money.

34.   *B.*   Misappropriation of Misdelivered Property (i.e., selection A) is only one of the statutes that would apply in Larry Kline's case. Credit Card Theft — Larceny in the Second Degree (i.e., 51.83-B) would apply as well.

35.   *B.*   The only statute that would apply in Ben Daily's case is Blackmail (i.e., 19.74-A). Under the circumstances given, Mr. Daily did not have a direct role in concealing or misappropriating the credit card stolen by Larry Kline.

36.   *C.*   Mr. Knolls, while not being directly responsible for the theft in question, did, in fact, willfully accept transportation in a vehicle that was stolen. Only statute 18.12-B would be applicable to Mr. Knoll's case. Selection A and B can be summarily eliminated because the statutes pertaining to First, Second, and Third Degree Larceny preclude motor vehicle theft.

37.   *C.*   Mr. Wells was responsible for stealing the vehicle in question. Therefore, the charge of Auto Larceny, or 18.12-A, would be applicable in his case.

38.   *C.*   The actual value of the watch was stated to be $2300, not $500. Consequently, Mr. Wallingford could be charged with statute 20.13-A — Receiving Stolen Property in the First Degree.

39.   *A.*   Mr. Bartlett utilized two months of cable service with full intent not to pay. Since the value of the services was $45, Mr. Bartlett would be guilty of larceny in the third degree. Selection D is irrelevant.

40.   *D.*   Selection A may initially seem the correct choice; however, blackmail is exclusive of public officials. This incident would be described as extortion, a term not given in the statutes provided.

41.   *A.*   Subject B has a wider face and different lips.

                 Subject C has different ears.

                 Subject D has a larger nose.

42.   *B.*   Subject A has smaller lips.

                 Subject C has fewer facial lines.

                 Subject D has a narrower face and different eyes.

43.   *C.*   Subject A has larger lips.

                 Subject B has higher cheekbone structures and smaller lips.

                 Subject D has deep-set dimples.

44.   *C.*   Subject A has different ears.

                 Subject B has different eyes as well as a cleft chin.

                 Subject D has fewer facial lines and a wider nose.

45.   *A.*   Subjects B, C, and D all lack the scar above the upper lip.

Your score for this exercise would rate as follows:

     41–45 correct — Excellent

     36–40 correct — Good

     31–35 correct — Fair

     Less than 31 correct — Poor

Chapter 5

DIRECTIONAL ORIENTATION

As mentioned earlier in this study guide, a superb memory is a real benefit to a State Police Officer. However, when this quality is coupled with a good sense of directional orientation, the police officer is an invaluable asset to his or her department. If a police officer is familiar with the directional layout of the city or district that encompasses his or her beat, he or she can respond to emergencies in a safer and more efficient manner. On the other hand, a misdirected approach to an emergency can waste valuable time and perhaps further endanger the lives of those involved and the public in general. For these reasons, State police departments are interested in determining a test applicant's directional abilities. Most of the directional orientation questions seen on past exams have been of three types. The first variety of question asks what would be the most efficient way of getting from one point on a street map to another. If a vehicle is involved, it is assumed that no traffic violations may be committed en route unless otherwise stipulated. For example, no U-turns are permitted, and it is prohibited to travel in the wrong direction on a one-way street. The alternatives provided for these kinds of question deserve close scrutiny. Don't immediately assume that the first possible answer found is the correct choice. Very often, two possible routes will be given, one of which will be shorter and more efficient. This fact can be easily overlooked if each of the four alternatives provided is not given equal consideration and the incorrect choices eliminated accordingly. Reaching premature conclusions on any question, for that matter, is an open invitation to poor test performance.

The second type of question examines how well you can follow explicit directions. A specific route is outlined, and you need to determine what or where the final destination is. This task may seem quite easy, but it is surprising how far off in the wrong direction you can go if you misinterpret any direction given even slightly.

The third type asks the directional location of an object in relation to a person or specific landmark. This could simply come in the form of someone asking how to get to a destination, or it may concern the relative location of two different buildings. This type of question is probably the easiest to solve because you can figure out any direction by looking at the legend of the illustration given (see compass at right).

Even if the legend specifies only one direction, you can easily extrapolate any other direction as needed.

On the exam, a city or precinct grid will be given on the basis of which questions will be asked. Be sure to read and follow the directions for each question word for word; do not assume anything. It is also important to approach these questions from the perspective of the person asking them. A northern heading from the questioner's standpoint may very well be an altogether different heading from you, depending on the way you look at the map. A right turn for the questioner could mean a left turn for you. To circumvent this confusion, simply rotate the diagram to view it from the same direction as the questioner. This will eliminate any disorientation when directions are discussed. As a final tip, you can more clearly determine correct answers by lightly sketching on the diagram provided all proposed or alternative routes in the question. This will allow for better contrast and easier discernment of the correct answer. If there are several questions relating to the same diagram, it is important to erase the previous sketching between questions. Otherwise, you will end up with a confusing array of lines, which can lead to a wrong answer.

SAMPLE QUESTIONS FOR DIRECTIONAL ORIENTATION

Answer questions 1–10 on the basis of Diagram A.

1. Where is the Library in reference to the Post Office?
   A. North
   B. South
   C. East
   D. West

2. Trooper Halverson was traveling south on Northern Avenue between McNeil and Lowell when she received a dispatch to investigate a two-car collision that occurred at the intersection of McDowell and Gibson. Assuming that all traffic regulations are obeyed, which of the following alternatives would be the most expedient means of reaching the scene of the accident?
   A. Commit a U-turn and proceed two blocks east and then one block north.
   B. Proceed east on Lowell Road for three blocks, north on Garfield Avenue for two blocks, and then one block west on McDowell Road.
   C. Proceed east on Lowell Road for two blocks and then two blocks north on Gibson Avenue.
   D. Proceed east on Lowell Road for two blocks and then two blocks south on Gibson Avenue.

3. Assume that State Patrol Officer Fuller was at the intersection of Country Club Road and Northern Avenue. If she drove east three blocks, south for two blocks, west for two blocks, and then south one block, which of the following locations would she end up in closest proximity to?
   A. Bank office
   B. City Administrative office
   C. Library
   D. Evergreen Towing and Impound

4. A late-model Volkswagen van parked on the southeast corner of McDowell Road and Northern Avenue had been tagged as an abandoned vehicle by the State Patrol three days earlier. Assuming that an Evergreen tow truck was dispatched from its office to impound the vehicle, which of the following routes would be the shortest, albeit legal, means of getting there?
   A. Left on Lowell Road to Garfield Avenue, left on Garfield Avenue to Country Club Road, left on Country Club Road to Northern Avenue, and then left on Northern Avenue and proceed one block south.
   B. Left on Lowell Road to Gibson Avenue, left on Gibson Avenue to McNeil Road, left on McNeil Road to Northern Avenue, then right on Northern Avenue and proceed one block north.
   C. Left on Lowell Road to Gibson Avenue, left on Gibson Avenue to McDowell Road, and then left on McDowell Road and proceed two blocks west.
   D. Right on Lowell Road to Northern Avenue, and then right on Northern Avenue and proceed two blocks north.

5. Where are the City Administrative offices in relation to State Patrol District Command?

    A. South

    B. Southeast

    C. North

    D. Northwest

6. Suppose a pedestrian were to ask a State Trooper who was taking a morning coffee break at Donuts-R-Us how to get from there to the Library. Which of the elicited responses would be correct?

    A. From Country Club Road, head south two blocks on Gibson Avenue and then turn right onto McNeil Road and go another three blocks west.

    B. Head south on Garfield Avenue to McNeil Road and then turn right on McNeil Road and go another four blocks west.

    C. Both selections A and B are correct.

    D. None of the above selections are correct.

7. Suppose Trooper Elmore had just passed the Broadway Avenue intersection heading west on Country Club Road when she received a dispatch to investigate a domestic dispute that occurred at Colonial Manor Apartments. What would be the quickest means to get there, assuming all traffic regulations were followed?

    A. Turn south on Northern Avenue, left at the next block, and then proceed approximately one and one-half blocks east.

    B. Turn north on Northern Avenue, right on the next block, and then proceed approximately one and one-half blocks west.

    C. Turn south on Broadway Avenue, left on McDowell Road, and then proceed approximately one-half block east.

    D. Turn south on Northern Avenue for two blocks and then proceed approximately one and one-half blocks east.

8. Referring to the previous question, where is Marston's Auto Repair in relation to where the domestic dispute was reported to have taken place?

    A. Southeast

    B. Southwest

    C. Northeast

    D. Northwest

9. Four juvenile gang members were seen by nearby residents to be involved in a serious fight at the northeast corner of Lindale Park. When one of the four juveniles spotted a State Patrol vehicle responding to the altercation, each of the four suspects took off in separate directions. The first suspect ran two blocks east, two blocks south, and then one block west. The second suspect ran one block north, two blocks east, and then three blocks south. The third suspect ran one block west, two blocks south, and then two blocks east. The fourth suspect ran one block west, one block north, and then three blocks east. On the basis of this information, which suspect would be nearest to the City Administrative Offices?

    A. Suspect 1

    B. Suspect 2

    C. Suspect 3

    D. Suspect 4

10. Referring to the information in the previous question, which suspect would end up in closest proximity to State Patrol District Command?

    A. Suspect 1

    B. Suspect 2

    C. Suspect 3

    D. Suspect 4

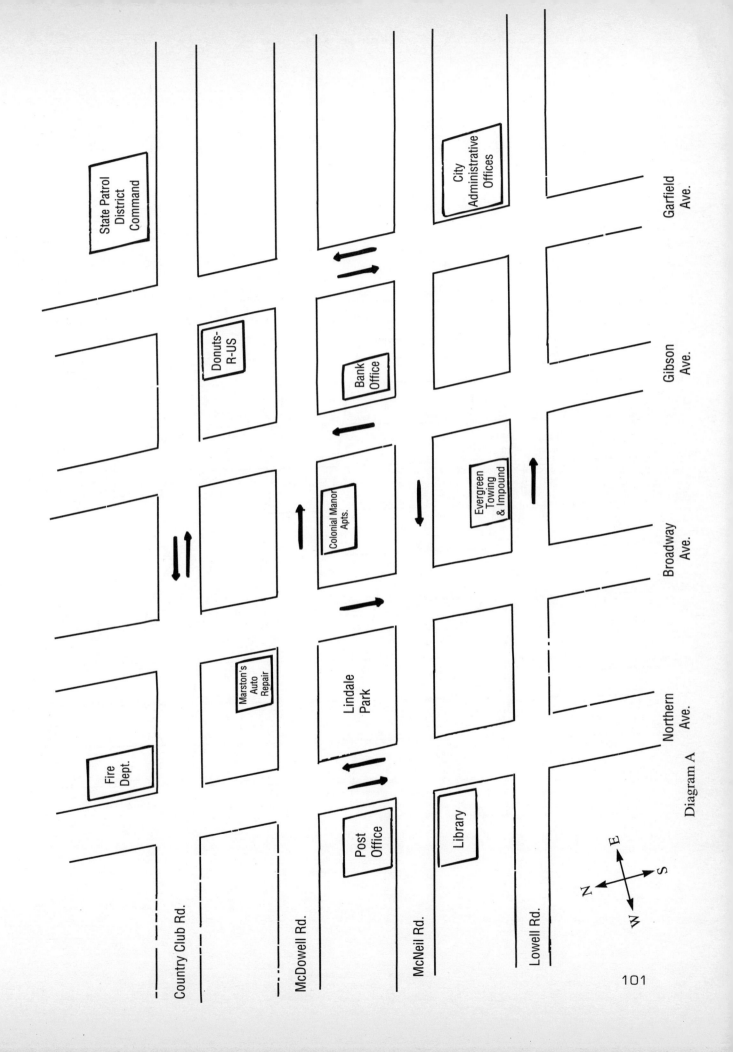

Diagram A

101

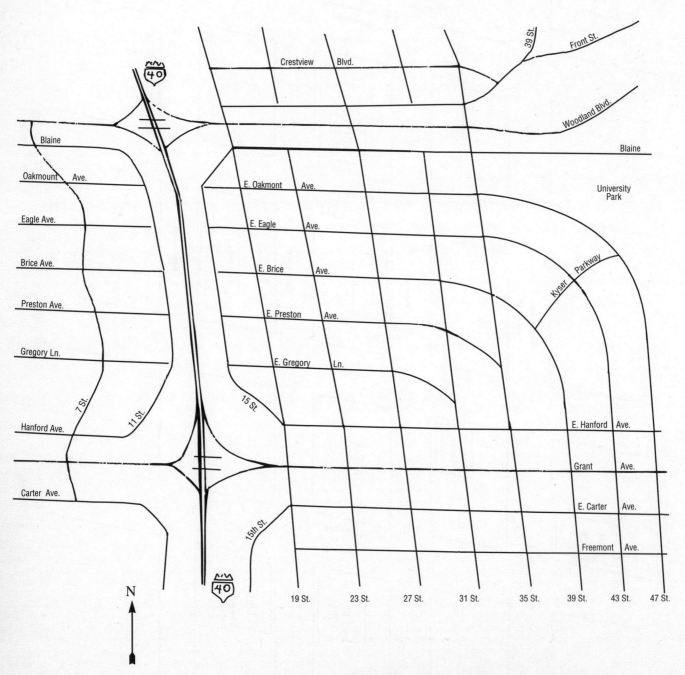

Diagram B

Diagram B illustrates four different law enforcement agency jurisdictions. The State Patrol is responsible for the area bounded by 11th Street and 15th Street (i.e., the interstate corridor). The County Sheriff is responsible for any and all areas west of Interstate 40. The 10th Precinct is responsible for the area bounded by 15th Street, E. Oakmont Avenue, 47th Street, and Freemont Avenue. The remaining area is assigned to the 5th Precinct.

Answer questions 11–18 on the basis of Diagram B.

11. Assuming a late-model sedan was abandoned along Interstate 40 between the Grant Avenue and Woodland Blvd. interchanges, which law enforcement agency bears primary responsibility for handling the matter?

    A. State Patrol

    B. County Sheriff

    C. 5th Precinct

    D. 10th Precinct

12. Officer Tina Morrow was at the intersection of E. Gregory Lane and 27th Street when she initiated pursuit of a northbound vehicle on 27th Street for failing to stop at a four-way stop. Officer Morrow traveled four blocks north and then another two blocks west before the driver in question responded by pulling over to the side of the road. Which of the locational references given below is most proximate to where Officer Morrow, in all likelihood, issued a citation for the violation observed?

    A. E. Oakmont Avenue and 35th Street

    B. E. Eagle Avenue and 15th Street

    C. E. Oakmont Avenue and 19th Street

    D. Eagle Avenue and 11th Street

13. According to the jurisdictional boundaries provided, the officer depicted in the previous question is most likely which of the following?

    A. County Sheriff

    B. State Patrol Officer

    C. City Police Officer from the 10th Precinct

    D. City Police Officer from the 5th Precinct

14. If a vehicle traveling north on E. Brice Avenue from E. Hanford Avenue makes a right turn onto Kyser Parkway, what direction is this particular vehicle now heading?

    A. East

    B. Northeast

    C. West

    D. Southwest

15. Assuming a motorist became stranded on 35th Street between Blaine and East Oakmont, which agency, according to the diagram, should respond to render roadside assistance?

    A. 5th Precinct

    B. 10th Precinct

    C. State Patrol

    D. County Sheriff

16. A vehicle traveling eight blocks north on 23rd Street from Freemont Avenue and then three blocks east, before continuing north three more blocks, would end up in whose jurisdiction?
    A. State Patrol
    B. 10th Precinct
    C. County Sheriff
    D. 5th Precinct

17. Assume State Trooper Mark Donahoe lived at a residence located on Front Street between 31st Street and 35th Street. If he just passed the Grant Avenue overpass while heading north on Interstate 40 and had the intention of taking his lunch break at home, which of the following routes would be the correct means of getting there?
    A. Take the off-ramp to Grant Avenue, proceed east to 35th Street, turn left on 35th Street and proceed to Front Street before turning left and traveling approximately one-half block.
    B Take the Woodland Blvd. off-ramp and proceed west three blocks before turning right and traveling approximately one-half block.
    C. Take the next available exit off the interstate, proceed east to the second intersection and then turn left, proceed north to the next street intersection and turn right, and then continue approximately one and one-half blocks east.
    D. Take the Woodland Blvd. off-ramp and proceed east two blocks before turning right and traveling approximately one-half block.

18. The driver of a stolen Sport Utility Vehicle heading south on Interstate 40 tried to elude the Highway Patrol by taking the Grant Avenue off-ramp and turning right at the first intersection encountered, and then continued to drive north another two blocks before abandoning the vehicle in a convenience store parking lot. An accurate locational reference made in subsequent police reports as to where the vehicle was recovered would be which of the following?
    A. 11th Street and Gregory Lane
    B. 7th Street and E. Gregory Lane
    C. 19th Street and Freemont Avenue
    D. 7th Street and Gregory Lane

19. If a motorist was heading south and then made two perpendicular right turns to get to a given destination, which direction is he or she now traveling?
    A. Southwest
    B. North
    C. East
    D. Northeast

20. Assume you are a State Patrol Officer traveling southeast on a given highway when you clock an oncoming vehicle doing 35 miles per hour over the speed limit. If you make a U-turn to initiate a pursuit, which direction would you now be traveling?
    A. Northeast
    B. Northwest
    C. Southwest
    D. North

21. If the same motorist described in the previous question attempts a right turn in an obvious bid to elude an inevitable citation, which direction would you now have to travel to effect an arrest?

    A. Northeast

    B. Northwest

    C. Southwest

    D. North

22. Trooper Glenn Howard was traveling northeast on Interstate 5 when he spotted two late-model Camaros drag racing in the opposite direction on a deserted frontage road that ran parallel to the interstate. Since Officer Howard was already en route to another emergency call, his only option at this point was to inform dispatch of the pair's location and the fact that they were last seen heading in which direction?

    A. Northeast

    B. Northwest

    C. Southwest

    D. North

23. Trooper Dan Holms was attempting to pull over an underage motorcyclist who was not wearing a helmet heading southwest on Highway 10. Initially, the young man was cooperative by pulling over to the shoulder. However, as soon as Officer Holmes got out of his troop car, the subject took off riding along the shoulder for approximately fifty yards before angling off to the right, jumping a drainage ditch, and headed diagonally across a hay field away from him. Assuming Officer Holmes radios for assistance and has to describe where the subject was last seen heading, which of the following directions would be an accurate description?

    A. Northwest

    B. Southwest

    C. West

    D. Northeast

24. Referring to the previous question, which of the following ways would allow Officer Holms to conduct an intercept, providing the subject maintains his present course of direction?

    A. Continue heading southwest on Highway 10 and take a left at the next exit that heads southeast.

    B. Continue heading southwest on Highway 10 and take a right at the next exit that heads northwest.

    C. Continue heading northwest on Highway 10 and take a left at the next exit that heads north.

    D. Continue heading northwest on Highway 10 and take a right at the next exit that heads northeast.

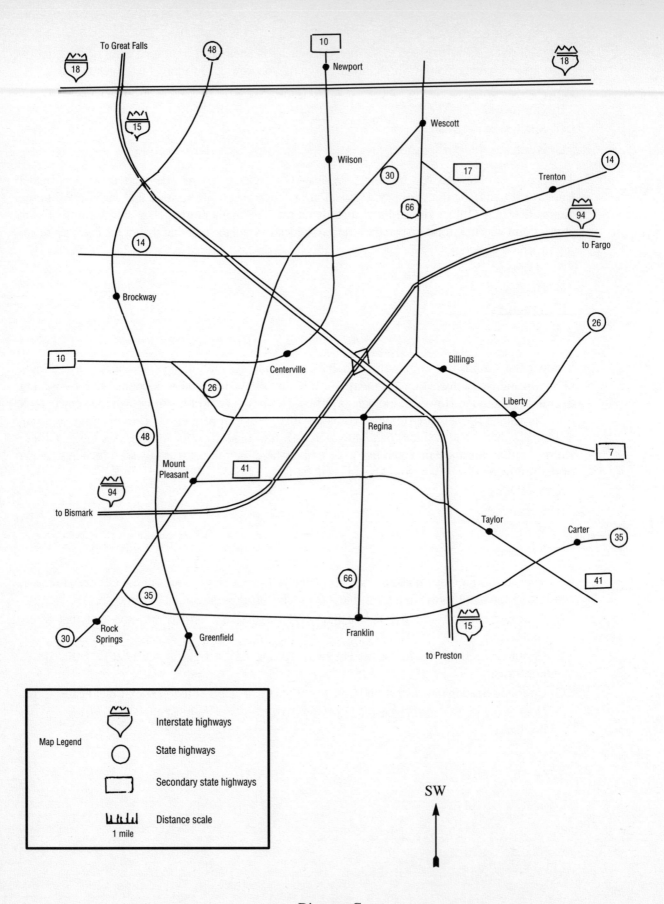

Diagram C

Answer questions 25–33 on the basis of Diagram C.

25. If a motorist intended to drive from Regina to Liberty on State Highway 26, which direction would he or she be traveling?

   A. Northwest

   B. West

   C. North

   D. Southeast

26. The stretch of secondary highway that effectively serves as a shortcut for motorists traveling between the towns of Wescott and Trenton has which of the following directional orientations?

   A. East–west

   B. Southwest–northeast

   C. Northwest–southeast

   D. North–south

27. Where is the town of Greenfield with respect to Mount Pleasant?

   A. Southwest

   B. North

   C. Southeast

   D. Northeast

28. All of the following statements are true with regard to Diagram C except:

   A. State Highway 48 intersects three different interstate highways.

   B. The most direct way of getting to Rock Springs from Liberty is to take State Highway 26 to State Highway 30 and turn west.

   C. The shortest secondary state highway shown is Route 17.

   D. The towns of Centerville, Newport, Taylor, Billings and Wilson are all located along various secondary state highways.

29. Trooper Beaumont was en route to a scheduled court appearance in Fargo. Assuming he had just turned onto Interstate 94 from State Highway 41, what direction would he initially be traveling?

   A. Southeast

   B. North

   C. West

   D. East

30. State Patrol Officer Kyle Talbott was heading northeast on State Highway 10 just outside of Newport when he received a dispatch to investigate a two-car collision approximately one mile southwest of Brockway. The shortest means of approach that Officer Talbott could take to get to the scene of the accident from his present location is which of the following?

   A. Stay on State Highway 10 until reaching State Highway 48, and then proceed southwest to the accident scene.

   B. Continue northeast on State Highway 10 to State Highway 14, turn right and follow Route 14 to State Highway 48, and then turn left and proceed to where the accident occurred.

   C. Continue northeast on State Highway 10 to State Highway 30, turn right and follow Route 30 to State Highway 14, turn right and follow Route 14 to State Highway 48, and then head northeast on Route 48 to where the accident occurred.

   D. Continue northeast on State Highway 10 to State Highway 30, turn right and follow Route 30 to State Highway 14, turn right and follow Route 14 to State Highway 48, and then head southwest on Route 48 to where the accident occurred.

31. According to an updated dispatch roster:

   State Police Unit #573 is presently located approximately five miles southwest of Franklin on State Highway 66.

   State Police Unit #301 is presently located approximately two miles northeast of Wescott on State Highway 66.

   State Police Unit #704 is presently located approximately three miles east of Mount Pleasant on State Highway 30.

   State Police Unit #187 is presently located at the intersection of Interstate 18 and State Highway 48.

   Based on these given locations, which particular unit would be in the best position to intercept, if not block, a suspect vehicle traveling north on Interstate 15 heading to Preston that had just passed the State Highway 30 interchange?

   A. Unit #573

   B. Unit #301

   C. Unit #704

   D. Unit #187

32. According to the same dispatch roster in the previous question, which particular unit would be in the best position to investigate a minor traffic accident that occurred on State Highway 48 approximately one mile northeast of Interstate 18?

   A. Unit #573

   B. Unit #301

   C. Unit #704

   D. Unit #187

33. Assuming State Police Officers Murry and Downs were patrolling the towns of Newport and Rock Springs respectively, if the pair wanted to meet at a halfway point to compare notes on an ongoing criminal investigation, what line of travel would be necessitated on Officer Murry's behalf to attend?

   A. West on State Highway 30 to Mount Pleasant.

   B. Northeast on Secondary State Highway 10 to Centerville.

   C. West on State Highway 30 to Secondary State Highway 10 and then northwest on Route 10 to Centerville.

   D. Northeast on Secondary State Highway 10 to Wilson.

Note: The following map symbols apply to questions 34–40.

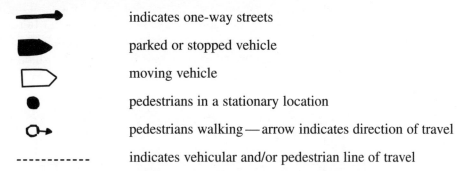

indicates one-way streets

parked or stopped vehicle

moving vehicle

pedestrians in a stationary location

pedestrians walking — arrow indicates direction of travel

indicates vehicular and/or pedestrian line of travel

34. The following information was taken from a State Police report detailing what happened when a motorist driving while under the influence of alcohol lost control of his vehicle. After you have read the report, determine which of the four sketches provided accurately depicts the incident described.

Ms. Tina Parkhurst was heading north on Kelso when the driver of a Chevrolet Iroc Z-28 came up from behind her at a high rate of speed, initiated a pass, and then cut directly in front to turn onto the off-ramp leading to Brice Street. Ms. Parkhurst was forced off the east shoulder into a ditch in the attempt to avoid a collision. The driver of the Iroc, however, could not slow down enough to prevent rear-ending a car that was waiting for a traffic light to change at the Brice Street intersection.

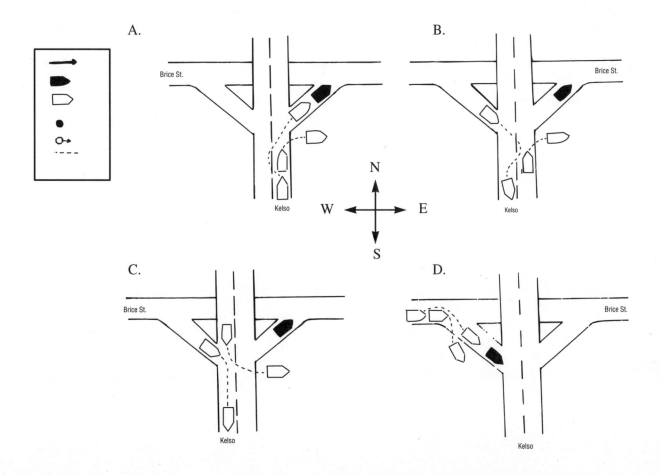

35. Teresa Goodwill claimed that she was standing on the southeast corner of Terrace and Ridgemont when she witnessed a Honda Accord traveling north on Terrace fail to stop for a red traffic light at the same intersection. In so doing, it clipped the right rear quarter panel of a Ford Probe heading east, and then swerved toward the northwest corner of the intersection, striking a street light standard. If these statements were to be incorporated into a State Police report, which of the four sketches shown below would serve as an accurate representation?

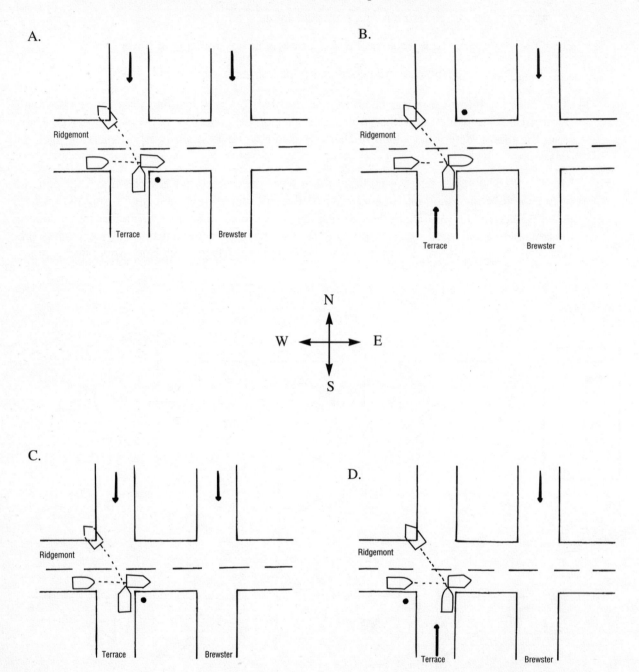

A.

B.

C.

D.

36. Teresa Billings was jogging South on Venetta and was about to cross 7th Street when she noticed that the driver of a Honda Prelude failed to stop for a stop sign on Hayward at the 7th Street intersection. Consequently, as the vehicle continued south on Hayward, it broadsided another vehicle, which had the right of way and was heading west on 7th Street. This story was corroborated by another witness standing at the southwest corner of 7th Street and Venetta. Which of the following sketches accurately depicts the circumstances just described?

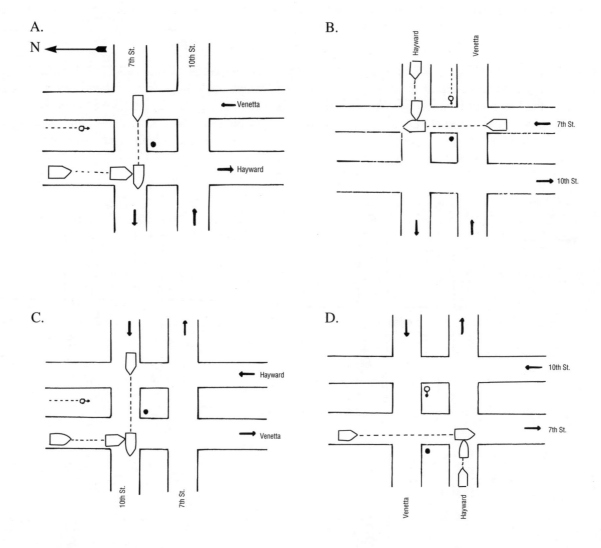

37. (Refer to Question 36.) After you have determined the correct map that depicts the incident described, where in relation to the jogger is the second witness?

    A. North
    B. East
    C. South
    D. West

38. In Question 36, in which direction was the vehicle that committed the traffic infraction headed?
    A. North
    B. East
    C. South
    D. West

39. The following information was taken from a State Police report detailing what happened when a teenager lost control of his vehicle. After you have read the report, determine which of the four sketches provided below accurately depicts the incident described.

    Blaine Williams was standing on the southeast corner of Piedmont and First Avenue when he noticed a Toyota pickup heading south on First Avenue begin to swerve erratically before entering the Piedmont intersection. The vehicle then went the wrong way on Piedmont (a one-way street), sideswiped a vehicle parked on Piedmont between First and Second Avenues, and then collided with another vehicle parked on the southeast corner of Second Avenue and Piedmont, narrowly missing two pedestrians waiting for a Metro bus.

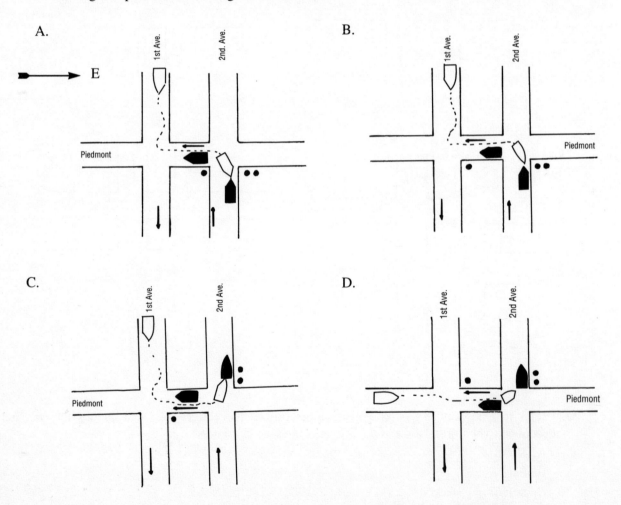

40. Bob Meinke claimed that he had been walking west on 20th Street and was halfway across the Aster Street crosswalk when a late-model Ford pickup traveling south on Aster Street failed to stop for the red light. It narrowly missed hitting Bob before swerving southwest and rear-ending a vehicle parked on the south side of 20th Street. If these statements were to be incorporated into a police report, which of the four sketches below would serve as an accurate representation?

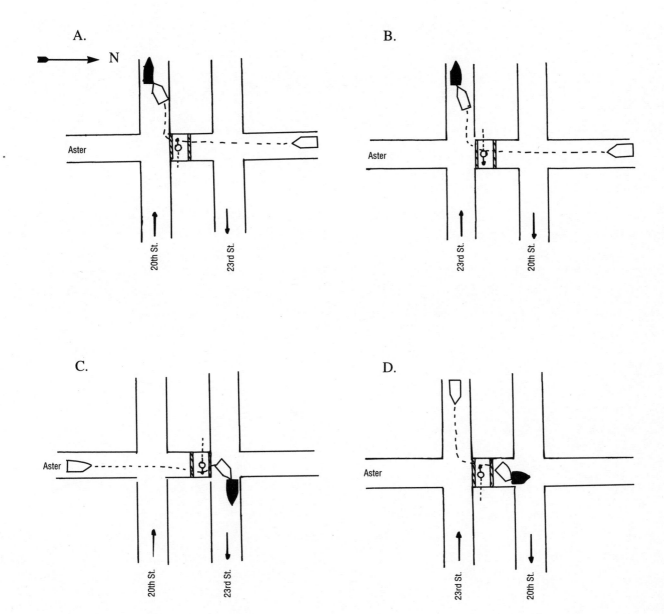

ANSWER SHEET TO DIRECTIONAL ORIENTATION QUESTIONS

1. (A) (B) (C) (D)	15. (A) (B) (C) (D)	29. (A) (B) (C) (D)
2. (A) (B) (C) (D)	16. (A) (B) (C) (D)	30. (A) (B) (C) (D)
3. (A) (B) (C) (D)	17. (A) (B) (C) (D)	31. (A) (B) (C) (D)
4. (A) (B) (C) (D)	18. (A) (B) (C) (D)	32. (A) (B) (C) (D)
5. (A) (B) (C) (D)	19. (A) (B) (C) (D)	33. (A) (B) (C) (D)
6. (A) (B) (C) (D)	20. (A) (B) (C) (D)	34. (A) (B) (C) (D)
7. (A) (B) (C) (D)	21. (A) (B) (C) (D)	35. (A) (B) (C) (D)
8. (A) (B) (C) (D)	22. (A) (B) (C) (D)	36. (A) (B) (C) (D)
9. (A) (B) (C) (D)	23. (A) (B) (C) (D)	37. (A) (B) (C) (D)
10. (A) (B) (C) (D)	24. (A) (B) (C) (D)	38. (A) (B) (C) (D)
11. (A) (B) (C) (D)	25. (A) (B) (C) (D)	39. (A) (B) (C) (D)
12. (A) (B) (C) (D)	26. (A) (B) (C) (D)	40. (A) (B) (C) (D)
13. (A) (B) (C) (D)	27. (A) (B) (C) (D)	
14. (A) (B) (C) (D)	28. (A) (B) (C) (D)	

Answers can be found on page 116.

ANSWERS TO DIRECTIONAL ORIENTATION QUESTIONS

1. *B.* South. Choice A would have been the correct answer had the question asked where the Post Office was in relation to the Library.

2. *C.* A is incorrect because it is stipulated within the question that traffic regulations must be followed. Not only is the U-turn illegal, but proceeding east on McNeil Road runs counter to traffic flow. B is incorrect because going west on McDowell Road runs counter to one-way traffic. Selection D is correct as far as proceeding east on Lowell Road for two blocks. However, turning south from that point would actually place the trooper at a location off the map.

3. *D.* The set of directions given would place Officer Fuller at the intersection of Lowell Road and Broadway Avenue which is closest to Evergreen Towing and Impound.

4. *B.* Selection A is a potential route that could be taken, however, it is not as short as selection B. C is incorrect because the left turn on McDowell runs counter to one-way traffic. Turning right on Lowell Road (i.e., heading west) from the tow truck office, as suggested by selection D, runs counter to east-bound one-way traffic.

5. *A.* South

6. *C.* As far as a pedestrian is concerned, directional traffic flow is irrelevant; that's what sidewalks are for. Therefore, both responses given will accomplish the same purpose.

7. *A.* B is incorrect because the direction would place Trooper Elmore at a point off the map. Selection C would necessitate the trooper to do a U-turn on Country Club Road to reach Broadway Avenue because she had already passed the intersection. Selection D would place the officer at a destination one block south of Colonial Manor Apartments, not to mention the fact that going east on McNeil Road runs counter to traffic flow.

8. *D.* Northwest

9. *B.* Suspect 2 (the escape route taken by the four suspects are highlighted in the diagram below).

10. *D.* Suspect 4

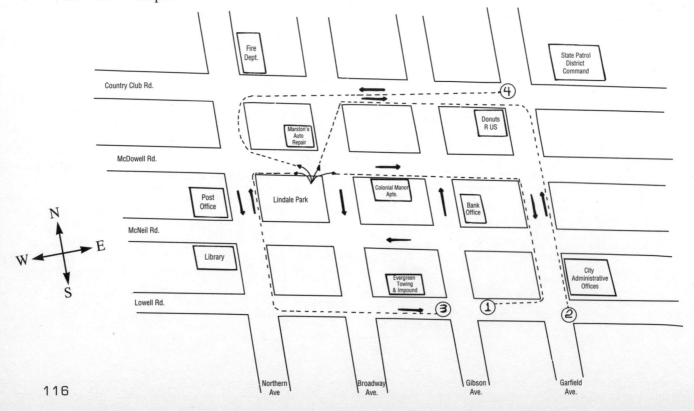

11. *A.* State Patrol has jurisdiction over the interstate corridor.

12. *C.* E. Oakmont Avenue and 19th Street

13. *C.* Even though the violator was stopped at a point that is considered a boundary line between two different jurisdictions (i.e., the 10th and 5th precincts) it would be reasonable to assume that Officer Morrow is assigned to the 10th Precinct because of where she was patrolling at the time of spotting the traffic infraction in question.

14. *B.* Northeast

15. *A.* 5th Precinct

16. *D.* The vehicle in question would end up close to Crestview Blvd. and 35th Street, which places it within the 5th Precinct's jurisdiction.

17. *C.* Selection A is not possible because the reading stipulated that Officer Donahoe had just driven past the Grant Avenue interchange. Selection B is a route that would actually take Officer Donahoe to a point that is not even on the map. Selection D would place Officer Donahoe close to 35th Street and Blaine, which is fairly close to home, but it is not the preferred destination.

18. *D.* According to the directions given, the vehicle was recovered at a location close to the intersection of 7th Street and Gregory Lane. Selection B does not exist.

19. *B.*

20. *B.* Northwest (see directional illustration below)

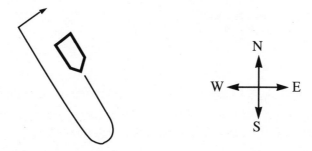

21. *A.* Northeast

22. *C.* Southwest. Despite the fact that the two Camaros were drag racing on a different road, the directional axis from the officer's point of view remains the same because it (i.e., the road they were on) was stated to run in tandem or parallel to the interstate. Since the pair was witnessed by the officer to be drag racing in the opposite direction that he was heading, southwest would be the correct description given over the radio.

23. C. West

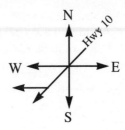

24. *B.*

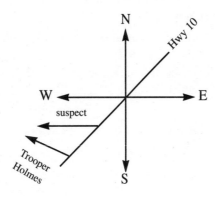

25. *A.* Northwest. To eliminate any potential confusion, it is strongly suggested that you extrapolate all of the major compass headings from what is provided in the map's legend. Then it will be easier to make directional references from any given point.

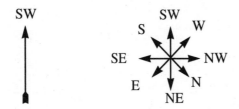

26. *D.* Secondary State Highway 17 has a north-south directional orientation.

27. *D.* Northeast. Selection A would have been the correct answer had the question asked been where was the town of Mount Pleasant with respect to Greenfield.

28. *B.* The directions in this selection are correct up until the point of heading west on State Highway 30. A right turn (i.e., western heading) would be a means of getting to Wescott instead of Rock Springs.

29. *C.* West

30. *C.* Selection D is correct up until the point of turning southwest on State Highway 48 in an attempt to reach the accident scene. Instead of going northeast towards the town of Brockway where the accident actually happened, Officer Talbott would, in fact, be headed towards Interstate 15.

31. *A.* Since State Police Unit #573 is proximate to the town of Regina, it would be in the best position to conduct an intercept of the suspect vehicle. The short distance from that point to

Interstate 15 via Route 66 or 26 would allow the officer in question sufficient time to place his or her unit in advance of the approaching vehicle.

32. *D.* Unit #187 is less than five miles away from the given accident; it would be in the best position to respond.

33. *B.* Centerville is as close to the halfway point as it gets between the officers' respective positions. Officer Murry would have to travel northwest on Route 10 to get there. Selection C is the correct means for Officer Downs to reach Centerville from Rock Springs, however, the question only concerns Officer Murry's perspective. Neither selection A or D (i.e., Mount Pleasant or Wilson) can serve as halfway points for the question.

34. *A.* Selection B correctly identifies Ms. Parkhurst's evasive actions and the stopped vehicle at the Brice Street Intersection waiting for a traffic light change. However, it incorrectly depicts the suspect's vehicular line of travel as well as not showing the rear end collision that occurred. Selection C compounds the inaccuracies by illustrating Ms. Parkhurst's line of travel as heading south on Kelso when, in fact, she was heading north. Selection D is wrong not only for directional reasons, but it portrays the accident as having occurred along Brice Street instead of Kelso.

35. *C.* Selection A is incorrect because it indicates the northbound Honda is running counter to one-way traffic flow. Running a red light in that direction precludes that assumption. Both selections B and D are correct in every aspect with exception to where Ms. Teresa Goodwill was standing at the time of the accident.

36. *B.* (*Note:* Frequently examiners provide questions that intentionally mix up points of reference. Don't let this confuse you. Analyze each map individually and determine the correct answer through the process of elimination. One other suggestion would be to establish compass points in each of the four sketches. This will tend to alleviate any directional errors.)

37. *C.* South

38. *C.* South

39. *B.* Selection A is incorrect because it fails to correctly identify the positioning of Blaine Williams. It places the witness at the southwest corner of 2nd Avenue and Piedmont. Selection C is incorrect because it places the accident at the northeast corner of 2nd Avenue and Piedmont. Selection D is wrong for the same reasons as C, as well as the fact that the vehicle in question did not enter Piedmont from 1st Avenue and that the witness location is misplaced as well.

40. *A.* Selection B is incorrect because it shows Mr. Meinke walking west on 23rd Street, not 20th Street, and the accident occurs on 23rd Street instead of 20th Street. Selection C is wrong for basically the same reasons as B, in addition to the fact that Mr. Meinke is walking due east, not west. Selection D is incorrect because here again the accident happens on 20th Street, not Aster. Additionally, Mr. Meinke is walking east, not west, across Aster on 23rd Street instead of 20th Street. (*Note:* This answer should have been fairly obvious because only Sketch A demonstrated an accident occurring on 20th Street.)

Your score for this exercise would rate as follows:
   37–40 correct — EXCELLENT
   33–36 correct — GOOD
   29–32 correct — FAIR
   Less than 29 correct — POOR

Chapter 6

Report Writing, Grammar, and Spelling

The ability of a State Police Officer to write authoritative investigative reports is important for several reasons. Probably among the most significant is that such reports serve as official, permanent records, which detail circumstances surrounding law-enforcement activity. Additionally, these same recorded facts may be used as potential leads by people outside of the initiating department (e.g., FBI, DEA, ATF, etc.) to further an investigation. The reports can also be forwarded to the criminal justice system to be used in determining what form of disciplinary action should be taken or to make a penalty assessment.

Police reports are also important at the administrative level. Data can be extrapolated and statistical correlations made regarding problem traffic areas, high crime districts, recurrent criminal trends, and the like. Departmental manpower can then be put to more effective use by focusing attention on such areas. Reports can also play a key role in promotion and budget recommendations. The ramifications of good report writing are considerable.

During the exam, you will not be expected to write an actual police report. However, the test questions will follow one of two different formats. One form involves reading a narrative. A blank report form of some kind is furnished in conjunction with the reading. You will then be required to find information within the reading pertinent to various sections of the report.

The second format is essentially the opposite of the first. You are provided with a report that has already been filled out. From it, you will need to extract information appropriate to the question asked. This exercise is not difficult, but a little care should be used in determining the who, what, when, where, why, and how factors of any particular incident. The reason for such caution is that there may be several facts in a crime scene that could go in one part of a report.

For example, there may be several *who's* contained in one report. For instance, who is the complainant (i.e., the victim or reportee of the purported crime)? Who is the witness, if there is one? Who responded to the incident? Who filed the report? It can be easy to misconstrue information inserted into a police report if close attention is not paid to the question at hand. The best advice here is to read either the narrative or prepared report through once to familiarize yourself with what has taken place. Then, read each question carefully and go back to the reading and discern what information is being requested. Once you have worked through the exercises provided in this study guide, you should be prepared for comparable questions on the actual exam.

The second part of this chapter involves basic grammar and spelling, two very important aspects of good report writing. Written police reports are essentially the official records of incidents. If the information contained in the report is vague, gramatically incorrect, or grossly misspelled, not only does it detract from the competence and professionalism of the officer in question, but it also reflects poorly on the department as a whole. Well-written reports communicate better and serve to expedite, not hinder, the complaint-issuing process.

It is not the intention of this book to provide instruction in basic grammar. If you feel that this may be one of your weaker areas, there are volumes of material dedicated to this subject available at your local library. Rather, test questions comparable to those seen on past exams are given with answers and explanations.

This chapter also reviews a few basic spelling rules that can lend substantial assistance to those who struggle in this area. Additionally, an extensive list of words that have been seen on past exams, as well as those studied at various training academies, have been compiled and included in this section. This does not guarantee that words other than those compiled will not be seen on your exam; however, it will offer a fairly comprehensive study of the word base you will most likely encounter on the actual exam.

Read the narrative provided below and then refer to the blank booking form that immediately follows to answer questions 1–10. (*Note:* Answer sheets for this exercise are placed at the end of this section.)

On September 17, 1992, Michael J. Connors was arrested at his home at 2025 Parker Boulevard, Auburn, Washington, for the manufacture of and intent to deliver a controlled substance and unlawful possession of a firearm by a felon, both of which are considered Class B felonies. Another person on the premises, Timothy Russell, who claimed to be a friend of the arrestee, was also arrested for conspiracy to distribute a controlled substance. He was booked in the Auburn County Jail (see arrest report #15-503).

Officer John Halden, Badge Number 363, was the arresting officer. Officer Halden currently resides on Creston Drive in Auburn, Washington. One hundred twenty grams of what is suspected to be cocaine and a .38-caliber pistol with the serial number 51105350 were placed in the evidence storage locker at Precinct 14 for future court exhibition. The arraignment of the suspect has been set for September 20, 1992, at 1:00 P.M. in Breston County District Court. Records indicate that the suspect has been convicted twice for assault and once for distribution of a controlled substance. He has served three years and two months in Humbolt Corrections and was paroled in October 1990, according to Officer Thurston Whitley, who was his probation officer at the time. Michael J. Connors has been known to have used the alias Mark E. Preston while engaging in drug-trade activity. Mr. Connors is a thirty-seven-year-old white male, 6', 195 pounds, with brown hair and hazel eyes. He is known to be a diabetic requiring insulin. One physical mark worth noting is a black eagle tattoo on his right forearm. Mr. Connors currently works for Hawthorne, Inc., located at 679 E. Marston Place, Auburn, Washington. His Social Security number is 508-27-4110, and another card found in his possession indicates that his stepmother, Andrea Stevens, who lives at 2042 Barrangton Avenue, Waverly, Iowa, should be contacted in case of an emergency. Her phone number is (319) 563-2751. Mr. Connors' two-tone white-on-blue 1990 Ford four-door station wagon was impounded by Hand K Towing at 4357 H Street, Auburn, Washington. Below are the names and addresses of people Mr. Connors asked to be notified pending his trial.

1. (Stepfather) George C. Nichols, 1459 E. Parkhurst, Federal Way, WA, home phone (206) 951-4321, business phone (206) 573-4444.

2. (Cousin) Arthur B. Gladstone, 160-D Magnuson Way Apartments, Colville, IA, home phone (515) 723-5678.

3. (Neighbor) Tina Weatherby, 2037 Parker Boulevard, Auburn, WA, home phone (206) 951-5541, business phone (206) 591-8741.

4. (Friend) Timothy Russell, 906 Forrest Drive, Auburn, WA, home phone (206) 933-5441.

① DATE OF REPORT	② BOOKING NO.	③ PRECINCT NO.	④ BADGE NO. OF ARRESTING OFFICER	⑤ TYPE F - FELONY M - MISDEMEANOR O - OTHER	⑥ EVIDENCE BOOKED ☐ YES ☐ NO

⑦ COMPLAINT FILED (CHARGES & COUNTS):

⑧ INVESTIGATING OFFICER'S NAME & ADDRESS:	⑨ ARRAIGNMENT DATE	⑩ TIME	⑪ COURT

㉕ ARRESTEE'S NAME:	㉗ SSN	⑫ ARREST DISPOSITION:

㉖ ARRESTEE'S ADDRESS:	⑬ D.A. FELONY REFERRAL:
	⑭ 72-HOUR RELEASE:

㉘ SEX	㊲ SCARS, PECULIARITIES:	⑮ FELONY WARRANT SERVED:
㉙ AGE/DOB	㊳ EMPLOYER'S NAME & ADDRESS:	⑯ MISDEMEANOR WARRANT SERVED:
㉚ RACE		⑰ FELONY COMPLAINT FILED:
㉛ HAIR	㊴ IN CASE OF EMERGENCY CALL: NAME: ADDRESS:	⑱ MISDEMEANOR COMPLAINT FILED:
㉜ EYES	RELATION: PHONE NO.:	⑲ OTHER:
㉝ HEIGHT	㊵ ARRESTEE'S VEHICLE: YR: MAKE: MODEL: COLOR:	⑳ PRIOR ARREST DISPOSITION:
㉞ WEIGHT	㊶ PRESENT LOCATION OR IMPOUNDMENT:	㉑ NAME OF PROBATION OFFICER:
㉟ MEDICAL PROBLEMS:		㉒ PRECINCT NO., IF AVAILABLE:
		㉓ TIME SERVED FOR OFFENSE:
㊱ ALIAS (AKAs):		㉔ PLACE WHERE TIME SERVED:

CODE	NAME	ADDRESS	HOME PHONE:	BUSINESS PHONE:

SEX:
O—MALE
Y—FEMALE

RACE:
1—CAUCASIAN
2—HISPANIC
3—AFRICAN AMERICAN
4—ASIAN AMERICAN
5—NATIVE AMERICAN

DATE OF BIRTH:
NUMERIC CODE SHOULD EXPRESS
MONTH-DAY-YEAR

EYES:
BROWN—BRO
BLUE—BE

GREEN—GE
HAZEL—HZ
GREY—GR
BLACK—B

HAIR:
BROWN—B
GREY—GE
BLACK—BA
BLONDE—BN
RED—R
BALD—NA

HEIGHT
WEIGHT
3 DIGIT NUMERIC CODE SHOULD
EXPRESS WEIGHT

SCARS/PECULIARITIES:
A—DEFORMITY
B—AMPUTATION
C—SCARS
D—TATTOO

LOCATION OF MARK:
1—FINGER
2—HAND
3—ARM
4—FOOT
5—LEG
6—CHEST
7—NECK
8—FACE

VEHICLE DESCRIPTION:
2 DOOR—2
4 DOOR—4
TRAILER—T
TRUCK—TK
VAN—N
STATION WAGON—W
CONVERTIBLE—K

CODES:
S—SPOUSE
A—BROTHER
D—SISTER
G—PARENT OR GUARDIAN
J—OTHER RELATIVE
M—FRIEND
O—ACCOMPLICE

ANY TIME ENTRIES IN THIS REPORT SHOULD BE EXPRESSED IN MILITARY FORM.

SAMPLE QUESTIONS FOR REPORT WRITING

1. According to the narrative, what information should be placed in Box 2 with regard to Mr. Connors' arrest?

    A. 15-503

    B. 511-05-5350

    C. 363

    D. None of the above

2. What information concerning Mr. Connors should be placed in Box 30 of this report?

    A. White

    B. Asian

    C. Black

    D. None of the above

3. What information concerning Mr. Connors should be placed in Box 33 of this report?

    A. 6'

    B. Brown

    C. 600

    D. 195 pounds

4. With regard to Mr. Connors' arrest, whose name should be inserted in Box 21?

    A. John Halden

    B. Thurston Whitley

    C. Arthur Gladstone

    D. Timothy Russell

5. The name Mark E. Preston would be appropriately inserted into what box on a booking report prepared for Mr. Connors?

    A. Box 36

    B. Box 39

    C. Box 42

    D. None of the above

6. What information would be placed in Box 10 with regard to Mr. Connors' arraignment?

    A. 9-17-92

    B. 9-20-92

    C. 1:00 P.M.

    D. None of the above

7. All of the following are true with respect to the booking report prepared on Mr. Connors except:

   A. 0, 1, 9-20-92, and B would be inserted in Boxes 28, 30, 29, and 31, respectively.

   B. Yes, Breston County District Court, 195 pounds, and HZ would respectively be inserted in Boxes 6, 11, 34, and 32.

   C. F, 363, Conspiracy to distribute a controlled substance, and 508-27-4110 would be inserted in Boxes 5, 4, 7, and 27, respectively.

   D. Both A and C

8. All of the following are true with respect to the booking report prepared on Mr. Connors' except:

   A. HZ, black-colored eagle tattooed on right forearm, 90-FORD-4-W-White/blue and Humbolt Corrections would be inserted in Boxes 32, 37, 40 and 24 respectively.

   B. Andrea Stevens would be inserted in Box 39.

   C. Diabetic, N/A, Hand K Towing-679 E. Marston Place, Auburn, WA, and the name George Nichols would be inserted in Boxes 35, 22, 41, and 42, respectively.

   D. All of the above are incorrect

9. What would be the appropriate report code used by the authorities to indicate Mr. Timothy Russell's relation to Mr. Connors?

   A. G

   B. M

   C. A

   D. None of the above

10. What would be the appropriate report code used by authorities to indicate Mr. Arthur B. Gladstone's relation to Mr. Connors?

   A. O

   B. A

   C. J

   D. None of the above

Look over the following Notice of Infraction (NOI) court docket. Answer questions 11–20 on the basis of the information provided in this report.

UNIFORM COURT DOCKET

☐ TRAFFIC INFRACTION   ☑ CRIMINAL TRAFFIC

☐ NON-TRAFFIC INFRACTION   ☐ CRIMINAL NON-TRAFFIC

☐ CITY/TOWN OF   ANKENY   PLAINTIFF VS. NAMED DEFENDANT

IN THE   ☑ DISTRICT   ☐ MUNICIPAL COURT OF   DES MOINES

STATE OF IOWA

COUNTY OF

THE UNDERSIGNED CERTIFIES AND SAYS THAT IN THE STATE OF IOWA

DRIVER'S LICENSE NO.	STATE	EXPIRES	SOCIAL SECURITY NUMBER
SANCHEZ 5214IP	NE	98	108-59-4832

NAME LAST	FIRST	MIDDLE	☐ INTERPRETER NEEDED
SANCHEZ	MICHAEL	P.	

ADDRESS   ☐ IF NEW ADDRESS
423 CRESTVIEW DR.

CITY	STATE	ZIP CODE	EMPLOYER
GRAND ISLAND	NE	65721	COMTRONICS LTD

SEX	RACE	DATE OF BIRTH	HEIGHT	WEIGHT	EYES	HAIR	RESIDENTIAL PHONE NUMBER
M	W	* 03-15-68	601	190	GR	BLK	(308) 513-1480

VIOLATION DATE	MONTH	DAY	YEAR	TIME (24 HRS)
ON OR ABOUT	MARCH	16	1996	2345 HRS

AT LOCATION	M.P.	CITY/COUNTY OF
INTERSTATE 35	162	POLK

DID OPERATE THE FOLLOWING VEHICLE/MOTOR VEHICLE ON A PUBLIC HIGHWAY AND

VEHICLE LICENSE NO.	STATE	EXPIRES	VEH. YR.	MAKE	MODEL	STYLE	COLOR
BLO 745	NE	97	94	FORD 2 DR		THUNDERBIRD	SIL/BLK

TRAILER #1 LICENSE NO.	STATE	EXPIRES	TR. YR.	TRAILER#2 LICENSE NO.	STATE	EXPIRES	TR. YR.

OWNER/COMPANY IF OTHER THAN DRIVER	ADDRESS	CITY	STATE	ZIP CODE
BUDGET RENTAL	1890 172ND ST.	OMAHA	NE	60711

ACCIDENT	BAC	COMMERCIAL	RENTAL	HAZARD	EXEMPT	
NO PD I F	READING	VEHICLE ☐YES ☑NO	VEHICLE ☑YES ☐NO	PLACARD ☐YES ☐NO	VEHICLE ☐FARM ☐FIRE ☐R.V. ☐OTHER	

DID THEN AND THERE COMMIT EACH OF THE FOLLOWING OFFENSES/INFRACTIONS

1. VIOLATION/STATUTE CODE	DESCRIPTION	VEHICLE SPEED	IN A	ZONE	
7.81.699	D.U.I.	92	65		☑RADAR ☐PACE ☐AIRCRAFT

2. VIOLATION/STATUTE CODE	DESCRIPTION
19.13.672	FIRST DEGREE RECKLESS DRIVING

PENALTY/BAIL
U.S. FUNDS $ 25,000

DATE NOTICE ISSUED	BOOKING DATE	TIME	APPEARANCE DATE	MO	DAY	YR.
03-16-96	03-17-96	0250 HRS		03	19	96

WITHOUT ADMITTING HAVING COMMITTED EACH OF THE ABOVE INFRACTIONS/OFFENSES, I PROMISE TO RESPOND AS DIRECTED ON THIS NOTICE

I CERTIFY (OR DECLARE) UNDER PENALTY OF PERJURY UNDER THE LAWS OF THE STATE OF IOWA THAT I HAVE REASONABLE GROUNDS/PROBABLE CAUSE TO BELIEVE AND DO BELIEVE THE ABOVE NAMED PERSON COMMITTED THE ABOVE INFRACTION(S) AND/OR OFFENSE(S) CONTRARY TO LAW.

OFFICER(S)	NUMBER
BEN WHITE	175
JILL FOSTER	189

X   *Michael Sanchez*
DEFENDANT'S SIGNATURE

DATE	PLACE
03-16-96	ANKENY, IA

	INFRACTION			COMPLAINT/CITATION					PENALTY		
INF	RESPONSE	DISPOSITION	CRG	PLEA	CNG	FINDING	FINE	SUSPENDED	SUB-TOTAL
1	C NC	C N D P	1	G NG		G NG D BF	$ 4700.00	$	$ 4700.00
2	C NC	C N D P	2	G NG		G NG D BF	$	$	$
							$	$	$

FINDING/ JUDGMENT DATE	03-19-96	TO SERVE	90 DAYS	WITH	60	DAYS SUSPENDED	CREDIT FOR TIME SERVE	2 DAYS	OTHER COSTS	$ 375.00
ABSTRACT MAILED TO ANKENY	03-21-96	RECOMMENDED NONEXTENSION OF SUSPENSION					LICENSE SURRENDER DATE	03-19-96	TOTAL COSTS	$5075.00

ABSTRACT OF JUDGMENT

11. When and where was the Notice of Infraction issued?

    A. March 3, 1996 – Polk County

    B. March 15, 1968 – Omaha, NE

    C. March 16, 1996 – Polk County

    D. March 17, 1996 – Des Moines, IA

12. According to the court docket, what was the defendant cited for?

    A. Traffic infraction

    B. Non-traffic infraction

    C. Criminal traffic

    D. Criminal non-traffic

13. According to the citation, the vehicle driven by the defendant was which of the following?

    A. State exempt vehicle

    B. Commercial vehicle

    C. Recreational vehicle

    D. Rental vehicle

14. The defendant was caught exceeding the posted speed limits by how much?

    A. 92 miles per hour

    B. 27 miles per hour

    C. 65 miles per hour

    D. 60 miles per hour

15. In which state was the defendant's license issued?

    A. Nebraska

    B. New Hampshire

    C. New Mexico

    D. Iowa

16. The defendant's date of birth was shown to be which of the following?

    A. March 21, 1996

    B. March 16, 1968

    C. March 15, 1968

    D. March 17, 1996

17. According to the NOI judgment abstract, Mr. Sanchez had how much time left to serve in lieu of posting bail?

    A. 28 days

    B. 30 days

    C. 60 days

    D. 90 days

18. When is the license of the vehicle in question due to expire?

    A. 1994

    B. 1998

    C. 1996

    D. 1997

19. According to the information shown, the applicable statute code for a DUI in the state of Iowa would be which of the following?

    A. 19.13.672

    B. 78.16.99

    C. 7.81.699

    D. Infraction statutes were not given.

20. All of the following statements are true except:

    A. The defendant was 28 years old at the time of his arrest.

    B. The defendant was a white male who was 6'1" tall and weighed 190 pounds.

    C. Milepost marker 162 on Interstate 35 is located in Polk County, IA.

    D. Sanchez's given home address is 1890 172nd St., Omaha, NE 60711.

ANSWER SHEET FOR SAMPLE REPORT-WRITING QUESTIONS

1. Ⓐ Ⓑ Ⓒ Ⓓ   8. Ⓐ Ⓑ Ⓒ Ⓓ   15. Ⓐ Ⓑ Ⓒ Ⓓ

2. Ⓐ Ⓑ Ⓒ Ⓓ   9. Ⓐ Ⓑ Ⓒ Ⓓ   16. Ⓐ Ⓑ Ⓒ Ⓓ

3. Ⓐ Ⓑ Ⓒ Ⓓ   10. Ⓐ Ⓑ Ⓒ Ⓓ   17. Ⓐ Ⓑ Ⓒ Ⓓ

4. Ⓐ Ⓑ Ⓒ Ⓓ   11. Ⓐ Ⓑ Ⓒ Ⓓ   18. Ⓐ Ⓑ Ⓒ Ⓓ

5. Ⓐ Ⓑ Ⓒ Ⓓ   12. Ⓐ Ⓑ Ⓒ Ⓓ   19. Ⓐ Ⓑ Ⓒ Ⓓ

6. Ⓐ Ⓑ Ⓒ Ⓓ   13. Ⓐ Ⓑ Ⓒ Ⓓ   20. Ⓐ Ⓑ Ⓒ Ⓓ

7. Ⓐ Ⓑ Ⓒ Ⓓ   14. Ⓐ Ⓑ Ⓒ Ⓓ

Answers can be found on page 149.

SAMPLE QUESTIONS FOR GRAMMAR

Questions 21–40 are specifically designed to test your knowledge of proper English usage and grammar. This section is meant only as a basic review of what is traditionally taught in high school. If you feel unsure about some of the rules, it is strongly advised that you study supplemental material that addresses this subject. A quick refresher course in writing can always be beneficial, regardless of the potential exam implications.

Each question will provide four complete sentences. You will have to determine which sentence, if any, is grammatically correct. The answers to these questions, complete with explanations detailing why the incorrect sentence structures are wrong, are provided at the end of this section.

21. A. The Policemen's Ball (an event established three years ago) has become a widely publicized festivity.

   B. These kinds of preparatory study guides are instructive.

   C. The grand jury has agreed on the verdict.

   D. All of the above sentences are grammatically correct.

22. A. Trooper Hanley is at his best in filing detailed field interview reports.

   B. Officer Briggs was upset at me.

   C. Rookie State Patrol Officer Dan Clemms only made one error on his first assignment.

   D. None of the above sentences are grammatically correct.

23. A. Sergeant Hill has arrested a woman identified by the victim's mother as the person she saw leaving the scene of the crime.

   B. The gang of juveniles fleed in several directions at the sight of Officer Jenkins.

   C. After completing the accident report, the rest of the day was easy.

   D. None of the above sentences are grammatically correct.

24. A. A gun was found lose in her purse.

   B. The mayor effected many changes in police personnel.

   C. The Thomas-Gains Community Service award was presented to both my partner and myself.

   D. All of the above sentences are grammatically correct.

25. A. Its about time they implemented that policy.

   B. The suspect was told to lay his gun down on the ground.

   C. Everyone shaked my hand at the conference.

   D. All of the above sentences are grammatically correct.

26. A. Trooper Bartelli's response was quick and emphatic.

   B. Steve Jones's nightstick was missing.

   C. In general, it's relatively quiet out there.

   D. All of the above sentences are grammatically correct.

27. A. To Lieutenant James, Patrolman Heath was borderline irresponsible.

 B. Each officer is bringing their own lunch.

 C. In summary: the prosecutor has proven a clear case of negligent homicide.

 D. None of the above sentences are grammatically correct.

28. A. The M.O. is very unique, but I cannot recall whom it is.

 B. This is the portable TV set that was knocked over during the argument.

 C. Detective Connelly remarked "that he felt fatigued."

 D. None of the above sentences are grammatically correct.

29. A. Richard and Sue said that their planning on a backpacking trip in October.

 B. "Your checkbook balance is wrong," she said, "add your deposit slips again."

 C. I have a partner who served three consecutive tours in Vietnam.

 D. All of the above sentences are grammatically correct.

30. A. To work effectively, a State Patrol Officer should keep his firearm cleaned and oiled.

 B. Bill was real livid.

 C. There isn't an unbroken window in the abandoned warehouse.

 D. All of the above sentences are grammatically correct.

31. A. Judith Merriweather chairwoman of Crime Stoppers Blockwatch has announced the merger.

 B. We shall always remember him as a compassionate police officer, said the minister.

 C. Where has John Carrington been at?

 D. None of the above sentences are grammatically correct.

32. A. The nature of police work both gave me excitement and satisfaction.

 B. The patrolman did not say whether he had completed the preliminary assessments.

 C. The applicant has had three years of undergraduate study at ohio state university.

 D. None of the above sentences are grammatically correct.

33. A. Steve and I attended the safety seminar sponsored by Kelso, Inc.

 B. Captain Felder has an leather recliner and an oak file cabinet he would like to sell.

 C. Carroll would like to join us to.

 D. All of the above sentences are grammatically correct.

34. A. The store manager payed little attention to the threat made by the suspect.

 B. How can you expect anyone to do his duty when you place them under intense scrutiny?

 C. Whom did you call?

 D. All of the above sentences are grammatically correct.

35. A. There is not no easy way of solving the problem of teenage drug abuse.

    B. Your official hiring date (once the background check proves satisfactory) will be the first Tuesday of next month.

    C. The new department policy was poorly planned, it lacked both insight and reality.

    D. None of the above sentences are grammatically correct.

36. A. Margarets new car has turned out to be a lemon.

    B. Talking, not arguing, is the best way to handle domestic disputes.

    C. That sort of trite remarks will ruin your career.

    D. All of the above sentences are grammatically correct.

37. A. Frank had a holier than thou attitude after tipping off authorities about an illegal gambling operation.

    B. A good police officer has courage, strength, and is patient.

    C. None of the administrators speaks well of Captain Martin.

    D. None of the above sentences are grammatically correct.

38. A. People seldom attend help sessions nevertheless they are proven to be extremely helpful for most.

    B. It almost seems impossible to meet the deadline established.

    C. Please fill out your job application form carefully, concisely, and truthfully.

    D. None of the above sentences are grammatically correct.

39. A. Before I worked for the department, I had never used a handgun.

    B. Officer Miller crouched besides the victim.

    C. Your going to the demonstration whether you like it or not.

    D. All of the above sentences are grammatically correct.

40. A. The Bill of Rights guarantees individual freedoms.

    B. The reason for Dave's absence was because he felt sick.

    C. Nobody else decisions are more respected than Sergeant Collin's.

    D. All of the above sentences are grammatically correct.

ANSWER SHEET FOR SAMPLE GRAMMAR QUESTIONS

21. Ⓐ Ⓑ Ⓒ Ⓓ
22. Ⓐ Ⓑ Ⓒ Ⓓ
23. Ⓐ Ⓑ Ⓒ Ⓓ
24. Ⓐ Ⓑ Ⓒ Ⓓ
25. Ⓐ Ⓑ Ⓒ Ⓓ
26. Ⓐ Ⓑ Ⓒ Ⓓ
27. Ⓐ Ⓑ Ⓒ Ⓓ

28. Ⓐ Ⓑ Ⓒ Ⓓ
29. Ⓐ Ⓑ Ⓒ Ⓓ
30. Ⓐ Ⓑ Ⓒ Ⓓ
31. Ⓐ Ⓑ Ⓒ Ⓓ
32. Ⓐ Ⓑ Ⓒ Ⓓ
33. Ⓐ Ⓑ Ⓒ Ⓓ
34. Ⓐ Ⓑ Ⓒ Ⓓ

35. Ⓐ Ⓑ Ⓒ Ⓓ
36. Ⓐ Ⓑ Ⓒ Ⓓ
37. Ⓐ Ⓑ Ⓒ Ⓓ
38. Ⓐ Ⓑ Ⓒ Ⓓ
39. Ⓐ Ⓑ Ⓒ Ⓓ
40. Ⓐ Ⓑ Ⓒ Ⓓ

Answers can be found on page 150.

SPELLING

Spelling questions can make up 5 to 10 percent of the State Patrol Officer exam. Consequently, this area warrants a degree of review even by those who have fairly good spelling skills. A basic list of guidelines that can be of assistance when the proper spelling of a word is in doubt is provided. Pay particular attention to any exceptions pointed out in these guidelines—test questions often center around such exceptions. As mentioned earlier, a list of words that have been seen on past exams has been compiled for your study. There is a good chance that most of the spelling questions that may be seen on your actual exam will be included in this list.

Once you have studied these spelling rules and the list, move on to the sample spelling test questions that follow. Do not use a dictionary for reference, because you will not be allowed to use one during the actual exam. The answers to these sample questions are provided at the end of this chapter.

SPELLING GUIDELINES

1. If you add a suffix that begins with a vowel to a word that ends in the letter *e* (silent), you should drop the final *e*. For instance, the word *dine* and the suffix *-ing* are combined to form the word *dining*. Other examples would be *coming, loving, continuous, deplorable*.

   However, if the word in question ends in soft *ge* or *ce*, the letter *e* may be kept before either *-able* or *-ous*. For instance, the word *manage* plus-*able* is spelled *manageable*. Other examples would include *traceable, enforceable, advantageous,* and *courageous*.

   One other exception is to keep the letter *e* in the present participle of the words *singe, due,* and *eye*: *singeing, dyeing,* and *eyeing*.

2. If you add a suffix that begins with a consonant (i.e., *-ment, -ly*), the spelling will not normally change. For instance, the words *movement, lonely, carelessness,* and *extremely,* illustrate this rule. Exceptions are *judgment, argument, acknowledgment,* and *truly*.

3. If a suffix is added to words that end in *y*, the *y* must be changed to *i* unless the suffix itself begins with *i*. For instance, *happy* and *-ness* are combined to spell *happiness*. Other examples include *business, merciless,* and *defiant*. However, words such as *study* or *carry* which end in *y* do not change with the addition of a suffix (*studying* and *carrying*).

4. The use of the suffix *-sede, -cede,* or *-ceed* is quite simple. *Supersede* is the only word spelled with *-sede. Succeed, proceed,* and *exceed* are the only words that incorporate *-ceed* as a suffix. All other comparable words are spelled with the *-cede* ending: *recede, intercede, precede,* etc.

5. In most cases, prefixes can be added to words without affecting the spelling of the word in question. For example, *mis-* added to *spell* produces *misspell*. Other examples would include *malcontent, unnecessary, inaccurate,* and *irreverent*.

6. Use *i* before *e* except after *c* or when it sounds like the name of letter *a*. For instance, the words *believe, chief, yield,* and *grief,* demonstrate the proper spellings in the absence of *c. Receive, perceive,* and *deceit* are a few examples that reverse the order of *i* and *e*. Some examples of words in which *ei* sounds like *a* are *neighbor, their,* and *weight*. They follow the same rules of spelling that apply to words having the letters *e* and *i* following *c*. Other words that seem to be an exception to these rules are *neither, seize, forfeit, either, leisure, weird, counterfeit,* and *foreign*.

7. If you intend to change the form of a single-syllable action word that ends in a consonant preceded by a vowel, you must double the final consonant. For instance, *plan, sad* and *sit* change to *planning, sadden,* and *sitting.*

    The final consonant must be doubled to change the form of a two-syllable word that ends in a consonant preceded by a vowel and that is accented on the second syllable. For instance, the words *refer, remit,* and *occur* can have their respective spellings changed to *referring, remittance,* and *occurring.* However, if you are using a two- or three-syllable word and the addition of a suffix results in the change of accent from the final syllable to a preceding one, you should not double the final consonant. For instance, the words *travel, refer,* and *cancel* would be spelled *traveling, reference,* and *cancelling* according to this rule.

8. Adjectives that end with the letter *l* may be changed to a corresponding adverb by simply adding *-ly* to the word. For instance, *legal, accidental,* and *unusual* may be changed to *legally, accidentally,* and *unusually.*

    If you desire to combine suffixes and prefixes that end in *ll,* usually one *l* is dropped from the word. For instance, the words *all together, all ready,* and *mind full* would appropriately be combined to spell *altogether, already,* and *mindful.*

9. If the intent is to change a singular to a plural, this can usually be accomplished by simply adding *s* to the word; for instance, *chips, rules,* and *times.* If the word in question ends in *s* or an *s*-like sound (i.e., *sh, ch, ss, x,* and *z*), then a plural may be formed by adding *es*; for instance, *crushes, annexes,* and *dishes.* Be aware, however, that some words require irregular changes to become plural. For instance, *alumnus* to *alumni, thief* to *thieves, woman* to *women,* and *crisis* to *crises,* just to name a few.

10. If you are unsure of whether a word's ending is properly spelled *-ise* or *-ize,* you can be relatively assured that the latter choice is correct more often than it is wrong. American usage (as opposed to British) seems to prefer *-ize* in most instances. *Advise, despise, surprise,* and *supervise* are just a few of the *-ise* exceptions. *Organize, utilize, centralize,* and *authorize* are typical words that incorporate *-ize.*

    There are, of course, other minor rules to spelling that have not been discussed here. However, this list of guidelines encompasses most of what will concern you on the actual exam. Keep this list in mind as you work through the sample questions provided.

SAMPLE QUESTIONS FOR SPELLING

41. Prior to the Miranda case, police officers felt that it was <u>unnecessery</u> to explain to a defendant his or her rights at the time of the arrest. How should the word underlined in this sentence be spelled?

    A. Unecesssary

    B. Unneccessary

    C. Unnecessary

    D. No change is required because the word in question is spelled correctly.

42. Most people probably <u>exsede</u> the speed limit by five to ten miles per hour. How should the word underlined in this sentence be spelled?

   A. Exceed

   B. Excede

   C. Exseed

   D. No change is required because the word in question is spelled correctly.

43. Kids learning to drive seem to have difficulty with the aspects of <u>parallel</u> parking. How should the underlined word be spelled?

   A. Parralel

   B. Paralell

   C. Pearallel

   D. No change is required because the word in question is spelled correctly.

44. Sex offenders need to be <u>superviced</u> closely. How should the underlined word be spelled?

   A. Supervized

   B. Supervised

   C. Supervizzed

   D. No change is required because the word in question is spelled correctly.

45. The witness claims to <u>reckinize</u> two of the three people we have in custody. How should the underlined word be spelled?

   A. Recognise

   B. Recognize

   C. Rekognize

   D. No change is required because the word in question is spelled correctly.

46. Howard wants the reports on his desk no later than <u>Wensday</u>. How should the underlined word be spelled?

   A. Wendsday

   B. Wedsday

   C. Wednesday

   D. No change is required because the word in question is spelled correctly.

47. It was very difficult to tell the difference between the <u>counterfiet</u> and the real thing. How should the underlined word in the sentence be spelled?

   A. Countorfeit

   B. Counterfit

   C. Counterfeit

   D. No change is required because the word in question is spelled correctly.

48. The defense attorney hoped that his client would receive a lenient judgement since it was a first-time offense. How should the underlined word in this sentence be spelled?

    A. Judgment

    B. Jugment

    C. Judgmente

    D. No change is required because the word in question is spelled correctly.

49. The whole incident proved to be embarrassing.

    A. Embarassing

    B. Embarrasing

    C. Emberrassing

    D. No change is required because the word in question is spelled correctly.

50. Only recently have repeat offenders receeved harsher sentences. How should the underlined word be spelled?

    A. Received

    B. Recieved

    C. Reccived

    D. No change is required because the word in question is spelled properly.

51. Considering the circumstances, her actions seemed justafiable. How should the underlined word be spelled?

    A. Justifyable

    B. Justefiable

    C. Justifiable

    D. No change is required because the word in question is spelled correctly.

52. Ocasionally, you will be required to put in overtime. How should the underlined word be spelled?

    A. Ocassionally

    B. Occasionally

    C. Occasionaly

    D. No change is required because the word in question is spelled correctly.

53. After chasing the suspect for several blocks, Officer Miller had to stop to catch his breathe. How should the underlined word in this sentence be spelled?

    A. Breath

    B. Breeth

    C. Braethe

    D. No change is required because the word in question is spelled correctly.

Questions 54–60 each have four numerically identified columns comprising various word sets. One of the word sets will contain an intentionally misspelled word. Select the column number that represents the misspelled word and mark your answer sheet accordingly.

54.

I	II	III	IV
penitentiary	bulletin	violation	bureau
mistaken	contraband	disciplin	disappear
district	attorney	conspiracy	security
coroner	commissary	fighting	committee

A. I
B. II
C. III
D. IV

55.

I	II	III	IV
infraction	mustache	negligent	intimidation
miscellanious	physical	retaliate	fracture
patient	obscene	disagree	incident
grievance	privilege	jury	felony

A. I
B. II
C. III
D. IV

56.

I	II	III	IV
medical	professional	informant	seize
parole	witness	penalty	proceedure
statute	vicinity	personnel	sincerity
sergeant	frequent	suspicion	testimony

A. I
B. II
C. III
D. IV

57.

I	II	III	IV
transferred	judicial	delusion	cigarette
inquiry	disoriented	dangerous	private
hazard	appoint	weapon	psychiatrist
observed	rehabilitate	planetiff	describe

A. I
B. II
C. III
D. IV

58.

I	II	III	IV
lethal	epileptic	narcotics	extortion
beleive	custody	knife	fugitive
apprehend	bail	obnoxious	investigate
courteous	molest	incriminate	laboratory

A. I
B. II
C. III
D. IV

59.

I	II	III	IV
forfeit	surveillance	thorough	muscle
indecent	realise	receipt	homicide
loiter	psychology	preliminary	forcibly
version	unconscious	prejudiced	opinion

A. I
B. II
C. III
D. IV

60.

I	II	III	IV
negotiable	insurance	interview	heroin
offender	metropolitan	hemorrhage	punitive
license	lieutenent	Wednesday	weight
exercise	parallel	schedule	subpoena

A. I
B. II
C. III
D. IV

ANSWER SHEET FOR SAMPLE SPELLING QUESTIONS

41. (A) (B) (C) (D)   48. (A) (B) (C) (D)   55. (A) (B) (C) (D)

42. (A) (B) (C) (D)   49. (A) (B) (C) (D)   56. (A) (B) (C) (D)

43. (A) (B) (C) (D)   50. (A) (B) (C) (D)   57. (A) (B) (C) (D)

44. (A) (B) (C) (D)   51. (A) (B) (C) (D)   58. (A) (B) (C) (D)

45. (A) (B) (C) (D)   52. (A) (B) (C) (D)   59. (A) (B) (C) (D)

46. (A) (B) (C) (D)   53. (A) (B) (C) (D)   60. (A) (B) (C) (D)

47. (A) (B) (C) (D)   54. (A) (B) (C) (D)

Answers can be found on page 152.

For your convenience, a reference list of words seen on various State Police Officer exams has been provided below. It should be noted that this list of words does not preclude the possibility of seeing other words or variations of the same word on the actual exam. However, this reference list should account for a majority of spelling questions most likely encountered on the test.

abandoned	article	carnal	cooperate
abduction	artificial	carrying	coordinate
academy	asked	cartridge	coroner
accelerator	asphyxiated	cashier	corporation
accessories	assault	casualty	corps
accident	assistance	ceiling	corpse
accomplice	assistants	cemetery	correctional
accountability	associate	chauffeur	corrective
accurate	assortment	chief	corroborate
acquaintance	athletics	cigarette	cough
acquitted	attorney	circle	council
across	attraction	circumstance	counsel
adjacent	attribute	citizen	counterfeit
administrative	authorization	coarse	coupon
admissible	automatic	cocaine	court
admission	available	coerce	courteous
admonition	backward	coherent	credibility
adultery	bail	collaborate	criminal
affidavit	bale	collar	criteria
affirmation	bandage	collision	cruising
aggravated	barricade	colonel	curfew
aggressive	beaten	combative	current
alcohol	beginning	coming	custody
allege	behavior	commercial	cylinder
always	beige	commissary	damage
ammunition	believe	commission	dangerous
analysis	belligerent	committed	deceased
anonymous	bicycle	committee	decent
answer	borderline	communication	decision
apparent	boulevard	community	defendant
appeal	brake	complainant	delinquent
application	break	comply	delusion
appoint	breathalyzer	concealed	demeanor
appraise	bruise	confusion	depression
apprehend	building	conscience	descent
approximately	bulletin	conscious	describe
argument	bureau	consent	description
arraignment	burglary	consistent	detached
arrangement	business	conspiracy	detention
arrest	cache	construction	deterrent
arson	calendar	continue	diabetic
arterial	campaign	contraband	diesel
artery	captain	conviction	different

disabled	feminine	implementation	knowledge
disagree	fighting	impossible	label
disappear	financial	impression	laboratory
disappointed	forcibly	incest	larceny
discipline	foreign	incident	latent
disoriented	forfeit	incorrigible	lawyer
dispatched	forgery	incriminate	legal
dispense	forth	indecent	leisure
disperse	forty	indicate	length
disposition	fourteen	indict	lethal
disseminate	fourth	indigent	liability
dissent	fracture	individual	likable
district	fraudulent	informant	liaison
disturbance	frequent	infraction	libel
duress	frequently	ingest	liberty
during	friend	inhaled	license
educational	frisk	inherent	lieutenant
eight	fugitive	inherit	liquor
elementary	furniture	initial	loiter
eliminate	gambling	injured	loose
embarrass	garbage	inquiry	lose
embezzlement	gauge	inscribed	loss
emergency	genuine	instead	malicious
emphasize	government	instinct	manipulate
employee	grabbed	institutional	manual
enforcement	grazed	insufficient	marijuana
epileptic	grease	insulted	marital
equipment	grievance	insurance	maximum
erratic	guardian	intelligent	medal
escape	gymnasium	intercourse	medical
escorted	handkerchief	interest	menace
evidence	hazard	interrogate	metal
examination	headache	intersection	metropolitan
exceed	hemorrhage	intervention	microfiche
excellent	heroin	interview	microphone
except	history	intimidation	mileage
excite	holster	intoxicating	minor
exclude	homicide	investigation	minute
exercise	horizontal	it's	Miranda
exhaust	hostage	its	miscellaneous
experience	hurrying	jealous	mischief
explanation	hydrant	jewelry	misdemeanor
explosion	identified	judge	misspelled
expression	illegal	judgment	mistaken
extension	illiterate	judicial	mitigate
extortion	imitation	jury	molest
extradite	immediately	juvenile	motorcycle
familiar	impact	khaki	municipal
felony	impaired	knife	muscle

mustache	penalty	prosecutor	respiration
naive	penitentiary	prostitution	responsible
narcotics	perform	provoke	restitution
nausea	perimeter	proximity	retribution
necessary	perjury	psychiatrist	request
negative	permanent	psychology	retaliate
neglect	permit	public	revoked
negligent	persecute	pulse	revolver
negotiable	persistent	pungent	rhythmic
neighbor	personal	punitive	riot
nervous	personnel	purpose	robbery
neurotic	perspiration	pursue	routine
niece	physical	pursuit	sacrifice
ninety	physician	putrefy	sanitary
noisy	piece	pyrotechnic	satisfactory
noticeable	plaintiff	quality	Saturday
notify	planning	quantity	scene
obligation	pneumatic	questionnaire	schedule
obnoxious	policies	quiet	scheme
obscene	polygamy	quite	schizophrenic
observed	polygraph	racial	search
obsolete	positive	radical	secretary
obstacle	possession	raid	security
occasion	potential	rally	seen
occupant	pregnancy	ramification	segregate
occur	prejudice	rationalization	seize
occurred	prejudiced	raucous	semiautomatic
odor	preliminary	react	sense
offender	premises	realize	sentence
official	prescription	receipt	sequester
operator	preservation	receive	sergeant
opinion	previous	reckless	serial
opportunity	principal	recognize	several
opposite	principle	recommendation	severely
ordinance	prisoner	recurrence	sexual
organize	private	reference	sheriff
original	privileges	refuse	shining
oxygen	probably	registration	shone
painful	probationary	regrettable	shown
parallel	procedure	rehabilitation	sieve
parole	proceeded	reimburse	signature
participate	process	relevant	silhouette
passed	profane	reliable	similar
passenger	professional	religious	simultaneous
past	prohibitive	remember	since
patience	promiscuous	renewal	sincerity
patients	promotional	representation	siphon
peace	proposition	reputation	skeleton
pedestrian	prosecute	resistance	skeptical

skidded
sleight
slight
sobriety
socialize
sodomy
sophisticated
specimen
spontaneous
sprain
statement
stationary
stationery
statute
sterilize
stomach
strangulate
strictly
striped
stripped
subject
submitting
subpoena
substantiate
subtle
succeed
successful
suffocate
suicidal
summons
superintendent
superior
supervisor
surveillance
susceptible
suspect
suspicion
symptom
tactical
tamper
tattoo
technician
telephone
temperature
temporary
terrorism
testimony
theater
theft

their
there
they're
thieves
thorough
thought
threaten
threw
throat
through
tier
tissue
to
together
tongue
too
tourniquet
toxicology
traffic
transferred
translucent
trespassing
truancy
Tuesday
two
typewriter
ultimatum
unconscious
uniform
unnecessary
urgent
using
utility
vacuum
vagrancy
valuable
vehicle
velocity
verify
version
vertical
vicinity
vicious
victim
violate
visible
volume
voluntary
waist

warehouse
warrant
waste
weapon
weather
Wednesday
weight
welfare
weather
whether
whiskey
whole
whore
witness
women
wounded
wrapper
wreck
yield
young
your
you're

ANSWERS TO SAMPLE REPORT-WRITING QUESTIONS

1. *D.* A booking report number had not been specifically given in the reading. Selection A represents an arrest report number for Mr. Russell.

2. *D.* Reference Code Number 1 should be used, according to the report. Selection A is a correct description; however, it is procedurally wrong to state the fact this way since applicable booking codes have been provided.

3. *C.* The report specifically mentions that height must be expressed as a three-digit number expressing both feet and inches. Therefore, C is the correct choice.

4. *B.* Thurston Whitley was Mr. Connors' probation officer. Selection A is the arresting officer involved.

5. *A.* This name is an alias used by Mr. Connors. Box 36 would be the correct place for this information.

6. *D.* Selection C is correct with respect to the appointed time; however, the booking report makes specific reference to the fact that all time entries must be expressed in military form. Therefore, 1300 hours would be the correct information to insert in Box 10.

   (*Note:* It should be mentioned here that many exams seen recently vacillate between the use of military time and regular [civilian] time. Many police departments utilize military time in filling out various reports. Therefore, you should be aware of both uses. Military time is figured on a 24-hour clock: 0100 hours represents 1:00 A.M., 0200 hours represents 2:00 A.M., 1200 hours represents noon, 1600 hours represents 4:00 P.M., 2200 hours represents 10:00 P.M., and so on. Minutes are figured the same as for civilian time. For instance, 0830 hours represents 8:30 A.M., 0945 hours represents 9:45 A.M., 1515 hours represents 3:15 P.M., etc. Be aware of both forms of time because invariably you will be expected to understand the differences.)

7. *D.* Selection A is incorrect in placing 9-20-92 in Box 29. This would reflect Mr. Connors' arraignment date, not his date of birth. Mr. Connors' age was given to be thirty-seven. Selection C is incorrect in the charges filed against Mr. Connors. Instead, this lists what was filed against Mr. Russell. Both manufacture of and intent to deliver a controlled substance, plus unlawful possession of a firearm by a felon, should be placed in Box 7.

8. *D.* Even though the description is correct, selection A is incorrect because it does not use the code D-3 to establish the location of the scar or peculiarity. Selection B is incomplete. Andrea Stevens' relation to Mr. Connors, home address and home phone number should be completed since the information is available. Selection C incorrectly states Hand K's impoundment yard as being located at 679 E. Marston Place; this is the address where Mr. Connors is employed. The correct insertion made into Box 41 is Hand K Towing, 4357 H Street, Auburn, WA.

9. *D.* Mr. Connors made reference to Mr. Russell as a friend. Mr. Russell was, in fact, arrested for conspiracy to distribute a controlled substance at the same time Mr. Connors was arrested. Therefore, from the authorities' perspective, Mr. Timothy Russell would be considered an accomplice. The code O was not offered as an option for the question.

10. *C.* Mr. Connors made reference to Mr. Gladstone as his cousin. Selection C best describes the relationship.

11. *C.* March 16, 1996 – Polk County

12. *C.* Criminal traffic

13. *D.* Rental vehicle

14. *B.* Mr. Sanchez was clocked doing 92 miles per hour in a 65 mile-per-hour zone. Therefore, 92 – 65 = 27 miles per hour over and beyond the posted speed limit.

15. *A.* Nebraska

16. *C.* March 15, 1968

17. *A.*   Mr. Sanchez was originally sentenced to ninety days for the pair of violations. Sixty days were suspended, and he was given credit for having already spent two days in jail. Therefore, the time remaining would be twenty-eight days.

18. *D.*   1997

19. *C.*   7.81.699

20. *D.*   The defendant's home address was shown to be 423 Crestview Drive, Grand Island, NE 65721. Selection D, on the other hand, is the business address for Budget Rental in Omaha, NE.

ANSWERS TO SAMPLE GRAMMAR QUESTIONS

21. *D.*   A. Parentheses can be used to enclose explanations within a sentence.

   B. The word *these* is plural and correctly modifies the plural noun *study guides*.

   C. *Grand jury* is considered a collective noun and therefore requires the singular verb *has*.

22. *A.*   The sentence correctly uses the present tense to illustrate a point.

   B. The word *at* exemplifies the incorrect use of a preposition. The word *with* would be considered appropriate.

   C. "Only made" exemplifies the incorrect placement of an adverb. It should be turned around to read "made only."

23. *A.*   This sentence correctly uses a subordinate clause in stating what happened.

   B. The word *fleed* does not exist; the appropriate word is *fled*.

   C. The sentence contains an inappropriate dangling modifier that fails to identify who filled out the accident report. One way to write this sentence correctly would be: After he completed the accident report, he found the rest of the day easy.

24. *B.*   *Affect* means "influence"; here *effect* ("cause," "bring about") is needed.

   A. The word *lose* is a verb that means the opposite of win. The proper adjective to use in this case is *loose*, which means unrestrained.

   C. *Myself* is a reflexive pronoun that should not be substituted for *I* or *me*.

25. *B.*   *Lay* is the correct transitive verb to be used in this statement.

   A. *It's* is a contraction of "it is." An apostrophe is needed between the letters *t* and *s*. *Its* is a possessive pronoun.

   C. *Shaked* is not recognized as a word. *Shook* is the appropriate word needed in this sentence.

26. *D.*   A. The apostrophe is correctly used to indicate possession.

   B. With a singular noun that ends in *s*, in this case *Jones*, it would be correct to indicate possession either by adding an apostrophe after *s* in *Jones (Jones')* or by adding an apostrophe and *s (Jones's)*. However, it would have been incorrect to write *Joneses*.

   C. The comma is appropriately used to set apart the introductory phrase, and the apostrophe is used correctly to indicate the contraction.

27. *A.*   The comma is appropriately used in the sentence after the introductory phrase. Without it, the sentence seems confused and may be misunderstood.

   B. There must be agreement between the pronoun and what it stands for. *His or her* would be considered correct instead of *their*.

   C. The colon is used correctly; however, the first word of a complete statement that follows a colon should be capitalized.

28. *B.*   *That* is the appropriate pronoun since it refers to an object, in this case a TV set.

   A. *Who* and *whom* can refer only to people. Since a method of operation instead of people is being described, the word *whose*, which is a possessive of *who*, would be considered the correct choice, referring to the person with that M.O.

   C. Quotation marks should not be used to set off indirect quotations. The absence of quotation marks would be acceptable.

29. *C.*   The adjective clause is appropriately introduced by the pronoun *who*.

A. *Their* is a possessive of *they*. Instead, the contraction *they're* is needed.

B. A comma splice should not be used in divided quotations. A period after *said* and capitalizing *add* would be one correct revision.

30. *C.*   The singular verb agrees with the singular noun.

A. This statement sounds ridiculous, not to mention that a modifier must modify something. A more appropriate statement would read, "The State Police officer should keep his firearm cleaned and oiled to make it work effectively."

B. Adverbs modify adjectives, verbs, and other adverbs. Therefore, it should read, "Bill is very livid."

31. *D.*   A. Commas were not used to set off words in parenthetical apposition. Commas should be placed at "Merriweather, chairwoman" and "Blockwatch, has."

B. Quotation marks should always be used to enclose a quotation. They should be placed prior to the word *We* and after the word *officer*.

C. "Where has John Carrington been?" This would be a more appropriate way of asking the question. *At* is unnecessary and ungrammatical.

32. *B.*   *Whether* is properly used as a conjunction in this statement.

A. A correlative conjunction was not appropriately placed next to the words it connects. A better way to restructure this sentence would be this: The nature of police work gave me both excitement and satisfaction.

C. Ohio State University is considered to be a proper name and should therefore be capitalized.

33. *A.*   *I* (instead of *me*) is the correct choice of first-person pronoun as subject of *attended*.

B. *A* instead of *an* should be used before "leather recliner."

C. *To* is a preposition that expresses motion or direction toward something. Instead, the adverb *too* should be used to indicate "in addition."

34. *C.*   *Whom* is the proper pronoun to use instead of *who*.

A. *Paid* is the correct substitute.

B. *His* is considered singular and, therefore, *them* should be replaced by *him*.

35. *B.*   Commas would have worked as well; however, parentheses are suitable to set off parenthetical expressions.

A. *Not* should be left out of the sentence. *Not* and *no* combined in a statement can render an expression ineffective.

C. A colon should be used instead of the comma when there is restatement of the idea.

36. *B.*   Commas are effectively used to set off contrasted phrases.

A. There is need for an apostrophe to demonstrate possession (*Margaret's*).

C. Plural adjectives must be used to modify plural nouns. Therefore, *that* should be replaced with *those*.

37. *D.*   A. *Holier than thou* is intended to be a single compound unit modifying *attitude* and therefore requires hyphenation (*holier-than-thou*).

B. Ideas within a sentence must be parallel or presented in the same form. The correct way of expressing the same idea is this: A good police officer has courage, strength, and patience.

C. *Speaks* fails to agree with the plural subject, administrators. *Speak* would be correct.

38. *C.*   The descriptive words in the statement are parallel in structure.

A. Any time there are two complete thoughts within a sentence that uses the connecting word *nevertheless*, it should be preceded with a semicolon and followed by a comma.

B. An adverb should be placed close to the word it modifies. *Seems* and *almost* should be reversed.

39. A. Punctuation and tense are correctly used in this statement.

B. *Besides* is an adverb that means "in addition to." In this sentence *beside,* a preposition that means "by the side of," is called for.

C. *Your* is a possessive of *you. You're,* which is a contraction of *you are,* is what is needed in this statement.

40. A. *Bill of Rights* is appropriately capitalized.

B. *Because* makes poor use of a conjunction. *That* would be more appropriate.

C. *Else* must illustrate possession by adding an apostrophe and *s (else's).*

ANSWERS TO SAMPLE SPELLING QUESTIONS

41. C. Unnecessary

42. A. Exceed

43. D. Parallel

44. B. Supervised

45. B. Recognize

46. C. Wednesday

47. C. Counterfeit

48. A. Judgment

49. D. Embarrassing

50. A. Received

(*Note:* Sometimes the very word that you are trying to determine the correct spelling for may appear elsewhere in the text. In this case, *received* was used in the previous question. While this may be atypical of the actual exam, be mindful of the fact that this method may serve as a cross-check of your word.)

51. C. Justifiable

52. B. Occasionally

53. A. *Breath* is the proper spelling of the noun that refers to respiration. *Breathe* is the proper spelling of the verb that refers to inhaling and exhaling. (*Note:* You may be given spelling questions that may require not only correct spelling, but vocabulary discernment as well. This question is a prime example of what could be involved. First, determine which word is applicable to the context of the sentence, and then select the correct spelling.)

54. C. Discipline

55. A. Miscellaneous

56. D. Procedure

57. C. Plaintiff

58. A. Believe

59. B. Realize

60. B. Lieutenant

Your score for this exercise would rate as follows:

54–60 correct — Excellent

47–53 correct — Good

40–46 correct — Fair

Less than 40 correct — Poor

Chapter 7

Mathematics

As a State Police Officer, you will need to have good mathematical ability to determine everything from property values to blood alcohol levels. Mathematics is important beyond your career, as well. The implications in your personal life can be as far-reaching as calculating depreciation values on real estate for tax purposes to simply balancing your checkbook.

Mathematics treats exact relations existing between quantities in such a way that other quantities can be deduced from them. In other words, you may know a basic quantity, but to derive further use from that quantity, it is necessary to apply known relationships (that is, formulas).

For example, let's say you wanted to know how many revolutions a tire would have to make to roll a distance of exactly 20 feet. Outside of physically rolling the tire itself and using a tape measure, it would be impossible to solve such a problem without mathematics. However, by applying math, we can exploit known relationships to derive the answer.

If we know that the diameter of the tire is 40 inches, we can easily determine the tire's perimeter or circumference. In geometric terms, the tire is a circle and the known formula for determining the circumference of a circle is to multiply the diameter by π (which is 3.1416). The symbol π is referred to in mathematics as *pi*. Therefore, our tire's circumference is $40 \times 3.1416 = 125.66$ inches.

Since we now know that the circumference of the tire is 125.66 inches, we can learn how many revolutions a tire with this circumference would need to go exactly 20 feet. However, we cannot simply divide 125.66 inches into 20 feet because we are dealing with two entirely different units of measure, inches and feet.

Therefore, we need to convert feet into inches. We know that there are 12 inches in 1 foot, so 20 feet $\times$ 12 inches = 240 inches. Now we can divide 125.66 inches into 240 inches to find the answer we need. In this case, the tire would have to make 1.91 revolutions to roll exactly 20 feet. You can see by this example how known relationships can help find an unknown.

This chapter is designed with the purpose of reviewing only those aspects of math that have been predominantly seen on past exams. If you find any areas of weakness after completing the exercises, it would be in your best interest to get additional reference material from your library.

The subjects reviewed in this section include fractions, decimals, ratios, proportions, and geometry. Each of these areas is discussed briefly, and some examples demonstrate its application. At the end of this section, there are practice exercises for you to complete. Answers and explanations are provided separately so you can check your performance.

MATHEMATICAL PRINCIPLES

A. FRACTIONS

Fractions are essentially parts of a whole. If you have $1/2$ of something, this means you have 1 of 2 equal parts. If you have $7/8$ of something, this means you have 7 of the 8 equal parts available.

The 1 of $^1/_2$ is the *numerator*, which tells the number of parts used. The 2 is the *denominator*, which tells how many parts the whole has been divided into. As a general rule, if the numerator is less than the denominator, the fraction is called *proper*. On the other hand, if the numerator is greater than or equal to the denominator, the fraction is called *improper*. See the examples below:

$^1/_3$ is a proper fraction.

$^2/_3$ is a proper fraction.

$^3/_3$ is an improper fraction (Note: this fraction has a value of 1).

$^7/_3$ is an improper fraction.

A mixed number is simply a whole number plus a fractional part. For example, $2^1/_3$ is a mixed number. If there is a need to change a mixed number into an improper fraction, simply multiply the whole number by the denominator of the fraction and add the resulting product to the numerator. For example:

$$2^1/_3 = (2 \times 3) + 1 \text{ divided by } 3 = {}^7/_3, \text{ an improper fraction}$$

If it is necessary to change an improper fraction into a mixed number, simply divide the numerator by the denominator. The quotient is the whole number; the remainder is left over the denominator, and this remaining fraction is reduced to its lowest terms. For example:

$$^{15}/_{10} = 1\,{}^5/_{10} = 1\,{}^1/_2$$

The fraction $^{15}/_{10}$ is improper, and 15 divided by 10 is 1 with 5 left over, so $1^1/_2$ is the resulting mixed number reduced.

When we need to add, subtract, divide, or multiply fractions, certain rules need to be understood and followed. One basic rule is that multiplication or division should be done prior to addition or subtraction.

To start, when you add or subtract fractional numbers, you must always use a common denominator. For example:

$$^1/_4 + {}^2/_4 = {}^3/_4$$
$$^3/_6 - {}^1/_6 = {}^2/_6$$

Notice that the solution's denominator remains the same, while the variable is the numerator (that is, $^1/_4 + {}^2/_4$ does not equal $^3/_8$, nor does $^3/_6 - {}^1/_6 = {}^2/_0$ or 0).

The same thing applies to mixed numbers as well.

$$2^1/_4 + 1^3/_4 = 3^4/_4$$

$^4/_4$ is an improper fraction that can be reduced to 1. Therefore:

$$2^1/_4 + 1^3/_4 = 4$$

But what happens when you have to add or subtract two fractions that have different denominators? Look at two such examples below:

$$^3/_7 + {}^1/_2 = X$$
$$^5/_8 - {}^1/_3 = X$$

Before anything can be figured out, it is essential that we find the least common denominator (LCD) for each problem. Looking at the former example ($^3/_7 + {}^1/_2 = X$), we need to find the LCD for 7 and 2. In this case, it happens to be 14 (that is, 7 and 2 each divide evenly into 14, and 14 is the smallest number for which that is true). Now that we are working the problem in units of fourteenths, it is easy to figure the values of the numerators involved. For example:

$$^3/_7 = {}^x/_{14}$$

To find X, you need to divide 7 into 14 and multiply the resulting quotient by the numerator:

$$14 \div 7 = 2, 2 \times 3 = 6; \text{ therefore, } 3/7 = 6/14$$

Work in a similar manner for all fractions.

$$1/2 = x/14, 14 \div 2 = 7, 7 \times 1 = 7, \text{ therefore } 1/2 = 7/14$$

Now that we have a common denominator, we can add or subtract numbers as we please. In this case,

$$6/14 + 7/14 = 13/14$$

This is a proper fraction that cannot be reduced any further.

Try your hand at the second example, $5/8 - 1/3 = X$. If you followed the format below to arrive at the answer of $7/24$, you were correct.

$$5/8 = x/24, 24 \div 8 = 3, 3 \times 5 = 15; \text{ therefore } 5/8 = 15/24$$
$$1/3 = x/24, 24 \div 3 = 8, 8 \times 1 = 8, \text{ therefore, } 1/3 = 8/24$$
$$15/24 - 8/24 = 7/24$$

This is a proper fraction that cannot be reduced further.

To add or subtract mixed numbers with different fractions, the same rule applies. The only difference is that whole numbers can be treated as fractions themselves if they need to be borrowed from. For example,

$$5\,2/8 - 3\,3/4 = X$$

First, we need to convert the fractions separately. The LCD for both fractions is 8. Therefore, we calculate that $3/4 = 6/8$.

Since $2/8 - 6/8$ would leave us with a negative number, we need to borrow from the whole number (which is 5). Therefore, we can look at $5\,2/8$ as $4\,10/8$. Thus, the problem now reads $4\,10/8 - 3\,6/8 = X$.

As the problem now reads, we can subtract the whole numbers (4 and 3) separately, thus $4 - 3 = 1$. The fractions $10/8$ and $6/8$ can be subtracted separately as well; thus $10/8 - 6/8 = 4/8$ or $1/2$.

Now, put the whole number answer and the fractional answer together and we arrive at the total solution, $X = 1\,1/2$.

To multiply fractions or mixed numbers it is not necessary to determine an LCD. Rather, the product of the numerators is divided by the product of the denominators. Several examples are shown below:

$$6/7 \times 5/8 = \frac{6 \times 5 = 30}{7 \times 8 = 56} = 30/56$$

which is equivalent to (or *reduces to*) $15/28$

$$4 \times 7\,1/3 = 4/1 \times 22/3 = \frac{4 \times 22 = 88}{1 \times 3 = 3} = 29\,1/3$$

When you need to divide fractions or mixed numbers, convert the divisor to its reciprocal (reverse numerator and denominator) and then multiply. For example:

$$7/8 \div 1/2 = X$$

($2/1$ is the reciprocal of $1/2$). Thus,

$$7/8 \times 2/1 = 14/8, \text{ or } 1\,3/4, \text{ reduced}$$

Another example involving mixed numbers is

$$6\,5/8 - 3\,1/3 = X$$

This equals $53/8 \times 3/10$ (reciprocal of $3\,1/3$) $= 159/80$, or $1\,79/80$, reduced.

B. DECIMALS

Decimals are basically another means to represent fractional numbers. The difference is that in decimals all fractions are expressed in factors of 10. The placement of the decimal point determines if it is a measure concerning tenths, hundredths, thousandths, ten thousandths, etc., and directly influences the size of the whole numbers involved. Look at the illustration below, which depicts the same number with different decimal placements, and examine the consequent change in value:

$$4,459.1340 = \text{Four thousand four hundred fifty-nine and one hundred thirty-four}$$
$$\text{thousandths}$$
$$44,591.340 = \text{Forty-four thousand five hundred ninety-one and thirty-four hundredths}$$
$$445,913.40 = \text{Four hundred forty-five thousand nine hundred thirteen and four tenths}$$
$$4,459,134.0 = \text{Four million four hundred fifty-nine thousand, one hundred thirty-four}$$

When conducting addition or subtraction of decimals, the place values (that is, decimal points) of decimals must be in vertical alignment. Just as mixed numbers require a common denominator, so decimals require this alignment. In this respect, the common denominator is that tenths are under tenths, hundredths are under hundredths, etc., so that you are adding or subtracting comparable units. For example:

$$
\begin{array}{r}
6.5432 \\
+ 73.43 \\
\hline
79.9732
\end{array}
\qquad \text{or} \qquad
\begin{array}{r}
50.432 \\
- 12.07 \\
\hline
38.362
\end{array}
$$

When multiplying decimals, it is necessary to treat them as whole numbers. Once you have determined the product, the decimal point is moved to the left the same number of places as there are numbers after the decimal point in both the decimals being multiplied. For example:

$$
\begin{array}{r}
5.678 \\
\times .02 \\
\hline
11356 \\
0000 \\
\hline
0.11356
\end{array}
$$

In this case, there are 5 numbers to the right of the decimal (678 and 02); therefore, 11356 should have the decimal placed in front of the first 1. The final number is 0.11356.

Dividing decimals is as simple as multiplication. When utilizing long division, simply move both place values to the right so that the divisor becomes a whole number. The decimal point then needs to be placed in the quotient above the place it has been moved to in the number being divided. At that point, each of the numbers can be treated as whole numbers and ordinary long division can be used. For example:

$$7.62 \div 3.11 = X$$

$$3.11\overline{)7.62} = X$$

We need to move the decimal point over two places to render the divisor a whole number. Note the placement of the decimal in the quotient.

$$311\overline{)762.} = X$$

Then,

$$
\begin{array}{r}
2.450 \\
311{\overline{\smash{\big)}\,762.}} \\
\underline{622} \\
1400 \\
\underline{1244} \\
1560 \\
\underline{1555} \\
5
\end{array}
$$

and $X = 2.450$

    With this rule in mind, it is very easy to convert fractions to decimals. Use the example below, and observe the placement value.

    The fraction $16/23$ is proper. But, when using long division to determine a decimal, we would divide 23 into 16.

$$
\begin{array}{r}
.6956 \\
23{\overline{\smash{\big)}\,16.0}} \\
\underline{138} \\
220 \\
\underline{207} \\
130 \\
\underline{115} \\
150 \\
\underline{138} \\
12
\end{array}
$$

or 0.696, rounded off

C. PERCENTAGES

The term *percentage* by itself means "divided by one hundred." For example, 15% means $15 \div 100$. A percentage shows what portion of 100 a given number constitutes. For example, if someone had 100 plants and gave away 20 to a friend, that would mean he or she gave away $20/100$ or 0.20 of the stock. To determine the percentage of plants given away, we would simply multiply 0.20 by 100, giving us 20%.

    Let's look at another problem and determine the percentages involved:

> If a fire truck had 300 feet of $1^1/2$ inch hose and 3 firefighters took 100 feet, 75 feet, and 125 feet respectively to attend to a fire, what percentage of hose did each firefighter carry?

Since we already know the total length of hose involved, it is a simple matter to determine the percentages.

Firefighter A	Firefighter B	Firefighter C
$\dfrac{100 \text{ feet}}{300 \text{ feet}} \times 100$	$\dfrac{75 \text{ feet}}{300 \text{ feet}} \times 100$	$\dfrac{125 \text{ feet}}{300 \text{ feet}} \times 100$
$= 33\%$	$= 25\%$	$= 42\%$

When you add these percentages together, you get 100% of hose used.

D. RATIOS AND PROPORTIONS

A ratio is simply two items compared by division. For instance, it is known that there are 3500 residents for every 1 patrolman in the city of Birmingham. If this were to be properly expressed as a ratio, it would be 3500:1 or 3500/1. As a rule, if a ratio is expressed as a fraction, it should be reduced. One other rule to remember is that a ratio should not be expressed as a mixed number.

A proportion, on the other hand, is an equation that shows that two ratios are equal. One of the more common types of questions seen on past exams concerns speed and distance proportions. For example, if a car can travel 5 miles in 6 minutes, how far can it travel in 30 minutes, assuming that the same speed is maintained? This kind of problem would first be set up as two separate ratios and then placed in a proportion to determine the unknown.

$$\text{RATIO 1 } \frac{5 \text{ miles}}{6 \text{ minutes}} \qquad \text{RATIO 2 } \frac{X \text{ miles}}{30 \text{ minutes}}$$

$$\text{In proportional form we then have: } \frac{5 \text{ miles}}{6 \text{ minutes}} = \frac{X \text{ miles}}{30 \text{ minutes}}$$

Once the proportion is established, you can cross multiply the proportion figures and obtain this:

$$6X = 5 \times 30$$

To solve for X, one of two basic algebraic laws needs to be applied. The addition law for equations states that the same value can be added or subtracted from both sides of an equation without altering the solution. The second basic law is the multiplication law for equations. This states that both sides of an equation can be multiplied or divided by the same number without changing the final solution.

These two laws are used to solve equations that have only one variable. In the case of $6X = 5 \times 30$, we will implement the multiplication/division law to determine X. If we divide both sides of the equation by 6, we can then figure how many miles the car would travel in 30 minutes.

$$\frac{6X}{6} = \frac{5 \times 30}{6}$$

$$X = \frac{150}{6}$$

$$X = 25 \text{ miles}$$

When working with direct proportions like this, you have to be careful not to confuse them with inverse proportions. An example would be two gears with differing numbers of teeth that run at a given number of revolutions per minute (rpm).

Let's say one gear has 30 teeth and runs at 60 rpm, while the other gear has 20 teeth and runs at X rpm. Find X.

We could set it up as a direct proportion:

$$\frac{30 \text{ teeth}}{20 \text{ teeth}} = \frac{60 \text{ rpm}}{X \text{ rpm}}$$

$$30X = 60 \times 20$$

$$X = \frac{1200}{30}$$

$$X = 40 \text{ rpm}$$

Since we recall from mechanical principles that a gear with fewer teeth turns faster than a gear with more teeth, we know that the ratios demonstrated by this proportion are incorrect. Rather, it should be inversely proportional. Therefore, it is important when coming across a question of this nature to utilize the reciprocal of one of the ratios in the equation to set up the proportion. For example:

$$\frac{20 \text{ teeth}}{30 \text{ teeth}} = \frac{60 \text{ rpm}}{X \text{ rpm}}$$

or

$$\frac{30 \text{ teeth}}{20 \text{ teeth}} = \frac{X \text{ rpm}}{60 \text{ rpm}}$$

Both of these are correct proportions.

$$20X = 30 \times 60$$

$$X = \frac{1800}{20}$$

$$X = 90 \text{ rpm}$$

$X = 90$ rpm is the correct answer, given the fact that this gear has the smaller number of teeth.

E. GEOMETRY

(*Note:* Even though geometry problems are rarely seen on State Police Officer exams, the review of very basic rules is warranted. If, by chance, you run across such questions on your exam, you will then be that much better prepared.)

Any object that requires space has dimensions that can be measured in length, width, and height. If all three of these measurements are used to quantify the size of a given object, it can be said that it is three-dimensional, or solid. If only two measurements, such as length and width, can be determined, it is considered to be two-dimensional, or a plane. A line is essentially a one-dimensional figure because it has no height or width, only length.

Two-dimensional objects frequently seen in geometry are:

1. *Rectangle:* a plane formed from two pairs of parallel lines that are perpendicular to one another. Its area can be determined by multiplying length by width. For example, a rectangle measuring 9 feet by 6 feet has an area of 54 square feet.

2. *Square:* a rectangle with sides of equal length. The area of a square is found in the same way as for a rectangle.

3. *Triangle:* a closed plane shape that has three sides. Its area can be determined by multiplying $1/2$ times the base times the height. For example, a triangle with a 10-foot base and 5-foot height has an area of 25 square feet ($1/2 \times 10 \times 5$). (A right triangle has one angle that is 90 degrees; that is, two sides are perpendicular.)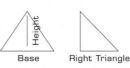

4. *Circle:* a closed plane curve whose circumference is equidistant from the center. A line from the center of the circle to its circumference is a radius. The diameter of a circle is the radius times two. The area of a circle is equal to πR^2 ($\pi = 3.1416$). For example, a circle with a radius of 10 feet has an area of $\pi \times 10^2 = 314.16$ square feet. If, on the other hand, we wanted to determine the circumference, we would multiply π by the diameter, or $\pi 2R$. In this case, the circumference $= 3.1416 \times 10 \times 2$, or 62.83 feet.

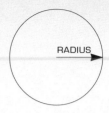

The space occupied by a three-dimensional object is called its volume. If we want to know the volume of a rectangular solid, we take the area of a rectangle times its height. For example, this rectangular solid has an area of 50 square feet (that is, 10 feet × 5 feet). When we multiply 50 square feet × 3 feet, we can determine its volume, which in this case is 150 cubic feet.

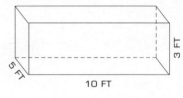

A square solid is a cube. Since all sides are equal in length, we can simply cube the length (L^3) to determine its volume.

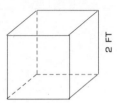

For example, let's say one side measures 2 feet in length. The volume of this cube would equal 2 feet × 2 feet × 2 feet, or 8 cubic feet.

The volume for a sphere is found by using the equation

$$V = \tfrac{4}{3} \pi R^3$$

For example, if the radius of a ball is 3 inches, what would its volume be?

$$(\tfrac{4}{3}) \times (3.1416) \times (3)^3 = \tfrac{4}{3} \times 3.1416 \times 27 = 113.1 \text{ cubic inches}$$

The volume of a cylinder is found by using the equation

$$V = \pi R^2 \text{ Height}$$

For example, if a tin can has a radius of 4 inches and a depth of 8 inches, what is its volume?

$$(3.1416) \times (4)^2 \times (8) = 3.1416 \times 16 \times 8 = 402.12 \text{ cubic inches}$$

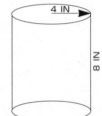

One other aspect of geometry that may be seen on Corrections Officer exams concerns right triangles. The Pythagorean theorem states that the square of the side opposite the right angle equals the sum of the squares of the other sides, or $C^2 = A^2 + B^2$. For example,

If side $A = 5$ feet and side $B = 10$ feet, then side C can be determined:

$$C^2 = 5^2 + 10^2$$
$$C^2 = 25 + 100$$
$$C^2 = 125$$

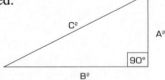

Therefore, C is equal to the square root of 125, or 11.2.

Next, you will find some sample questions on mathematical principles so you can test your skills in this area. Solutions to the problems are given at the end of the exercise to verify your work.

SAMPLE QUESTIONS FOR MATHEMATICS

1. $17^{3}/_{4} - 8^{1}/_{4} = X$. Which of the following equals X?

   A. $9^{2}/_{4}$ B. $9^{1}/_{8}$ C. $9^{1}/_{2}$ D. 9

2. $9 - {}^{3}/_{8} = X$. Which of the following equals X?

   A. $8^{3}/_{8}$ B. $8^{5}/_{8}$ C. 9 D. $7^{3}/_{8}$

3. $9^{1}/_{4} + 18^{2}/_{4} + 20^{1}/_{4} = X$. Which of the following equals X?

   A. $48^{1}/_{4}$ B. $48^{1}/_{2}$ C. $43^{1}/_{4}$ D. 48

4. $6^{1}/_{3} - 4^{5}/_{6} = X$. Which of the following equals X?

   A. $1^{1}/_{4}$ B. $1^{1}/_{2}$ C. $1^{3}/_{4}$ D. $1^{3}/_{6}$

5. $4^{2}/_{3} + 1^{1}/_{6} - 2^{1}/_{8} = X$. Which of the following equals X?

   A. $3^{17}/_{24}$ B. $3^{1}/_{4}$ C. $3^{3}/_{16}$ D. $3^{5}/_{18}$

6. $12^{3}/_{8} \times 2^{5}/_{7} = X$. Which of the following equals X?

   A. $32^{33}/_{25}$ B. $32^{17}/_{18}$ C. $33^{33}/_{56}$ D. $34^{1}/_{3}$

7. $7 \times {}^{1}/_{2} \times {}^{3}/_{7} = X$. Which of the following equals X?

   A. $1^{3}/_{7}$ B. $1^{1}/_{4}$ C. $1^{3}/_{4}$ D. $1^{1}/_{2}$

8. $8^{3}/_{4} \div 2^{1}/_{2} = X$. Which of the following equals X?

   A. $1^{7}/_{8}$ B. $3^{1}/_{8}$ C. $3^{1}/_{2}$ D. $4^{1}/_{10}$

9. If the number $5^{2}/_{3}$ is changed from a mixed number to a decimal, which of the following is correct, assuming it is rounded off to hundredths?

   A. 5.67   B. 5.66   C. 5.6   D. 5.7

10. $6.71 \times 0.88 = X$. Which of the following equals X?

    A. 5.0948   B. 5.887   C. 5.91   D. 5.9048

11. $132.069 - 130.69 = X$. Which of the following equals X?

    A. 0.379   B. 1.379   C. 1.739   D. 1.793

12. $8.53 + 17.671 = X$. Which of the following equals X?

    A. 16.524   B. 23.102   C. 26.201   D. 25.012

13. $15.75 \div 4.12 = X$. Which of the following equals X?

    A. 3.823   B. 3.283   C. 3.023   D. 3.803

14. $6.75 + 8.372 \times 3.14 = X$. Which of the following equals X?

    A. 47.48   B. 33.04   C. 37.48   D. 34.03

15. $9 \times 5.2 \div 18.76 = X$. Which of the following equals X?

    A. 0.40   B. 15.75   C. 28.06   D. 2.49

16. $17 - 14.87 \div 2.5 + 3.61 = X$. Which of the following equals X?

    A. 4.46   B. 0.35   C. 14.66   D. 4.64

17. If 23.6 were changed into a percentage of its relationship to the number 1, which of the following would be correct?

    A. 23.6%   B. 0.236%   C. 236%   D. 2360%

18. The fraction $3/7$ represents what percentage?

    A. 41.85%   B. 42.85%   C. 48.25%   D. 43.35%

19. If someone were to withdraw $237.00 from a savings account that totaled $3,000.00, what percent of the money would be left in the account?

    A. 92.1%   B. 83.7%   C. 94.1%   D. 89.7%

20. The number 13 is 75% of what number?

    A. 15.49   B. 16.35   C. 16.99   D. 17.33

21. If a screw has a pitch that requires it to be turned 30 times to advance it 2 inches, what ratio correctly reflects the relationship?

    A. 2:30   B. 30:2   C. 2:15   D. 15:1

22. According to the directions on a bottle of liquid fertilizer, it is supposed to be mixed in water at the rate of 3 tablespoons per gallon before applying to a garden. How many tablespoons of fertilizer would be required for 20 gallons of water?

    A. 20   B. 40   C. 60   D. 80

23. $\dfrac{5}{8} = \dfrac{X}{32}$ Which of the following equals X?

    A. 10   B. 20   C. 25   D. 30

24. $\dfrac{3/5}{1/2} = \dfrac{X}{15}$ Which of the following equals X?

    A. 18   B. 16.5   C. 19.2   D. 16

25. What is the area of a rectangle if it is 6 feet long by 4 feet wide?

    A. 10 square feet

    B. 64 square feet

    C. 24 cubic feet

    D. 24 square feet

26. If a township is a square section of territory and one side is known to be 6 miles in length, how many square miles does the township occupy?

    A. 16 square miles

    B. 18 square miles

    C. 36 square miles

    D. 42 square miles

27. What is the circumference of a gear that has a 5 7/8 inch diameter?

    A. 18.05 inches

    B. 16.57 inches

    C. 19.45 inches

    D. 18.46 inches

28. If a triangle had a base of 8 feet and a height of 3.5 feet, what would its area be?

    A. 12 square feet

    B. 14 square feet

    C. 16 square feet

    D. 20 square feet

29. If a rectangular object is 20 feet long by 15 feet wide and has a height of 4 inches, what is its approximate volume?

    A. 1200 cubic feet

    B. 1200 square feet

    C. 100 cubic feet

    D. 100 square feet

30. If one side of a cube measures 36 inches, what is its volume?

    A. 46,000 cubic inches

    B. 46,656 square inches

    C. 46,656 cubic yards

    D. 1 cubic yard

31. If a fully inflated basketball has a diameter of 12 inches, how much volume does it occupy?

    A. 904.78 cubic inches

    B. 673.54 cubic inches

    C. 509.78 cubic inches

    D. 475 cubic inches

32. If a can has a height of 16 inches and a volume of 1256.64 cubic inches, what is its diameter?

    A. 10 inches

    B. 11 inches

    C. 12 inches

    D. 12.5 inches

33. The Pythagorean theorem concerns what kind of geometric shape?

    A. Equilateral triangle

    B. Scalene triangle

    C. Right triangle

    D. Acute triangle

34. If the length of side *A* of a right triangle is 8 feet and the length of side *C* (the hypotenuse) is 12.8 feet, what is the length of side *B*?

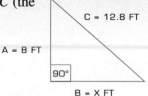

A. 8 feet

B. 10 feet

C. 12 feet

D. 12.3 feet

35. What is the area of the figure below?

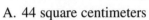

A. 44 square centimeters

B. 46 square centimeters

C. 48 square centimeters

D. 50 square centimeters

36. If a basement's floor plan has the dimensions shown below, how many square feet would it cover?

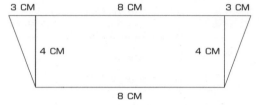

A. 1000

B. 995

C. 988

D. 984

37. What is the length of a diagonal line inside a square that measures 81 square feet?

A. 9.82 feet

B. 10.38 feet

C. 12.73 feet

D. 14.71 feet

38. If 34 inches represents 34% of the diameter of a particular circle, what is the area of the circle?

A. 4,891 square inches

B. 5,432 square inches

C. 6,971 square inches

D. 7,854 square inches

39. If you were told that a specific tire could roll 200 yards in 27.28 revolutions, what is the radius of the tire?

A. 42 inches

B. 84 inches

C. 37.5 inches

D. 75 inches

40. What is the volume of the figure shown below? (Hint: Look at this diagram as half of a cylinder on top of a rectangular solid.)

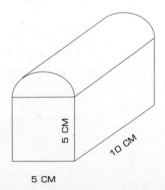

A. 376.7 cubic centimeters

B. 348.2 cubic centimeters

C. 336.7 cubic centimeters

D. 329.8 cubic centimeters

ANSWER SHEET FOR SAMPLE MATHEMATICS

1. Ⓐ Ⓑ Ⓒ Ⓓ   15. Ⓐ Ⓑ Ⓒ Ⓓ   29. Ⓐ Ⓑ Ⓒ Ⓓ

2. Ⓐ Ⓑ Ⓒ Ⓓ   16. Ⓐ Ⓑ Ⓒ Ⓓ   30. Ⓐ Ⓑ Ⓒ Ⓓ

3. Ⓐ Ⓑ Ⓒ Ⓓ   17. Ⓐ Ⓑ Ⓒ Ⓓ   31. Ⓐ Ⓑ Ⓒ Ⓓ

4. Ⓐ Ⓑ Ⓒ Ⓓ   18. Ⓐ Ⓑ Ⓒ Ⓓ   32. Ⓐ Ⓑ Ⓒ Ⓓ

5. Ⓐ Ⓑ Ⓒ Ⓓ   19. Ⓐ Ⓑ Ⓒ Ⓓ   33. Ⓐ Ⓑ Ⓒ Ⓓ

6. Ⓐ Ⓑ Ⓒ Ⓓ   20. Ⓐ Ⓑ Ⓒ Ⓓ   34. Ⓐ Ⓑ Ⓒ Ⓓ

7. Ⓐ Ⓑ Ⓒ Ⓓ   21. Ⓐ Ⓑ Ⓒ Ⓓ   35. Ⓐ Ⓑ Ⓒ Ⓓ

8. Ⓐ Ⓑ Ⓒ Ⓓ   22. Ⓐ Ⓑ Ⓒ Ⓓ   36. Ⓐ Ⓑ Ⓒ Ⓓ

9. Ⓐ Ⓑ Ⓒ Ⓓ   23. Ⓐ Ⓑ Ⓒ Ⓓ   37. Ⓐ Ⓑ Ⓒ Ⓓ

10. Ⓐ Ⓑ Ⓒ Ⓓ   24. Ⓐ Ⓑ Ⓒ Ⓓ   38. Ⓐ Ⓑ Ⓒ Ⓓ

11. Ⓐ Ⓑ Ⓒ Ⓓ   25. Ⓐ Ⓑ Ⓒ Ⓓ   39. Ⓐ Ⓑ Ⓒ Ⓓ

12. Ⓐ Ⓑ Ⓒ Ⓓ   26. Ⓐ Ⓑ Ⓒ Ⓓ   40. Ⓐ Ⓑ Ⓒ Ⓓ

13. Ⓐ Ⓑ Ⓒ Ⓓ   27. Ⓐ Ⓑ Ⓒ Ⓓ

14. Ⓐ Ⓑ Ⓒ Ⓓ   28. Ⓐ Ⓑ Ⓒ Ⓓ

Answers can be found on pages 167–172.

ANSWERS TO MATHEMATICS SAMPLE QUESTIONS

1. *C.* $3/4 - 1/4 = 2/4$ and should be reduced to $1/2$.
   $17 - 8 = 9$; therefore, $X = 9\,1/2$.

2. *B.* $9 - 3/8 = X$; $9 = 8\,8/8$; then, $8/8 - 3/8 = 5/8$;
   therefore, $X = 8\,5/8$.

3. *D.* $9\,1/4 + 18\,2/4 + 20\,1/4 = X$;
   $1/4 + 2/4 + 1/4 = 1$; $9 + 18 + 20 = 47$; therefore,
   $X = 47 + 1 = 48$.

4. *B.* $6\,1/3 - 4\,5/6 = X$; $1/3 = 2/6$, therefore,
   $5\,8/6 - 4\,5/6 = X$; $5 - 4 = 1$ and $8/6 - 5/6 = 3/6$;
   $3/6$ is reduced to $1/2$; therefore, $X = 1\,1/2$. Choice D is the correct answer also, but it is not in reduced form.

5. *A.* $2/3$, $1/6$, $1/8$ have the LCD of 24; therefore,
   $2/3 = 16/24$, $1/6 = 4/24$, $1/8 = 3/24$

   $$\frac{16}{24} + \frac{4}{24} = \frac{20}{24} \qquad \frac{20}{24} - \frac{3}{24} = \frac{17}{24}$$

   $(4 + 1) = 5$; $(5 - 2) = 3$; therefore $X = 3\,17/24$.

6. *C.* $12\,3/8 = 99/8$; $2\,5/7 = 19/7$;
   $99/8 \times 19/7 = 1881/56 = 33\,33/56$

7. *D.* $\dfrac{7}{1} \times \dfrac{1}{2} = \dfrac{7}{2} \qquad \dfrac{7}{2} \times \dfrac{3}{7} = \dfrac{21}{14}$
   $21/14 = 1\,7/14$; when this is reduced, $X = 1\,1/2$.

8. *C.* $8\,3/4 = 35/4$; $2\,1/2 = 5/2$;
   $35/4 \div 5/2 = 35/4 \times 2/5 = 70/20$;
   $70/20 = 3\,10/20$, or $3\,1/2$ when reduced; therefore, $X = 3\,1/2$.

9. *A.* The whole number 5 remains unchanged; however, $2/3$ is the same as saying 2 divided by 3. Therefore, when rounded off to hundredths, the fraction is 0.67. Thus, the decimal should be 5.67. Choice B is correct, except that it has not been rounded off as requested. Choices C and D are not correct because both are rounded off to tenths, not hundredths.

10. *D.* $6.71 \times .88 = X$; therefore, $X = 5.9048$

11. *B.* $\begin{array}{r} 132.069 \\ -\ 130.690 \\ \hline 1.379 \end{array}$

    Therefore, $X = 1.379$.

12. *C.* $\begin{array}{r} 17.671 \\ +\ 8.53 \\ \hline 26.201 \end{array}$

    Therefore, $X = 26.201$.

13. *A.* 15.75 divided by 4.12 should be looked at as 1575 divided by 412; then, the decimals are reinserted. The answer is 3.8223, or 3.822 rounded off to thousandths.

14. *B.* You should remember that multiplications and divisions are always carried out before additions or subtractions. Another similar rule states that when several multiplications and divisions occur together, you should do them in the order they are given. In this case, we first multiply 8.372 by 3.14, giving us 26.29. Now, add 26.29 to 6.75. Therefore, $X = 33.04$.

15. *D.* Multiply $9 \times 5.2 = 46.8$; $46.8 \div 18.76 = 2.4946695$; therefore, $X = 2.49$ rounded off to hundredths.

16. *C.* Remembering the rules discussed in answer 14, division must be done first; 14.87 divided by 2.5 should be looked at as 148.7 divided by 25, or 5.95. Thus,

$$17 - 5.95 + 3.61 = X$$

$$\begin{array}{ll} 17.00 & 11.05 \\ -5.95 & +3.61 \\ \hline 11.05 & 14.66 \end{array}$$

$$X = 14.66$$

17. *D.* 23.6 multiplied by $100 = 2360\%$.

18. *B.* 3.0 divided by $7 = 0.4285$; then, 0.4285 multiplied by $100 = 42.85\%$.

19. *A.*
$$\begin{array}{l} 3000.00 \\ -237.00 \\ \hline 2763.00 \end{array}$$

then, 2763.0 divided by $3000 = 0.921$. Finally, 0.921 multiplied by $100 = 92.1\%$.

20. *D.* This kind of percentage problem needs to be worked as a proportion. We would get the following:

$$\frac{75}{100} = \frac{13}{X}; \quad 75X = 1300$$

$$X = \frac{1300}{75} = 17.33$$

21. *D.* Since the ratio is 30/2, as with fractions, it should be reduced as low as possible, preferably to 1. In this case, 30:2 can be reduced to 15:1.

22. *C.* The ratio is 3:1 in this problem. Therefore,

$$\frac{3 \text{ Tbsp}}{1 \text{ gal}} = \frac{X \text{ Tbsp}}{20 \text{ gal}}$$

$$X = 3 \times 20, \text{ which is } 60.$$

23. *B.* $\dfrac{5}{8} = \dfrac{X}{32}$

$8X = 160$

$X = \dfrac{160}{8} = 20$

24. *A.* $\dfrac{3/5}{1/2} = \dfrac{X}{15}$; $\tfrac{1}{2}X = 9$; thus, $\tfrac{1}{2}X \times 2 = 9 \times 2$;

therefore, $X = 18$.

25. *D.* A rectangular area is determined by the following equation:

A = length × width

Therefore, 6 feet × 4 feet = 24 square feet.

26. *C.* Since the area of a square is equal to the length of one side squared, we simply square 6 miles (that is, 6^2), giving us 36. Therefore, the township occupies 36 square miles.

27. *D.* The first step in this problem is to change the fraction $7/8$ into a decimal since π is in decimal form. Thus, we divide 7 by 8, giving us .875. The gear's diameter is 5.875 in decimal form. Circumference = diameter × π (3.1416). Therefore,

5.875 diameter × 3.1416 = 18.4569 inches, or 18.46 inches (rounded to hundredths).

28. *B.* Since the area of a triangle is equal to $1/2$ × base × height, we can plug in the numbers accordingly, giving us the following:

$(1/2)(8)(3.5) = 14$ square feet

The area is 14 square feet.

29. *C.* The volume of a rectangle is found by using the formula A = length × width × height. Before we use this equation, all units must be the same (that is, inches or feet). In this case, it is easier to convert the height to feet.

$$\dfrac{4 \text{ inches}}{12 \text{ inches/feet}} = .3333 \text{ feet}$$

Area = 20 feet × 15 feet × .33 feet = 99.90 cubic feet, or approximately 100 cubic feet.

30. *D.* The easiest way to solve this problem is to recognize that 36 inches = 1 yard. Since 36^3 is a sizable number to multiply, we will use the simpler alternative of 1^3. Therefore, $1^3 = 1$ cubic yard. This is a common unit of measure in the construction field when ordering specific volumes of dirt, rock, concrete, etc. Choice B would be correct if the number were in cubic inches. Square inches determine only the area of a two-dimensional shape.

31. *A.* A basketball fully inflated can be thought of as a sphere. To determine its volume, we need to use the equation

$$4/3 \times \pi \, (3.1416) \times R^3$$

The diameter is given as being 12 inches; therefore, its radius is equal to 1/2 the diameter (that is, 6 inches).

$$\frac{4}{3} \times \frac{3.1416}{1} = \frac{12.5664}{3} = 4.1888$$

$6^3 = 6 \times 6 \times 6 = 216$ cubic inches;
$4.1888 \times 216 = 904.78$ cubic inches, rounded to hundredths.

32. *A.* Since the geometric shape in the question is a cylinder, we need to examine the equation volume $= \pi R^2 H$. If we plug our known values into this equation, it would read

$$1256.64 = \pi \, (3.1416)(X)^2 \, (16 \text{ inches})$$

$$\frac{1256.642}{3.1416 \times 16} = X^2$$

$25 = X^2$; therefore, $X = 5$.

Remember, 5 inches represents only the radius; the diameter would equal $5 \times 2 = 10$ inches.

33. *C.* Right triangle

34. *B.* Implementing the Pythagorean theorem, $A^2 + B^2 = C^2$, we can determine X with simple algebra to solve for one variable.

$$A^2 = 8^2 = 64$$
$$C^2 = 12.8^2 = 163.84$$
$$64 + X^2 = 163.84$$
$$X^2 = 163.84 - 64$$
$$X = \sqrt{99.84}$$

Therefore, $X = 10$ feet.

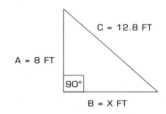

35. *A.* In geometric terms this is considered to be a trapezoid, which is a quadrilateral with two sides parallel and the other two sides not parallel. To figure the area, we can see it as one rectangle (*A*) and two triangles (*B*) and (*C*).

The rectangular area is equal to length × width; therefore,

$8 \times 4 = 32$ square centimeters (cm)

The triangle areas are equal to $1/2 \times$ base × height

$1/2 \times 3 \times 4 = 6$ square cm

Since triangles B and C have the same dimension, we just multiply $6 \times 2 = 12$ to determine their total area combined. Therefore, $A + B + C =$ total area of trapezoid.

32 square cm $+ 12$ square cm $= 44$ square cm

36. *D.* With the dimensions given, we can assume it has a rectangular shape. The easiest way to approach this question is to figure the total area of the basement as a rectangle and subtract the area missing in the corner.

$$40 \text{ feet} \times 25 \text{ feet} = 1,000 \text{ square feet}$$
$$\text{Side } A = 25 \text{ feet} - 21 \text{ feet, or 4 feet}$$
$$\text{Side } B = 40 \text{ feet} - 36 \text{ feet, or 4 feet}$$

The area of the missing corner is 4 feet × 4 feet, or 16 square feet. Therefore, this basement's total area is

$$1000 \text{ square feet} - 16 \text{ square feet} = 984 \text{ square feet}$$

37. *C.* The area of a square is the length of one side squared. If the square given is 81 square feet in area, then the square root of 81 will give us the length of the square's side, which, in this case, is equal to 9. Since we are dealing with right angles in the square, we can apply the Pythagorean theorem to determine the length of the diagonal. Therefore,

$$9^2 + 9^2 = X^2$$

$$81 + 81 = X^2$$

$$162 = X^2; \text{ therefore, } X = 12.73 \text{ feet.}$$

38. *D.* First, we need to figure the diameter. If we know that 34 inches is 34% (that is, .34) of the diameter, we can set up a proportion to solve it. Our proportion would be

$$\frac{34 \text{ inches}}{.34} = \frac{X}{1.00}$$

$$\frac{.34X}{.34} = \frac{34}{.34}$$

Therefore, $X = 3,400$ divided by 34.

Since the diameter is 100 inches, the following formula can be applied to determine the area of the circle in question.

$$A = \pi R^2$$

The radius is equal to $\frac{1}{2}$ the diameter, or, in this case, $100 \times .50 = 50$ inches.

Therefore,

$$A = 3.1416 \times 50^2 \text{ inches}$$
$$A = 3.1416 \times 2,500 \text{ square inches}$$
$$A = 7,854 \text{ square inches.}$$

39. *A.* First, if we divide 27.28 revolutions into 200 yards, we can determine how many yards (or inches) this tire would travel after 1 revolution. We arrive at 7.33 yards. Then, since the diameter of this tire is referred to in inches, not yards, we simply multiply 7.33 yards × 36 inches/yard to give us 263.88 inches. In other words, for every 1 revolution this tire makes, it can travel 263.88 inches. This number is the tire's circumference. If we know the tire's circumference, using the equation

diameter × 3.1416 = circumference

we can easily figure the tire's diameter.

$$X \times 3.1416 = 263.88 \text{ inches}$$

$$\frac{X \times 3.1416}{3.1416} = \frac{263.88 \text{ inches}}{3.1416}$$

$$X = 83.99, \text{ or } 84 \text{ inches, in diameter}$$

Since the question asked for the radius of the tire, we can simply divide the diameter by 2, giving us an answer of 42 inches.

40. *B.* The volume of the rectangular solid is equal to its length × width × height.

10 cm × 5 cm × 5 cm = 250 cubic centimeters

The volume of a cylinder is equal to π × radius squared × height. Since the width of the rectangular solid can be considered the diameter of the cylinder, the radius is ½ the diameter, or, in this case, 5 cm divided by 2 = 2.5 cm. The length of the rectangular solid can be considered the height of the cylinder. Therefore,

3.1416×2.5^2 cm × 10 cm = volume of cylinder
3.1416 × 6.25 cm × 10 cm = 196.35 cubic cm

However, there is only half of a cylinder on top of the rectangular solid, so the cylinder represents only 98.2 cubic cm volume in the illustration shown. Now, add both volumes to give the total volume of this geometric shape.

250 cubic cm + 98.2 cubic cm = 348.2 cubic cm

Chapter 8

Practice Exam 1

The time allowed for the entire examination is two and a half hours. Each question has four answers, lettered A, B, C, and D. Choose the best answer and then, on the answer sheet provided on pages 217–218 (which you can remove from the study guide), find the corresponding question number and darken the circle corresponding to the answer you have selected.

Study the following narrative for three minutes. Do not exceed the time allowed; if you do, you will forfeit the true sense of how an exam is actually conducted. When your time is up, turn to questions 1–8 without making further reference to this reading.

Mr. James Emery Hall was arrested November 13, 1996, by State Patrol Officer Lt. Pete Kendrick, badge number 1515, on charges of aggravated assault of an officer (NCIC Code 13501-A) and resisting arrest (NCIC Code 13721-B). Mr. Hall's erratic driving pattern on Interstate 199 prompted Officer Kendrick to pull him over to conduct a field sobriety check. Pursuant to Officer Kendrick's request to submit to a breathalyzer test, Mr. Hall became agitated and struck the officer in the face. There was a brief struggle, but Mr. Hall was subdued, handcuffed, and Mirandized (i.e., read his rights). During the course of the arrest, Mr. Hall (the suspect in question) maintained that his name was Jeffrey T. Beaumont. A computer-records search of what apparently was a forged ID indicated that no such person existed. However, his physical description—Caucasian, 6'2", approximately 215 pounds, black hair and brown eyes—matched that of a Mr. James Emery Hall, who was the legally registered owner of the vehicle pulled over. There was also an existing warrant out for his arrest for failure to appear in court over two unrelated misdemeanor charges. Lakeview Police Officer Harry M. Stevens, badge number 503, took custodial responsibility for transporting Mr. Hall to Lewis County Detention for booking and intake. Corrections Officer John Cornwall, badge number 181, received Mr. Hall at 0937 hours on the same day of his arrest and inventoried his personal effects for property storage. Mr. Hall was issued receipt number 1517 for his personal belongings. Mr. Hall was much more compliant during the booking and intake process than he was during his arrest. Not only was he cooperative with being fingerprinted, he additionally provided Officer Cornwall his true identity, including his Social Security number (555-22-0557), place of birth (Cedar Rapids, IA), and birth date (October 3, 1957). He remains in detention pending an arraignment hearing scheduled on November 19, 1996, in Lewis County Superior Court. Mr. Hall's case file reference number is 26-07A.

Answer questions 1–8 on the basis of the narrative just studied. *Do not refer to the reading.*

1. Assuming the Lewis County Deputy Prosecutor's office needed to review file information pertinent to the defendant (i.e., the person arrested), which of the following case file numbers would be used for proper reference?

    A. 62-71C

    B. 15-17A

    C. 26-07A

    D. 50-01E

2. The arresting officer in this particular incident was whom?

    A. Lewis County Sheriff Harry M. Stevens

    B. Lakeview Police Officer James E. Hall

    C. State Patrol officer Sergeant John Cornwall

    D. State Patrol officer Pete Kendrick

3. According to the narrative, the defendant in question tried to use which of the following names as an alias?

    A. Jeffery T. Beaumont

    B. James E. Hall

    C. Jeffery M. Kendrick

    D. John A. Cornwall

4. Fingerprint Processing Reports have a standard entry for applicable NCIC code detailing charges against the person arrested. Since the defendant in question was charged with resisting arrest and aggravated assault of an officer, the respective NCIC codes entered into such a report would be which of the following?

    A. 13501-A and 13721-B

    B. 1515-B and 0937-A

    C. 13503-A and 13215-C

    D. 13721-B and 13501-A

5. Pursuant to the defendant's release after posting the required bail, he was scheduled to appear when for an arraignment hearing in Lewis County Superior Court?

    A. 9-19-96

    B. 11-19-96

    C. 10-3-96

    D. None of the above

6. All of the following selections are accurate physical descriptions of the defendant except?

    A. Black hair

    B. Blue eyes

    C. Caucasian

    D. 6'2"

7. Who took custodial responsibility of transporting the defendant to Lewis County Detention for booking and intake?

    A. State Patrol officer John Cornwall

    B. Lakeview Police officer Harry M. Stevens

    C. County Sheriff Lieutenant Pete Kendrick

    D. Corrections officer James E. Hall

8. According to the narrative, what was the defendant's Social Security number?

    A. 222-55-0257

    B. 552-55-0227

    C. 555-22-0557

    D. 252-55-0227

Below are sketches of items taken from four people immediately following their arrest by State Patrol officers and subsequent incarceration. Study the items shown and to whom they belong for a period of ten minutes. Do not exceed the time allowed. When time is up, turn to questions 9–15 without making further references to the sketches just studied.

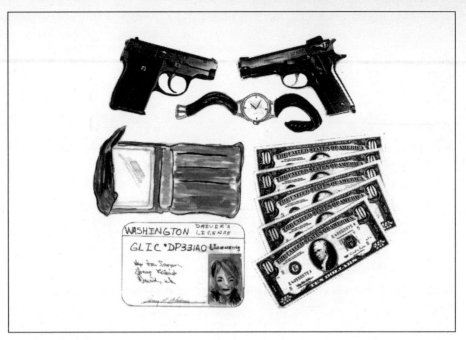

A. Danny P. Glickman

B. Christine L. Thomas

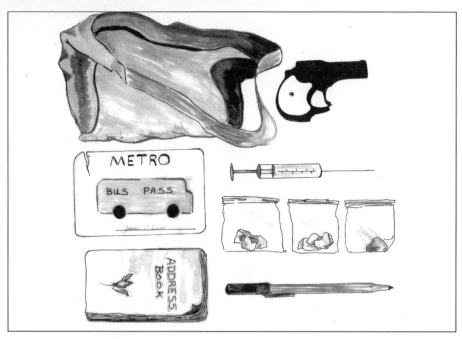

C. Joanne C. Lewis

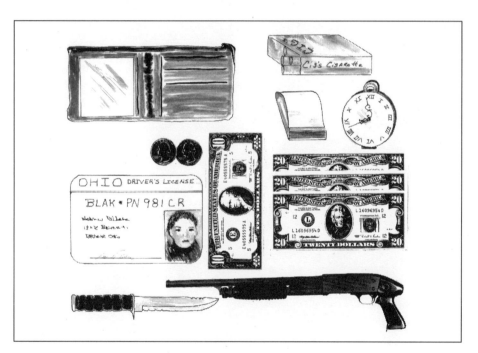

D. Pat N. Blake

9. Which of the four suspects given was not carrying a firearm at the time of his or her arrest?

A. Joanne C. Lewis

B. Pat N. Blake

C. Christine L. Thomas

D. Danny P. Glickman

10. Which of the suspects had obvious connections with the drug trade?

A. Suspect A

B. Suspect B

C. Suspect C

D. Suspect D

11. Which individual did not have a watch among the inventoried personal effects shown?

A. Joanne C. Lewis

B. Christine L. Thomas

C. Danny P. Glickman

D. Pat N. Blake

12. Between the four individuals given, who was an apparent smoker?

A. Suspect A

B. Suspect B

C. Suspect C

D. Suspect D

13. Who did not have a driver's license in their possession at the time of their arrest?

A. Joanne C. Lewis

B. Danny P. Glickman

C. Christine L. Thomas

D. All four suspects had various state driver's licenses at the time of their arrest.

14. Who had $30.00 cash on their person at the time of their arrest?

A. Danny P. Glickman

B. Pat N. Blake

C. Christine L. Thomas

D. Joanne C. Lewis

15. New Jersey license number THOM*CL245BT belonged to whom?

A. Suspect A

B. Suspect B

C. Suspect C

D. Suspect D

Assume you are a State Patrol officer who has fifteen minutes to spare prior to beginning a given patrol assignment. Before leaving Post Command you devote that time to studying the most recent composite list of wants and warrants posted on a squadron bulletin board. Four particular suspects garner your attention because they were last seen in the district you have been assigned to patrol. Keeping the fifteen-minute time frame in mind, study the information pertinent to the four individuals given and then proceed to answer questions 16–25 without further reference to the files.

Suspect 1

Name:	Sarah H. Spangler
Alias:	Jane Webber, Renee Stoner
Date of Birth:	April 15, 1973
Height:	5'5"
Weight:	120 pounds
Hair:	Blonde
Eyes:	Hazel
Sex:	Female
Race:	Caucasian
Scars or Marks:	None
Social Security No.:	187-38-7419
Wants and Warrants:	Second-degree arson, burglary, and grand theft
Criminal Record:	First-degree malicious mischief

Automated Want and Warrant System (AWWS) Number: 187-43

Suspect 2

Name:	Ben L. Morris
Alias:	None
Date of Birth:	December 18, 1965
Height:	6'3"
Weight:	230 pounds
Hair:	Black
Eyes:	Brown
Sex:	Male
Race:	Caucasian
Scars or Marks:	Dime-size birthmark on right forearm
Social Security No.:	981-66-4216
Wants and Warrants:	Second-degree murder and first-degree kidnapping
	Considered armed and dangerous
Criminal Record:	No priors

Suspect 3

Name: Marilyn D. Kinslow

Alias: None

Date of Birth: August 2, 1976

Height: 5'4"

Weight: 110 pounds

Hair: Black

Eyes: Brown

Sex: Female

Race: African American

Scars or Marks: None known

Social Security No.: 351-48-1578

Wants and Warrants: First-degree bribery, extortion, and petty larceny

Criminal Record: First-degree malicious mischief, aggravated assault of a police officer, and resisting arrest

NCIC File Number: 124-15

Suspect 4

Name: Don E. Hudspeth

Alias: James H. Humphrey

Date of Birth: July 23, 1970

Height: 5'11"

Weight: 170 pounds

Hair: Brown

Eyes: Brown

Sex: Male

Race: African American

Scars or Marks: One-inch vertical scar on chin

Social Security No.: 505-44-8113

Wants and Warrants: Interstate flight, first-degree assault, and kidnapping
Considered armed and dangerous

Criminal Record: Criminal trespass and third-degree assault

NCIC File Number: 125-14

16. Which of the following composite sketches is representative of the individual who is wanted for kidnapping, interstate flight, and first-degree assault?

A.

B.
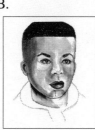

C.

D.

17. Which of the following individuals shown was described as being 5'5" tall and weighing 120 pounds?

A.

B.
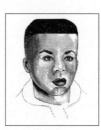

C.

D.

18. Which of the dates given below represents Ben Morris's date of birth?

A. 12-18-65

B. 5-15-73

C. 7-23-66

D. 8-2-76

19. The individual pictured had past convictions for which of the following offenses?

A. First-degree malicious mischief, aggravated assault, and kidnapping

B. First-degree malicious mischief

C. Third-degree assault and criminal trespass

D. This suspect did not have any prior convictions.

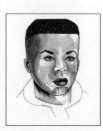

20. Social Security number 351-48-1579 belongs to which of the individuals shown below?

A.    B.    C.    D.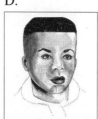

21. Which of the following four suspects utilized multiple aliases in the commission of his or her crimes?

    A. Suspect 1

    B. Suspect 2

    C. Suspect 3

    D. Suspects 1 and 4

22. According to the criminal files provided, which suspect(s) is (are) considered by authorities to be armed and dangerous?

    A. Suspect 1

    B. Suspects 2 and 3

    C. Suspects 3 and 4

    D. Suspects 2 and 4

23. Which of the following composite sketches is representative of the individual that had a case file number posted in the Automated Want and Warrant System?

A.    B.    C.    D.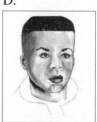

24. According to NCIC file number 124-15, the suspect in question has a criminal record that encompasses all of the following offenses except:

    A. First-degree malicious mischief

    B. Criminal trespass

    C. Resisting arrest

    D. Aggravated assault of a police officer

25. The individual pictured utilized which of the following names as an alias?

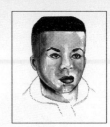

A. Ben L. Morris

B. Don E. Humphrey

C. Don E. Hudspeth

D. James H. Humphrey

Answer questions 26–28 on the basis of the reading below.

If a State Police officer witnesses a traffic infraction or elects to issue a citation during the investigation of a traffic accident, the violator can do one of two things. He or she may accept the citation with the promise to respond, or he or she may refuse to sign the citation. If the violator refuses to sign, the officer may charge him or her with failure to sign and effect an arrest for a misdemeanor. If the violator elects the former, he or she will have ten days to respond, provided the officer filed the infraction notice with the court within forty-eight hours from the time of issuance. Otherwise, the court dismisses the citation without prejudice. Provided the officer is in compliance with this dictate, a violator may respond by either requesting a hearing to contest the infraction, paying the appropriate penalties as assessed by state law, or requesting a hearing to explain any mitigating circumstances. A violator who does not respond may be faced with nonrenewal of his or her driver's license until all penalties are paid in full; or, worse, the prosecutor may institute a criminal complaint for failure to respond that can result in incarceration.

If a State Police officer recognizes that an infraction has been committed, but through either indecisiveness or the fact that the violator in question was not present at the time of the officer's arrival, he may file a written citation with the court at a later point. The officer must explain in the citation the reasonable grounds why he or she believes that an infraction was committed. If the infraction notice is filed with a court within forty-eight hours, and the court elects to send the citation via the U.S. Mail, the violator in question has fourteen days to respond. If, on the other hand, the court elects to have the violator served directly, then he or she has only eight days to respond. The forms of response which may be used by the violator at this point are the same as described earlier.

If the officer witnesses a standing, stopping, or parking violation, he or she may issue a citation and display it conspicuously on the vehicle. If the officer involved files the citation with the court within the time specified earlier, the violator in question will have nine days to respond in the same manner as noted previously.

26. Trooper Davis observes a vehicle double parked in front of a loading zone. Trooper Davis issues a citation for the infraction and leaves a copy under the windshield wiper on the driver's side. She files the notice of infraction with the court three days later. Under these circumstances, how many days does the violator in question have to respond?

A. 10

B. 9

C. 8

D. None of the above

27. State Patrol Officer Stone witnesses a driver go through a stop sign in an apparent attempt to merge into traffic when the opportunity availed itself. Trooper Stone pulls the driver over and issues a citation for failure to stop. The driver is adamant that a tree partially obstructed his view of the sign and consequently refuses to sign the issuance. At this point, which of the following is considered to be true?

   A. The violator has the right to request a mitigating circumstance hearing.

   B. The violator may contest the infraction in municipal court.

   C. The driver may be charged with a misdemeanor and subsequently arrested.

   D. The violator in question has ten days to determine the means to address the charge.

28. Mr. Harold Phelps receives a notice in the mail that regards a traffic infraction he had incurred earlier in the week. Assuming that the officer involved was in compliance with court standards for issuance and that the postmark on the envelope was March 10, 1992, which of the dates provided below represents the day by which Mr. Phelps has to respond to the notice or face possible prosecution for failure to respond?

   A. March 18, 1992

   B. March 19, 1992

   C. March 20, 1992

   D. March 24, 1992

Answer questions 29–32 on the basis of the reading below:

The month expiration tab on a passenger vehicle or a truck displays the month in which the vehicle's registration expires. A color-code scheme has been implemented to identify the part of the year that registrations need to be renewed.

   Yellow: January, February, and March

   Green: April, May, and June

   Red: July, August, and September

   Black: October, November, and December

Anything other than a passenger vehicle or a truck follows the scheme presented below:

   Red: January, February, and March

   Yellow: April, May, and June

   Black: July, August, and September

   Green: October, November, and December

The year expiration tab displays the year in which the vehicle registration expires. This identification needs to be present only on the rear plate. All tab numbers are recorded on the vehicle registration form. Government vehicles are exempt from registration fees and expiration tabs, and are identified accordingly. Corporations that own fleet vehicles are exempt as well; a vehicle that falls into that category is issued a permanent fleet registration tab that is renewed in October of each year.

29. The color code for identifying month expiration tabs on recreational vehicles (e.g., snowmobiles) is regulated by what type of system?

    A. Monthly

    B. Quarterly

    C. Semi-annual

    D. Yearly

30. Fleet vehicles owned by corporations are on what type of registration renewal system?

    A. Monthly

    B. Quarterly

    C. Annual

    D. Exempt

31. If Joe Collier owned a new 1993 Buick LeSabre whose vehicle registration was due to expire in September of the year following its purchase, which of the following descriptions would be considered true?

    A. The month expiration tab would be black, and the year expiration tab would indicate 93.

    B. The month expiration tab would be black, and the year expiration tab would indicate 94.

    C. The month expiration tab would be red, and the year expiration tab would indicate 93.

    D. The month expiration tab would be red, and the year expiration tab would indicate 94.

32. Shawn Turner drove a 1980 Ford Fairlane to and from various state departments to conduct official business. If the vehicle was purchased in July by the government agency he worked for, what would be the correct color code and year tab for the eight-year-old vehicle?

    A. Red and 88, respectively, placed on both the front and back license plates

    B. Black and 88, respectively, placed on both the front and back license plates

    C. Red and 88, respectively, placed on the rear plate only

    D. None of the above

Answer questions 33–35 on the basis of the reading given below:

State Patrol Public Affairs Officer Dan Sweeny was told by a joint steering committee of community block watch leaders that a rash of crime had recently been affecting participating neighborhoods. Specifically, Meadowlark Estates, on Humbolt Avenue and 7th Street, had seen an increase in vehicular prowling. Farmington Community Club, located on Elmhurst Boulevard and Crescent, had experienced an increase in residential burglaries. Carver Center Apartments, on Bridgeview Lane and Center Road, had seen a higher incidence of malicious mischief, and the Port Herrington Center for the Disabled, at Wilmont and Chester Boulevard, had seen a rise in petty larceny. The participants at the meeting also claimed that vehicular prowling and larceny seemed to occur more often on weekends between 8:30 P.M. and 1:30 A.M. and again between 12:30 and 6:30 P.M. Malicious mischief and residential burglary seemed to occur more often on weekdays between 6:30 and 10:30 P.M. and between 8:00 and 11:30 P.M.

33. If Officer Sweeny was in a position to delegate patrol assignments, which of the following actions would most likely reduce the incidence of residential burglary?

    A. Assign additional patrols to Crescent Street and Elmhurst Boulevard Monday through Friday between 6:30 and 10:00 P.M.

    B. Assign additional patrols to Elmhurst and Wilmont Monday through Friday between 8:00 and 11:30 P.M.

    C. Assign additional patrols to Elmhurst and Crescent on Saturday and Sunday between 8:30 P.M. and 1:30 A.M.

    D. Assign additional patrols to Crescent and Elmhurst Boulevard Monday through Friday between 8:00 and 11:30 P.M.

34. Assuming Officer Sweeny wanted to reduce the incidence of malicious mischief in the area of concern, it would probably prove most effective to:

    A. Assign additional patrols to Wilmont and Chester Monday through Friday between 6:30 and 10:30 P.M.

    B. Assign additional patrols to Bridgeview Lane and Center Road Saturday and Sunday between 12:30 and 6:30 P.M.

    C. Assign additional patrols to Center Road and Bridgeview Lane Monday through Friday between 6:30 and 10:30 P.M.

    D. Assign additional patrols to 7th Street and Humbolt Avenue Saturday and Sunday between 8:30 P.M. and 1:30 A.M.

35. All of the following statements are true except:

    A. Additional patrols on Chester Boulevard and Wilmont on Saturday and Sunday between 12:30 and 6:30 P.M. would most likely reduce the incidence of petty larceny.

    B. Additional patrols on 7th Street and Humbolt Avenue on Saturday and Sunday between 8:30 P.M. and 1:30 a.m. would most likely reduce the incidence of malicious mischief.

    C. Additional patrols in Meadowlake Estates on Saturday and Sunday between 8:30 P.M. and 1:30 A.M. would most likely reduce the incidence of vehicular prowling.

    D. The incidence of residential burglary and malicious mischief would most likely remain unchanged by assigning extra patrols to work during the weekends.

36. Detective Brad Jones was sent to investigate a homicide in a low-income housing project. Four witnesses each claimed to have gotten a relatively good view of the suspect as he fled the crime scene. Mrs. Dorothy Williams claimed that the suspect was a Caucasian male of light complexion with reddish-blonde hair and blue eyes, standing approximately 5'11", weight 175 pounds. Mrs. William French described the suspect as being a Latin male of light complexion, approximately 6' tall, 180 pounds, with light brown hair and green eyes. Mr. William Becket described the suspect as being a Caucasian male, approximately 5'11" tall, weight 190 pounds, with sandy blonde hair and hazel eyes. Mr. Howard Werner described the same person as a Caucasian male with medium complexion, standing approximately 5'6" tall, weight 175 pounds, with brown hair and blue eyes. Judging from these descriptions, which witness probably offered the most accurate description of the suspect in question?

    A. Mr. Becket

    B. Mrs. Williams

    C. Mr. Werner

    D. Mrs. French

Answer questions 37–43 on the basis of the information provided below.

Effective July 1, 1998, by order of Commander Jamison, Post Command District 18, assigned work schedules are as follows:

Personnel Roster/ Sector 14
Badge No.

	M	T	W	TH	F	S	S
Wiggins - 521	521-C	329-B	417-C	521-C	670-A	521-B	145-B
Hershberger - 145	329-A	131-C	145-B	612-A	521-B	152-C	802-A
Brown - 976	670-B	976-A	612-A	802-B	152-C	802-A	521-C
Vanderpool - 329							
Klinger - 131			**Sector 12**				
Bateman - 670							
Locke - 563	670-C	314-B	329-A	417-C	131-C	718-B	314-A
Santoya - 802	976-B	718-C	131-C	131-B	145-B	314-A	718-B
Tyson - 718	145-A	802-A	976-B	314-A	802-A	612-C	152-C
Unger -314							
Ryzek - 612			**Sector 9**				
Pratt - 152	802-A	670-B	670-B	145-B	417-B	329-A	329-A
Powell - 417	718-C	145-A	314-A	152-C	976-A	417-B	417-C
Hudson - 410	314-B	612-C	718-C	670-A	612-C	131-C	976-B

Annual Leave postings:		**Vacation Relief:**
July 1–7	(976)	(410)
July 1–14	(131)	(563)
July 7–21	(612)	
July 14–21	(314)	
July 21–26	(329)	**Tours:**
July 21–31	(145)	

A 6:30 A.M. – 2:30 P.M.
B 2:30 P.M. – 10:30 P.M.
C 10:30 P.M. – 6:30 P.M.

37. According to the duty roster, which trooper drew a part-time (i.e., less than forty hours) work assignment?

    A. Santoya

    B. Vanderpool

    C. Pratt

    D. Klinger

38. Assuming that Tour A was the preferred shift among trooper personnel, which of the following individuals received the best schedule presumably due to his or her seniority status?

    A. Brown

    B. Ryzek

    C. Powell

    D. Unger

39. Who was assigned to work the Monday 10:30 P.M. – 6:30 A.M. shift in Sector 9?

    A. Tyson

    B. Santoya

    C. Unger

    D. Bateman

40. On the presumption that District 18 did not have a serious shortage of patrol personnel, who seems to be the subject of an apparent scheduling error?

    A. Locke

    B. Bateman

    C. Hudson

    D. Wiggins

41. If Independence Day fell on a Saturday, who would be working Tour C on July 6 in Sector 12?

    A. Hudson

    B. Tyson

    C. Vanderpool

    D. Hershberger

42. If Independence Day fell on a Friday, who would be working the Tour A detail on July 18 in Sector 14?

    A. Klinger

    B. Brown

    C. Ryzek

    D. Bateman

43. If July 22 fell on a Thursday, who is scheduled to work Tour C detail in Sector 14 on July 13?

    A. Klinger

    B. Pratt

    C. Locke

    D. Wiggins

Answer questions 44–46 based on the information provided below:

The number located at the top of a driver's license consists of the first five letters of the last name, the first letter of the first name, and the first letter of the middle name. The birth year, when subtracted from 100, produces the first two numerical digits. A check digit inserted by the computer produces the third numerical digit. A code for the month of birth and a code for the day of birth are inserted toward the end. Month and day codes are represented below:

MONTHS		DAYS	
January – A	01 – A	13 – M	25 – Y
February – B	02 – B	14 – N	26 – Z
March – D	03 – C	15 – 0	27 – 1
April – F	04 – D	16 – P	28 – 2
May – G	05 – E	17 – Q	29 – 3
June – H	06 – F	18 – R	30 – 4
July – J	07 – G	19 – S	31 – 5
August – L	08 – H	20 – T	
September – 0	09 – I	21 – U	
October – P	10 – J	22 – V	
November – R	11 – K	23 – W	
December – T	12 – L	24 – X	

44. According to the formula prescribed, John Doe Smith, born 10-26-56, would be issued which of the following driver's license numbers?

   A. JDSMITH44ZP9

   B. SMITHJD449PZ

   C. DJSMITH449PZ

   D. SMITHJD44PZ

45. According to the formula prescribed, Jason Lowell Halvorson, born June 16, 1975, would be issued which of the following driver's license numbers?

   A. HALVOJL251HP

   B. HALVEJL523PH

   C. HALVOLJ25H1P

   D. HALVOJL521HP

46. According to the formula prescribed, Vicki Jean Bartenolli, born August 30, 1963, would be issued which of the following driver's license numbers?

   A. VJBARTE378L4

   B. JVBART837L4

   C. BARTEJV371L4

   D. BARTEVJ378L4

47. Often it is said that law enforcement officers are their own worse enemies. Minor oversights and complacency in procedures and situations can often result in violence to officers. Those who have been spared or survived a particular incident are amazed at their own negligence in times of stress. What would it be reasonable to deduce from this?

    A. Law enforcement officers should guard themselves against complacency at all times.

    B. Law enforcement officers should avoid stressful situations altogether.

    C. Compared to veteran officers, rookie law enforcement officers are probably at more of a risk of making such mistakes.

    D. The element of danger involved in an arrest can be completely eliminated by following certain basic operational safeguards.

48. During a routine traffic stop, the placement of a police vehicle is important to the safety of the officer. All of the following procedures would be considered correct in this respect, except:

    A. Pull approximately 10–15 feet behind the violator's vehicle.

    B. Park offset approximately half the vehicle width to the right.

    C. Park the police vehicle with the front angled to the left.

    D. All of these will afford some degree of protection for the officer.

49. Many state legislatures have changed laws in an effort to decriminalize minor traffic offenses while making no change for the more serious offenses. All of the following support this action except:

    A. Such changes may reduce the traffic warrant backlog by offering alternative penalties.

    B. Court-issued civil penalties and potential jail time are viewed by law enforcement officials as being a comparable deterrent.

    C. The time spent in court by police officers will be significantly reduced as a result of changing the hearing procedures.

    D. Both A and C would be considered the exceptions.

50. Trooper Bill Mason was transporting a prisoner to the station house for processing when he observed the vehicle ahead of him being driven in a flagrantly negligent manner. As the only law enforcement officer in the area, what should Trooper Mason do?

    A. Allow the incident to pass since his primary duty is to transport the person he already has in custody to the station house.

    B. Pull the violator over and issue an oral warning before continuing on.

    C. Pull the violator over and issue a citation for the infraction before continuing on.

    D. Pull the violator over and effect a custodial arrest, and then have backup transport the individual to the station for booking.

51. State Patrol Officer Nichols is following a late-model Chevrolet pickup that has a broken taillight. Both vehicles are in the middle lane of Interstate 12, which is crowded with commuters attempting to get home. Which of the following would be considered the most appropriate action for Officer Nichols to take?

    A. Tap his brakes to indicate to the vehicle behind him that he intended to slow to a stop, and then issue the driver of the pickup a ticket for the infraction.

    B. Activate his emergency lights and siren and attempt to pull the driver of the truck over to the shoulder of the road, where it would be relatively safe to issue a notice of infraction.

    C. Follow the vehicle, regardless of how far it may go, until it takes an exit ramp off the highway, and then pull the driver over to the side of the road and issue a ticket.

    D. Allow the vehicle to pass without issuing a ticket.

52. Assume you are a State Patrol officer working traffic enforcement at a busy intersection and you witness two people emerge armed from a credit union adjacent to your post. They run toward a vehicle being driven by an accomplice to effect escape. What would be your best reaction to this situation?

    A. Draw your weapon and order the suspects to freeze.

    B. Run into the credit union to assess what had been taken.

    C. Get a physical description of the suspects and their vehicle, then notify dispatch.

    D. Attempt to maneuver in front of the vehicle and confront the suspects directly.

53. Which of the following alternatives would be considered the most effective way for police to suppress criminal activity in general?

    A. Educate the public as a whole and seek citizen cooperation.

    B. Conduct patrol tours in a systematically unsystematic manner.

    C. Have police officers become fully aware of their jurisdictional boundaries and alternate routes (i.e., shortcuts) which can significantly reduce response times.

    D. Aggressively patrol neighborhoods that are known to be problem areas.

54. Trooper Bradshaw (a one-officer primary unit) pulled over a suspect van wanted in connection with a felony. Which of the following actions would be considered most appropriate in clearing the suspect vehicle?

    A. Walk up to the driver door and request identification from the driver.

    B. Move along the passenger side of the vehicle in a crouched position, take a quick peek through the window to assess the number of occupants present, and then command everyone to get out of the vehicle.

    C. After the driver removes himself from the vehicle, conduct a pat-down search and arrest of the suspect to the rear of the vehicle.

    D. Call for backup and wait for assistance before attempting to clear the suspect vehicle.

55. Facts pertinent to a traffic accident investigation are given below. On the assumption that you have to complete an accident report regarding the matter, select from the four lettered statements that follow the one which most concisely describes what happened.

    ■   Victim's name is Mrs. Jerome Wilson

    ■   Victim's vehicle: 1985 Monte Carlo

    ■   Accident occurred at 5:30 P.M. on the Charleston Overpass

- ■ Nature of crime: Hit and run

- ■ Associated property damage: Sideswiped left rear quarter panel

- ■ Description of suspect vehicle: light-colored, two-door sedan; license plate number unknown

A. At 5:30 P.M., Mrs. Jerome Wilson was driving her 1985 Monte Carlo across the Charleston Overpass when she was sideswiped by another vehicle, which did not stop. The suspect vehicle was described by Mrs. Wilson as a light-colored, two-door sedan, license plate number unknown. Mrs. Wilson's 1985 Monte Carlo sustained damage to the left rear quarter panel.

B. At 5:30 P.M., Mrs. Jerome Wilson was crossing the Charleston Overpass when she was sideswiped by the driver of a light-colored, two-door sedan that failed to stop. Damage was strictly limited to the left rear quarter panel of her car. The license plate number of the suspect vehicle is unknown.

C. A 1985 Monte Carlo driven by Mrs. Jerome Wilson was sideswiped on the Charleston Overpass at 5:30 P.M. Damage to the victim's vehicle was confined to the left rear quarter panel. The suspect vehicle was a two-door sedan, license plate number unknown, which did not stop.

D. A light-colored, two-door sedan, license plate number unknown, sideswiped Mrs. Jerome Wilson at 5:30 P.M. on the Charleston Overpass. The suspect vehicle did not stop. Vehicle damage was restricted to the left rear quarter panel.

56. Facts pertinent to a burglary investigation are given below. On the assumption that you have to complete an accident report regarding the matter, select from the four lettered statements that follow the one which most concisely describes what happened.

- ■ Victim's name is Ms. Sarah Oppenheimer

- ■ Victim's address is 1507 W. Chestnut Avenue

- ■ Nature of crime: Burglary

- ■ Approximate time of occurrence: 11:30 P.M. to 7:00 A.M.

- ■ Associated property damage: Back door windowpane broken

A. Sometime between 11:30 P.M. and 7:00 A.M., the residence at 1507 W. Chestnut Avenue, owned by Ms. Sarah Oppenheimer, was burglarized.

B. Ms. Sarah Oppenheimer's residence was burglarized between 11:30 P.M. and 7:00 A.M. It is located at 1507 W. Chestnut Avenue and sustained damage to the back door.

C. Between 11:30 P.M. and 7:00 A.M., the residence of Ms. Sarah Oppenheimer, located at 1507 W. Chestnut Avenue, was burglarized after access had been gained by breaking a back door windowpane.

D. After gaining entry through a back door windowpane, Ms. Sarah Oppenheimer's house, located at 1507 W. Chestnut Avenue, was burglarized between 11:30 P.M. and 7:00 A.M.

57. During a statewide emphasis patrol one weekend, troopers arrested 380 individuals for driving while under the influence (DUI). Ninety percent of those cases were attributed to alcohol while the remaining involved drug-impaired driving. According to a State Patrol Toxicologist, approximately 5 percent of the latter group of cases actually involved prescription or over-the-counter medication. On the basis of this information, how many people were cited for driving while being impaired by illegal drugs?

   A. 2

   B. 5

   C. 36

   D. 38

58. One of the reform bills various state legislatures have approved to toughen drunk driving laws involves changing the legal blood-alcohol threshold to .0008 from .001. Quantitatively speaking, this reflects what kind of modification?

   A. 20% increase

   B. .02% increase

   C. .02 % decrease

   D. 20% decrease

59. For the purpose of this question, assume that a direct proportional correlation exists with regard to different individuals' ability to metabolize alcohol; variances are not an issue here. If a 130-pound woman could consume $3^1/_3$ glasses per hour of wine on an empty stomach and remain legally sober, how many glasses of wine could a 156-pound woman consume under the same circumstances and do likewise?

   A. 4

   B. $4^1/_4$

   C. $4^1/_2$

   D. $4^2/_3$

60. Assume that a trooper-cadet had to take the following course work in academy training the first month following appointment.

   ■ Civil Rights and Constitutional Law

   ■ Law Enforcement Ethics

   ■ Crisis Intervention

   ■ Executive Security Management

   ■ Criminal Justice

   Additionally, academic standards mandate cadets to maintain an overall average of 85% to continue in the program toward graduation. If a cadet had scored a 90%, 70%, 88%, and 94% in the first four classes given, what would he or she have to achieve in Criminal Justice studies to satisfy the scholastic requirement given?

A. 96%

B. 89%

C. 83%

D. 78%

61. If the State Patrol responded to 129 traffic accidents for the month and the other 14% of its calls were attributed to stranded motorists, how many calls did the State Patrol receive altogether?

    A. 150

    B. 163

    C. 169

    D. 173

62. Suppose a State Patrol ballistics expert made the claim that a bullet from a .22-250 rifle would travel 2²/₃ yards in the same time it takes a .22-caliber rifle bullet to travel 16 inches. How could this information be best expressed in terms of a ratio?

    A. 1:3

    B. 3:1

    C. 2.66:1

    D 6:1

63. Suppose you were at the scene of a winter traffic accident and for the record you had to state how cold it was in Fahrenheit degrees. If you knew it was 25° Celsius and the conversion formula F = ⁹/₅ (C°) + 32
was handy, which of the following would be the correct entry for the incident report?

    A. 102.6°

    B. 77°

    C. 67.3°

    D. 59.4°

64. If a rectangular area of 14.2 feet by 37.5 feet were roped off on a given road for a traffic accident investigation, how many square feet would that encompass?

    A. 523 square feet

    B. 530.5 square feet

    C. 531 square feet

    D. 532.5 square feet

65. Troopers Trent and Fairmont live at locations equidistant to the post at which they are both head-quartered. If Officer Trent can commute to work in 40 minutes doing an average speed of 35 miles per hour, how fast could Officer Fairmont get to work driving at an average speed of 45 miles per hour, assuming all other factors remain constant?

    A. 63.7 minutes

    B. 51.42 minutes

    C. 31.1 minutes

    D. 25.61 minutes

Answer question 66 on the basis of the chart provided.

TRAFFIC INFRACTIONS PERCENTAGE INDEX

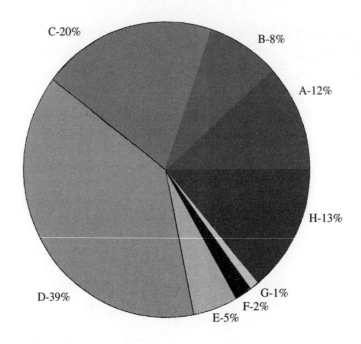

A. Operation of a motor vehicle with a suspended or revoked license.

B. Operation of a non-highway vehicle on public roads.

C. Reckless driving

D. Driving while under the influence.

E. Vehicular theft

F. Attempted felony elude of police vehicles

G. Vehicular assault

H. Driving with an invalid driver's license

66. If there were a total of 560 traffic infractions reported and the percent distribution of offenses was as indicated in the chart, how many actual reckless driving and vehicular theft cases would there be respectively?

   A. 218 and 11

   B. 137 and 17

   C. 112 and 28

   D. 105 and 39

67. According to a recently released government Crime Index Offense report, nationally one murder is committed every 30 seconds, one robbery occurs every 15 seconds, and one aggravated assault occurs every 12 seconds. If this information was translated into crimes committed per hour, which of the following selections would be correct?

    A. 60, 120, and 280, respectively

    B. 120, 240, and 300, respectively

    C. 140, 220, and 290, respectively

    D. 150, 240, and 300, respectively

68. The sketch below depicts the path taken by a vehicle that was traveling northeast on CY-15 at a high rate of speed. When the vehicle reached the point where CY-15 turns north (point A), it lost control by failing to negotiate the curve. Consequently, it continued on a northeast heading, hurtling across Deer Creek, and coming to rest on the south shoulder of CY-40 (point C). If Trooper Halverson measured off the distance between points B and C and points B and A (point B represents the right angle intersection of CY-40 and CY-15) as 59.5 meters and 62.5 meters respectively, what would the distance be that the vehicle traveled off-road (i.e., between points A and C)?

    A. 86.3 meters

    B. 79.1 meters

    C. 72.8 meters

    D. 67.5 meters

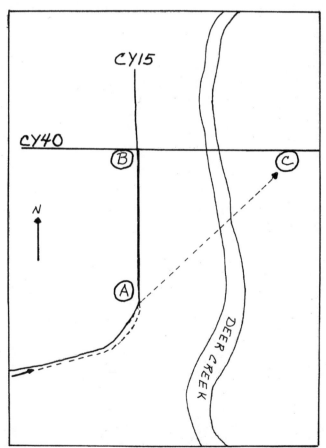

Study the following Uniform Crime Report to answer questions 69–72.

	Males				Females			
	Total		Under 18		Total		Under 18	
Criminal Offense	1993	1998	1993	1998	1993	1998	1993	1998
Motor Vehicle Theft	1,896	2,070	807	1,003	1,209	1,315	107	113
Larceny	5,482	4,681	1,892	1,340	3,110	2,801	1,188	1,247
Forcible rape	173	215	39	63	23	27	12	19
Shoplifting	6,852	8,957	5,060	5,783	4,090	5,679	3,491	3,687
Vandalism	4,008	4,639	3,407	3,960	3,242	3,360	2,352	2,799
Burglary	2,980	2,712	1,678	1,702	983	1,204	381	438
Robbery	1,444	1,230	480	322	506	213	157	120
Aggravated assault	11,512	12,185	8,502	9,100	6,806	7,314	4,700	4,777
Murder	105	121	61	52	47	56	13	17
Narcotics	7,412	7,760	5,430	7,010	7,042	7,664	4,112	4,871
Arson	432	475	118	142	162	168	137	153

69. According to the most recent statistics, how many more times is a man likely to commit burglary than a woman?

    A. 2:1

    B. 2.25:1

    C. 2.5:1

    D. 3.25:1

70. Shoplifting accounts for what percentage of the total crimes committed by female juveniles in 1998?

    A. 31%

    B. 25%

    C. 20%

    D. 17%

71. In the five-year period indicated in the survey, which of the following criminal offenses committed by male adults experienced the second-highest percentage increase?

    A. Murder

    B. Arson

    C. Vandalism

    D. Forcible rape

72. Which category of offenders demonstrates the second-highest percentage decrease in robbery?

    A. Adult males

    B. Adult females

    C. Juvenile males

    D. Juvenile females

73. State Patrol forensics expert Don Miller employed a wheel search pattern in his investigation of a case involving a homicide. In searching for thread, fiber, and hair samples that could potentially help the case, he meticulously searched an area that extended 12 feet in all directions from the victim. How many square feet of area did this search pattern account for?

    A. 376.5 square feet

    B. 397.69 square feet

    C. 438.1 square feet

    D. 452.39 square feet

Questions 74–82 pertain to spelling. Each question has four numerically identified columns, each comprising various word sets. One of the word sets given will contain an intentionally misspelled word. Select the column number that represents the misspelled word and mark your answer sheet accordingly.

74.

I	II	III	IV
intervention	fraudulent	Wednesday	leisure
privilege	raucous	intimidation	schedule
responsable	skeptical	homicide	pungent
hemorrhage	velocity	erratic	revolver

    A. I

    B. II

    C. III

    D. IV

75.

I	II	III	IV
quite	proximity	indigent	illiterate
sequester	semiautomatic	persistant	district
authorization	occupant	signature	neurotic
criteria	grievance	judicial	simultaneous

    A. I

    B. II

    C. III

    D. IV

76.

I	II	III	IV
municipal	superior	bulletin	juvinile
pedestrian	toxicology	arraignment	opinion
retaliate	admonition	sequester	insufficient
version	description	parallel	government

A. I
B. II
C. III
D. IV

77.

I	II	III	IV
mustache	vicious	liaison	obsolete
prosecutor	excellent	relevent	intersection
psychiatrist	khaki	inhaled	illegal
unconscious	forcibly	discipline	epileptic

A. I
B. II
C. III
D. IV

78.

I	II	III	IV
marital	prejudice	weather	incident
frequent	skidded	succeed	marijuana
preliminary	yield	hazardous	escape
sacrifice	transfered	foreign	initial

A. I
B. II
C. III
D. IV

79.

I	II	III	IV
silhouette	secretary	impaired	complaint
reputation	official	renewal	acquitted
persperation	mitigate	sobriety	utility
pursuit	mischievous	belligerent	substantiate

A. I
B. II
C. III
D. IV

80.

I	II	III	IV
proposition	gauge	deterrent	religious
receipt	embarrass	approximate	parole
simultaneous	perimeter	chauffeur	nausea
medical	baricade	court	impression

A. I
B. II
C. III
D. IV

81.

I	II	III	IV
muscle	representation	mileage	disappear
experienced	segregation	exhaust	misdemeaner
larceny	permanent	adjacent	corroborate
opposite	intoxicated	coroner	cocaine

A. I
B. II
C. III
D. IV

82.

I	II	III	IV
analysis	quality	obscene	liquor
coherent	marital	psycology	feminine
ramification	infraction	disoriented	employment
scheme	forgery	emergency	proceeded

A. I

B. II

C. III

D. IV

Questions 83–94 pertain to vocabulary proficiency. Each question will pose a statement that will have a particular word(s) in italics. You must determine from the four choices given which one correctly defines the word(s) in question and then mark your answer accordingly.

83. The choice of a concealed weapon is pretty much left up to the *discretion* of the individual officer involved. Discretion most nearly means:

   A. Prudence

   B. Implementation

   C. Initiative

   D. Disposition

84. The problems were *alleviated* with the new filing system. Alleviated most nearly means:

   A. Intensified

   B. Exacerbated

   C. Aggrandized

   D. Mitigated

85. It was a thinly *veiled* attempt to *placate* his immediate supervisor. *Veiled* and *placate* respectively mean:

   A. Open and infuriate

   B. Calculated and mollify

   C. Disguised and appease

   D. Masqueraded and annoy

86. The defender in question has some peculiar *mannerisms*. *Mannerisms* most nearly means:

   A. Idiosyncrasies

   B. Benefits

   C. Thoughts

   D. Conclusions

87. *Irrespective* of public perception, high-speed pursuit policies followed by this department demonstrate *unequivocal* restraint. *Irrespective* and *unequivocal* respectively mean:

    A. Contrary and borderline

    B. Disregarding and clear

    C. Supportive and ambiguous

    D. Cognizant and certain

88. Officer Hendricks was *appalled* by the *exorbitant* interest rate currently being charged by her credit union for an auto loan. *Appalled* and *exorbitant* respectively mean:

    A. Content and average

    B. Gratuitous and reasonable

    C. Shocked and excessive

    D. Enthralled and lofty

89. Lieutenant Givens seemed uncharacteristically *reticent* when the topic of departmental hiring practices was broached. *Reticent* most nearly means:

    A. Assertive

    B. Anxious

    C. Reserved

    D. Expressive

90. The feeling of *resignation* was particularly *pervasive* among the younger cadets. *Resignation* and *pervasive* respectively mean:

    A. Acquiescence and permeative

    B. Resiliency and present

    C. Persistence and obvious

    D. Resolve and manifest

91. State Patrol officers in charge of protecting the Governor try to be as *unobtrusive* as possible. *Unobtrusive* most nearly means:

    A. Noticeable

    B. Secure

    C. Prepared

    D. Inconspicuous

92. A well-written traffic accident report *precludes superfluous* details. *Precludes* and *superfluous* respectively mean:

    A. Includes and pertinent

    B. Excludes and excessive

    C. Exemplifies and redundant

    D. Evaluates and all

93. Virtually every person that has shared a work assignment with Officer Milton will attest to his *magnanimous* nature. *Magnanimous* most nearly means:

   A. Unforgiving

   B. Malicious

   C. Unselfish

   D. Incompetent

94. Despite the *incontrovertible* evidence presented in court, the defendant was *exonerated* of all charges because of a legal technicality. *Incontrovertible* and *exonerated* respectively mean:

   A. Indisputable and blameless

   B. Contradictory and freed

   C. Fabricated and excused

   D. Relevant and vindicated

Questions 95–106 relate to grammar, punctuation, and spelling. Each question will provide a written statement that may or may not contain specific errors. From the choices provided, select the answer that represents an accurate assessment of the statement in question and then mark your answer sheet accordingly.

95. Many states explicitly prohibit the placement of some or all types of juveniles in adult institutions.

   The statement, in terms of English usage,

   A. Is structurally incorrect.

   B. Contains one or more misspellings.

   C. Lacks necessary punctuation and/or capitalization.

   D. Is correct in all aspects.

96. A legal obligation against the state is an obligation that would form the basis of a judgement against the state in a court of competant jurisdiction should the legislature permit the state to be sued.

   The statement, in terms of English usage,

   A. Is structurally incorrect.

   B. Contains one or more misspellings.

   C. Lacks necessary punctuation and/or capitalization.

   D. Is correct in all aspects.

97. The evidentiary value of labratory tests on fibers varies greatly depending on the quantity of fibers collected and the uniqueness of the characteristics found during the examination.

   The statement, in terms of English usage,

   A. Is structurally incorrect.

   B. Contains one or more misspellings.

   C. Lacks necessary punctuation and/or capitalization.

   D. Is correct in all aspects.

98. It is not uncommon in many jurisdictions for felony cases to be referred by the district attorneys office to a city attorneys office for the purpose of reducing the charges to a misdemeanor.

    The statement, in terms of English usage,

    A. Is structurally incorrect.

    B. Contains one or more misspellings.

    C. Lacks necessary punctuation and/or capitalization.

    D. Is correct in all aspects.

99. Larceny is defined as the felonious taking and carrying away of someone else's personal property, without they're consent, with the intention of permanently depriving that person of its use or possession.

    The statement, in terms of English usage,

    A. Is structurally incorrect.

    B. Contains one or more misspellings.

    C. Lacks necessary punctuation and/or capitalization.

    D. Is correct in all aspects.

100. Police personnel in most jurisdictions are percieved by the general public as being spread too thin to fulfill all the responsibilities that come with serving the community.

    The statement, in terms of English usage,

    A. Is structurally incorrect.

    B. Contains one or more misspellings.

    C. Lacks necessary punctuation and/or capitalization.

    D. Is correct in all aspects.

101. One of the areas that have been affected by budgetary constraint is job training.

    The statement, in terms of English usage,

    A. Is structurally incorrect.

    B. Contains one or more misspellings.

    C. Lacks necessary punctuation and/or capitalization.

    D. Is correct in all aspects.

102. Drug Awareness and Resistance Education programs are designed for juveniles contemplating the use of drugs and their parents.

    The statement, in terms of English usage,

    A. Is structurally incorrect.

    B. Contains one or more misspellings.

    C. Lacks necessary punctuation and/or capitalization.

    D. Is correct in all aspects.

103. Undercover investigators must exercise a great deal of caution in planning and affecting communication with supervisory personnel.

    The statement, in terms of English usage,

    A. Is structurally incorrect.

    B. Contains one or more misspellings.

    C. Lacks necessary punctuation and/or capitalization.

    D. Is correct in all aspects.

104. It is recommended that, when at all possible, apparent suicides should be handled with the same degree of attention given a homicide.

    The statement, in terms of English usage,

    A. Is structurally incorrect.

    B. Contains one or more misspellings.

    C. Lacks necessary punctuation and/or capitalization.

    D. Is correct in all aspects.

105. State Police Officer Harris eluded to the hazards of joining a gang when he referred to a list of juveniles who have been killed in gang-related incidents.

    The statement, in terms of English usage,

    A. Is structurally incorrect.

    B. Contains one or more misspellings.

    C. Lacks necessary punctuation and/or capitalization.

    D. Is correct in all aspects.

106. Involuntary commitment is possible through a mental health professional when the suspect refuses appropriate treatment, is a danger to him or herself or others, and can be detained for fourteen to sixty days.

    The statement, in terms of English usage,

    A. Is structurally incorrect.

    B. Contains one or more misspellings.

    C. Lacks necessary punctuation and/or capitalization.

    D. Is correct in all aspects.

Answer questions 107–109 on the basis of the reading below:

Malicious mischief is defined in *Black's Law Dictionary* as "the willful destruction of personal property from actual ill will or resentment toward its owner or possessor." This crime was formerly considered trespass by common law, but most states have made penalties for this kind of crime more severe. The spectrum of malicious mischief is sketched out below:

First-degree malicious mischief involves knowingly and maliciously damaging property that belongs to another where the sum of the damages exceeds $1700, or willfully interrupting a public service by damaging or tampering with a utility, a public conveyance, communications equipment, or an emergency vehicle. First-degree malicious mischief is a Class B felony.

Second-degree malicious mischief involves knowingly and maliciously damaging property that belongs to another where the sum of the damages exceeds $300 but does not exceed $1700, or willfully creating a substantial risk of interrupting a public service by damaging or tampering with a utility, a public conveyance, communications equipment, or an emergency vehicle, or willfully causing the injury or death of any livestock owned by another. Second-degree malicious mischief is a Class C felony.

Third-degree malicious mischief involves knowingly and maliciously damaging property that belongs to another where the sum of the damages is beneath the limits imposed by the first two statutes. Third-degree malicious mischief is a gross misdemeanor if the sum of damages caused exceeds $75. Otherwise, the crime is deemed a misdemeanor.

107. For the lack of something better to do, Billy White decided to key-scratch the front right fender of a Cutlass Supreme parked in front of a small convenience store. Two people across the street witnessed the event that led to Billy's arrest. A claims adjuster from the vehicle owner's insurance firm estimated the damage would cost approximately $850 to fix. According to the reading and under the circumstances given, what should Billy White be charged with?

　A. Class B felony

　B. Class C felony

　C. Gross misdemeanor

　D. Misdemeanor

108. Robert Blakemore was considered a genius by most computer experts. For the challenge of it, Mr. Blakemore had gained unauthorized access to county courthouse records. He planted a tailor-made virus in the county's computer system that would methodically eliminate certain information from the electronic database. Assuming that Mr. Blakemore had left some sort of trail that resulted in his arrest, which of the crimes described in this reading would apply to this case?

　A. First-degree computer trespass

　B. Second-degree computer trespass

　C. Class C felony

　D. Class B felony

109. Vicki Thurston wanted revenge against a classmate who embarrassed her in front of her friends at school. Vicki knew where this person lived. After school, she went to a local hardware store and bought a can of black spray paint. That same evening, Vicki went to this person's house and spray painted graffiti on the exterior of the garage. Police had little difficulty in determining the motive and who was responsible for the incident. The initial damage estimate from the homeowner's insurance carrier was approximately $300. According to the guidelines established in the reading, Ms. Thurston could be prosecuted for what crime?

　A. First-degree malicious mischief

　B. Second-degree malicious mischief

　C. Third-degree malicious mischief

　D. Class B felony

Answer questions 110–112 on the basis of the reading provided below:

> *Black's Law Dictionary* defines assault as "any willful attempt or threat to inflict injury upon the person of another, when coupled with an apparent present ability to do so, and any intentional display of force such as would give the victim reason to fear or expect immediate bodily harm." According to one state's criminal statutes, the crime of assault is further subclassified depending on the severity of the offense committed. First-degree assault involves the use of a firearm or deadly weapon or any other means which is likely to result in the victim being severely harmed or killed. This form of assault is considered a Class A felony.
>
> Second-degree assault involves intentional assault that consequently inflicts substantial bodily harm to the victim or assault of another for reason of committing a felony or with the intent to cause bodily harm, inadvertently passing a pathogen on to the victim. This form of assault is considered a Class B felony.
>
> Third-degree assault involves the assault of any law enforcement officer or public employee while performing their assigned duties, or any criminal negligence that results in bodily harm to the victim, or the willful intent to assault another to avoid lawful apprehension or detention. This form of assault is considered a Class C felony.
>
> Fourth-degree assault involves any kind of assault except for those already described. This form of assault is simply considered a gross misdemeanor.
>
> It should be noted that if there are multiple assaults of varying degrees committed, the defendant shall be charged with the most severe offense.

110. Paul goes to his estranged wife's apartment knowing that her boyfriend, John, is visiting. When John opens the front door to let Paul in, Paul immediately starts a physical altercation that results in a small facial laceration and two broken ribs to John. Accordingly, if John has intentions to prosecute, Paul may be charged with which of the following:

   A. Class A felony

   B. Class B felony

   C. Class C felony

   D. Gross misdemeanor

111. As Trooper Beaumont was attempting to place Margaret Williams into the back of his patrol car for transport and subsequent booking into the county jail for suspected prostitution, Ms. Williams stomped on his right foot with her high-heeled shoe. Officer Beaumont sustained injuries to his right toe resulting in light duty desk assignment for three weeks. Ms. Williams should be charged with which of the following crimes, according to the reading:

   A. First-degree assault

   B. Second-degree assault

   C. Third-degree assault

   D. No crime, because she was already being charged with prostitution

112. Tom Briggs, a reputed cocaine addict, was confronted by Bill Evans, a store manager, and accused of shoplifting two cameras. Mr. Briggs, feeling cornered, produced a syringe that he claimed was contaminated with the AIDS virus. He indicated he would, without reservation, stick Mr. Evans with it if Mr. Evans failed to get out of the way. The State Police, who had been summoned earlier, arrived and quickly subdued the suspect. Toxicology reports later confirmed that the syringe was, in fact, clean. Outside of shoplifting, Mr. Briggs should be additionally charged with which crime, according to the reading? (*Note:* Disregard aspect of robbery.)

    A. First-degree assault

    B. Second-degree assault

    C. Third-degree assault

    D. Mr. Briggs can't be charged with anything besides shoplifting because lab results on the syringe turned out to be negative for the AIDS virus.

Answer questions 113–115 on the basis of the narrative provided below.

    There are specific guidelines that law enforcement officers follow when making an arrest at a suspect's home. Officers should identify themselves as law enforcement officers, state the express purpose of their visit, and wait a reasonable time for a response or an incontrovertible refusal to allow entry. This is referred to as the "knock and announce" rule. If the officer has a warrant and is refused entry by the suspect, the officer retains the right to break and enter to effect an arrest. Most state courts will not issue no-knock warrants. However, there are certain exceptions to the "knock and announce" rule. If the officer suspects that evidence crucial to the case may be destroyed while the police are waiting and complying with these standards, he or she may bypass the knock and announce rule. If the rule creates the risk of imminent escape for the suspect or risk to the public, there again is valid reason to circumvent such procedural guidelines. Three important court cases established precedent with regard to this procedure. *Payton v. New York* (1980) established that an arrest warrant must be in an officer's possession prior to entering a person's premises when permission to enter is denied and exigent circumstances (i.e., exceptions to the rules) do not exist. *Steagold v. U.S.* (1981) dictated that if the suspect is in a home other than his own, both an arrest warrant and a search warrant would be required to effect an arrest. *Watson v. U.S.* (1976) was definitive as to what constitutes a private area and what constitutes a public domain. Any place or space which is basically open to the public at large is considered to be an area that does not require a warrant to effect an arrest. The difference established in this court case is that a doorway to a person's home is considered to be a private area, thus falling under the guidelines prescribed. However, a person's porch is considered to be a public domain.

113. From both a legal and a practical perspective, the implementation of the knock and announce policy in conducting an arrest does all of the following except:

    A. Reduce the possibility of violence

    B. Serve as a prelude to using any means necessary to effect an arrest

    C. Avert property damage

    D. Protect the suspect's/occupant's constitutional right to privacy

114. State Patrol Officer Jake Talbott and his partner go to the home of Barry Livermore to execute an arrest warrant. After they spend a few moments waiting on the porch for the suspect to answer his door, a passing neighbor mentions that Barry was next door visiting a close friend. Officer Talbott then goes to the home next door, and after being refused admission, he enters forcibly and promptly places Mr. Livermore under arrest. According to the reading, Officer Talbott's actions were:

   A. Legal, because the warrant was served after correctly following knock and announce guidelines.

   B. Illegal, because the owner of the home was reluctant to permit the officer to enter.

   C. Legal, because Mr. Livermore was outside his home and the situation thus did not require full compliance with knock and announce policy.

   D. Illegal, because a search warrant was not obtained in addition to the arrest warrant prior to arresting Mr. Livermore at his neighbor's house.

115. Trooper Blake Anderson went to a suspect's home prior to seeking an arrest warrant signed by a magistrate and by good fortune saw the suspect standing in the driveway. Officer Anderson identified himself prior to placing the suspect under arrest. Under the circumstances, according to the reading, Trooper Anderson's actions were:

   A. Illegal, because he failed to have an arrest warrant for the suspect in his possession.

   B. Legal, because the driveway would be considered a public area and therefore would not require Trooper Anderson to have a warrant to effect an arrest.

   C. Illegal, because Trooper Anderson did not specifically ask for permission to come onto the property.

   D. Legal, because Trooper Anderson did identify himself.

Questions 116–120 involve composite sketch cross comparison. Look at the original sketch of the subject and then try to discern which of the four other sketches provided is the same individual attempting to disguise his or her appearance. Unless otherwise stated, assume the individual in question has not undergone any surgery.

116.

A.    B.    C.    D.

117.

A.  B.  C.  D.

118.

A.  B.  C.  D.

119.

A.   B.   C.   D.

120.

A.   B.   C.   D.

Answer questions 121–125 on the basis of the map provided below.

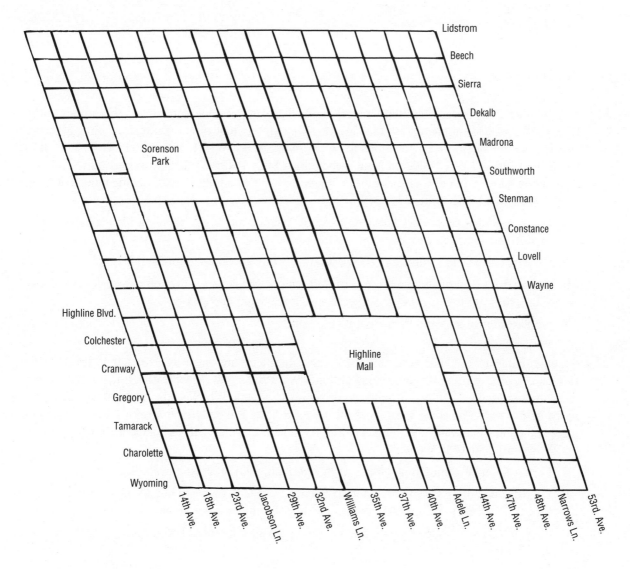

121. If Trooper Kim Peterson were conducting traffic enforcement at Highline Blvd. and 44th and received a call to investigate suspected vehicular prowling in the southeast vicinity of Sorenson Park, in what general direction must she head?

   A. Northeast

   B. Southeast

   C. Southwest

   D. Northwest

122. Assume that Constance, Highline, Gregory, and Charolette are one-way streets that direct traffic flow north; all odd-numbered avenues are one-way streets that direct traffic flow east; all other streets not referenced can be presumed to be two-way streets. Which of the alternative routes provided below would be considered legal means for a State Police Officer working traffic enforcement at the intersection of Charolette and 35th Avenue to respond to a traffic accident that occurred on Constance and 29th Avenue?

   A. Go from 35th Avenue on Charolette to 32nd Avenue, turn right, go eight blocks before turning left and driving one block.

   B. Go east one block, south four blocks, west nine blocks, and then north one block.

   C. Go north on Charolette one block, turn left, go one block west, turn left again, go five blocks south, turn right, go seven blocks west, turn right again and go one block north.

   D. Go east four blocks and then eight blocks south.

123. Assume that Wayne, Constance, Tamarack, and Charolette are one-way streets that direct traffic flow north; all even-numbered avenues are one-way streets that direct traffic flow east; all other streets not referenced can be presumed to be two-way streets. Which of the alternative routes provided below would be considered legal means for a State Police Officer working traffic enforcement at the intersection of Wyoming and 40th Avenue to respond to a traffic accident that occurred on Southworth and 14th Avenue?

   A. Go south on Wyoming nine blocks, turn right, and then proceed eleven blocks west.

   B. Go from Wyoming to Gregory on 40th Avenue, turn left, go seven blocks, turn right, go eight blocks west before turning left and proceeding two more blocks south.

   C. Go south on Wyoming seven blocks, turn right, go eleven blocks before turning right and proceeding two more blocks.

   D. Go south on Wyoming one block, turn right, go three blocks west, turn left, go six blocks south, turn right, go eight blocks west before turning left and proceeding south two more blocks.

124. If State Patrol Officer Alex Kimbell is presently positioned at Dekalb and 29th Avenue and is dispatched to investigate a vehicular assault that allegedly took place at the northeast corner of the Highline Mall parking lot, which of the alternative routes provided below would afford him the quickest means to respond? (Assume all streets are two-way and have identical speed limits—all other factors remain constant.)

    A. Go ten blocks east on 28th Avenue before turning left and proceeding approximately six more blocks; the scene should be in view on the left.

    B. Go seven blocks north on Dekalb before turning left and proceeding approximately nine blocks; the scene should be in view on the right.

    C. Go ten blocks north on Dekalb, nine blocks east on Narrows Lane, and then three blocks south on Cranway; the scene should be in view directly ahead.

    D. Go two blocks north on Dekalb and then ten blocks east on Williams before turning left and proceeding approximately four more blocks; the scene should be in view on the left.

125. Assume that Sierra, Southworth, Wayne, Dekalb, and Colchester are one-way streets that direct traffic flow south; all even-numbered avenues are one-way streets that direct traffic flow west; all other streets not referenced can be presumed to be two-way streets. Other situations of concern involve a repaving project on 44th and 47th Avenues between Stenman and Wayne that will necessitate closure to thru traffic for the entire day; the intersection of Lovell and 48th Avenue will be closed between 10:30 A.M. and 1:45 P.M. for an underground natural gas line repair; and a tanker truck transporting anhydrous ammonia experiences a minor valve leak at the intersection of Madrona and 40th Avenue. As a safety precaution, a hazardous materials team working under the auspices of the local fire department cordons off all streets within a four-square block area surrounding the site. The chemical spill occurred at 8:45 A.M. and it's expected to take approximately five hours to clear and reopen to public transit. Under the given circumstances, if Trooper Joe Blakemore was dispatched from his district post located at Beech and 35th Avenue at 1330 hours to investigate a traffic fatality that occurred at the intersection of Wayne and 48th Avenue, which of the routes given below would serve as a viable means of response?

    A. Go north on Beech to 48th Avenue, turn right and then drive eight blocks east.

    B. Go five blocks north on Beech, turn right, go eight blocks east before turning left and proceeding one more block.

    C. Go three blocks north on Beech, turn right, go nine blocks east, turn left, go three blocks north before turning west and proceeding one more block.

    D. Go eight blocks north on Beech, turn right, go eight blocks east before turning south and proceeding two more blocks.

ANSWER SHEET TO PRACTICE EXAM 1

1. Ⓐ Ⓑ Ⓒ Ⓓ
2. Ⓐ Ⓑ Ⓒ Ⓓ
3. Ⓐ Ⓑ Ⓒ Ⓓ
4. Ⓐ Ⓑ Ⓒ Ⓓ
5. Ⓐ Ⓑ Ⓒ Ⓓ
6. Ⓐ Ⓑ Ⓒ Ⓓ
7. Ⓐ Ⓑ Ⓒ Ⓓ
8. Ⓐ Ⓑ Ⓒ Ⓓ
9. Ⓐ Ⓑ Ⓒ Ⓓ
10. Ⓐ Ⓑ Ⓒ Ⓓ
11. Ⓐ Ⓑ Ⓒ Ⓓ
12. Ⓐ Ⓑ Ⓒ Ⓓ
13. Ⓐ Ⓑ Ⓒ Ⓓ
14. Ⓐ Ⓑ Ⓒ Ⓓ
15. Ⓐ Ⓑ Ⓒ Ⓓ
16. Ⓐ Ⓑ Ⓒ Ⓓ
17. Ⓐ Ⓑ Ⓒ Ⓓ
18. Ⓐ Ⓑ Ⓒ Ⓓ
19. Ⓐ Ⓑ Ⓒ Ⓓ
20. Ⓐ Ⓑ Ⓒ Ⓓ
21. Ⓐ Ⓑ Ⓒ Ⓓ
22. Ⓐ Ⓑ Ⓒ Ⓓ
23. Ⓐ Ⓑ Ⓒ Ⓓ
24. Ⓐ Ⓑ Ⓒ Ⓓ
25. Ⓐ Ⓑ Ⓒ Ⓓ
26. Ⓐ Ⓑ Ⓒ Ⓓ
27. Ⓐ Ⓑ Ⓒ Ⓓ
28. Ⓐ Ⓑ Ⓒ Ⓓ
29. Ⓐ Ⓑ Ⓒ Ⓓ
30. Ⓐ Ⓑ Ⓒ Ⓓ

31. Ⓐ Ⓑ Ⓒ Ⓓ
32. Ⓐ Ⓑ Ⓒ Ⓓ
33. Ⓐ Ⓑ Ⓒ Ⓓ
34. Ⓐ Ⓑ Ⓒ Ⓓ
35. Ⓐ Ⓑ Ⓒ Ⓓ
36. Ⓐ Ⓑ Ⓒ Ⓓ
37. Ⓐ Ⓑ Ⓒ Ⓓ
38. Ⓐ Ⓑ Ⓒ Ⓓ
39. Ⓐ Ⓑ Ⓒ Ⓓ
40. Ⓐ Ⓑ Ⓒ Ⓓ
41. Ⓐ Ⓑ Ⓒ Ⓓ
42. Ⓐ Ⓑ Ⓒ Ⓓ
43. Ⓐ Ⓑ Ⓒ Ⓓ
44. Ⓐ Ⓑ Ⓒ Ⓓ
45. Ⓐ Ⓑ Ⓒ Ⓓ
46. Ⓐ Ⓑ Ⓒ Ⓓ
47. Ⓐ Ⓑ Ⓒ Ⓓ
48. Ⓐ Ⓑ Ⓒ Ⓓ
49. Ⓐ Ⓑ Ⓒ Ⓓ
50. Ⓐ Ⓑ Ⓒ Ⓓ
51. Ⓐ Ⓑ Ⓒ Ⓓ
52. Ⓐ Ⓑ Ⓒ Ⓓ
53. Ⓐ Ⓑ Ⓒ Ⓓ
54. Ⓐ Ⓑ Ⓒ Ⓓ
55. Ⓐ Ⓑ Ⓒ Ⓓ
56. Ⓐ Ⓑ Ⓒ Ⓓ
57. Ⓐ Ⓑ Ⓒ Ⓓ
58. Ⓐ Ⓑ Ⓒ Ⓓ
59. Ⓐ Ⓑ Ⓒ Ⓓ
60. Ⓐ Ⓑ Ⓒ Ⓓ

61. Ⓐ Ⓑ Ⓒ Ⓓ
62. Ⓐ Ⓑ Ⓒ Ⓓ
63. Ⓐ Ⓑ Ⓒ Ⓓ
64. Ⓐ Ⓑ Ⓒ Ⓓ
65. Ⓐ Ⓑ Ⓒ Ⓓ
66. Ⓐ Ⓑ Ⓒ Ⓓ
67. Ⓐ Ⓑ Ⓒ Ⓓ
68. Ⓐ Ⓑ Ⓒ Ⓓ
69. Ⓐ Ⓑ Ⓒ Ⓓ
70. Ⓐ Ⓑ Ⓒ Ⓓ
71. Ⓐ Ⓑ Ⓒ Ⓓ
72. Ⓐ Ⓑ Ⓒ Ⓓ
73. Ⓐ Ⓑ Ⓒ Ⓓ
74. Ⓐ Ⓑ Ⓒ Ⓓ
75. Ⓐ Ⓑ Ⓒ Ⓓ
76. Ⓐ Ⓑ Ⓒ Ⓓ
77. Ⓐ Ⓑ Ⓒ Ⓓ
78. Ⓐ Ⓑ Ⓒ Ⓓ
79. Ⓐ Ⓑ Ⓒ Ⓓ
80. Ⓐ Ⓑ Ⓒ Ⓓ
81. Ⓐ Ⓑ Ⓒ Ⓓ
82. Ⓐ Ⓑ Ⓒ Ⓓ
83. Ⓐ Ⓑ Ⓒ Ⓓ
84. Ⓐ Ⓑ Ⓒ Ⓓ
85. Ⓐ Ⓑ Ⓒ Ⓓ
86. Ⓐ Ⓑ Ⓒ Ⓓ
87. Ⓐ Ⓑ Ⓒ Ⓓ
88. Ⓐ Ⓑ Ⓒ Ⓓ
89. Ⓐ Ⓑ Ⓒ Ⓓ
90. Ⓐ Ⓑ Ⓒ Ⓓ

91. Ⓐ Ⓑ Ⓒ Ⓓ   103. Ⓐ Ⓑ Ⓒ Ⓓ   115. Ⓐ Ⓑ Ⓒ Ⓓ
92. Ⓐ Ⓑ Ⓒ Ⓓ   104. Ⓐ Ⓑ Ⓒ Ⓓ   116. Ⓐ Ⓑ Ⓒ Ⓓ
93. Ⓐ Ⓑ Ⓒ Ⓓ   105. Ⓐ Ⓑ Ⓒ Ⓓ   117. Ⓐ Ⓑ Ⓒ Ⓓ
94. Ⓐ Ⓑ Ⓒ Ⓓ   106. Ⓐ Ⓑ Ⓒ Ⓓ   118. Ⓐ Ⓑ Ⓒ Ⓓ
95. Ⓐ Ⓑ Ⓒ Ⓓ   107. Ⓐ Ⓑ Ⓒ Ⓓ   119. Ⓐ Ⓑ Ⓒ Ⓓ
96. Ⓐ Ⓑ Ⓒ Ⓓ   108. Ⓐ Ⓑ Ⓒ Ⓓ   120. Ⓐ Ⓑ Ⓒ Ⓓ
97. Ⓐ Ⓑ Ⓒ Ⓓ   109. Ⓐ Ⓑ Ⓒ Ⓓ   121. Ⓐ Ⓑ Ⓒ Ⓓ
98. Ⓐ Ⓑ Ⓒ Ⓓ   110. Ⓐ Ⓑ Ⓒ Ⓓ   122. Ⓐ Ⓑ Ⓒ Ⓓ
99. Ⓐ Ⓑ Ⓒ Ⓓ   111. Ⓐ Ⓑ Ⓒ Ⓓ   123. Ⓐ Ⓑ Ⓒ Ⓓ
100. Ⓐ Ⓑ Ⓒ Ⓓ   112. Ⓐ Ⓑ Ⓒ Ⓓ   124. Ⓐ Ⓑ Ⓒ Ⓓ
101. Ⓐ Ⓑ Ⓒ Ⓓ   113. Ⓐ Ⓑ Ⓒ Ⓓ   125. Ⓐ Ⓑ Ⓒ Ⓓ
102. Ⓐ Ⓑ Ⓒ Ⓓ   114. Ⓐ Ⓑ Ⓒ Ⓓ

Answers can be found on pages 219–228.

ANSWERS TO PRACTICE EXAM 1

1. *C.* 26-07A
2. *D.* State Patrol Officer Lieutenant Pete Kendrick
3. *A.* Jeffery T. Beaumont
4. *D.* 13721-B and 13501-A. Selection A is the correct chronology of NCIC codes given in the narrative, however, one has to pay particular attention to how a question is worded. In this case, the order of the charges against the defendant were revised, thus changing the respective order of the applicable NCIC codes.
5. *D.* Selection B is the correct date for the scheduled arraignment hearing, but the reading stipulated that the defendant remained in detention; he was not released after posting bail.
6. *B.* The subject was described as having brown eyes.
7. *B.* Lakeview Police Officer Harry M. Stevens
8. *C.* 555-22-0557
9. *C.* Christine L. Thomas
10. *C.* Suspect C, i.e., Christine L. Thomas
11. *A.* Joanne C. Lewis did not have a watch at the time of her arrest.
12. *D.* Suspect D, i.e., Pat N. Blake, has possession of cigarettes along with a book of matches.
13. *A.* Joanne C. Lewis
14. *C.* Christine L. Thomas
15. *B.* Suspect B, i.e., Christine L. Thomas' driver's license number
16. *B.* Don Hudspeth
17. *D.* Sarah Spangler
18. *A.* December 18, 1965
19. *C.* Third-degree Assault and Criminal Trespass
20. *A.* Marilyn D. Kinslow
21. *A.* Suspect 1. Selection D is incorrect because Suspect 4 had only one alias.
22. *D.* Suspects 2 and 4 were considered to be armed and dangerous.
23. *C.* Sarah Spangler's case file number 187-43 was an AWWS posting.
24. *B.* Marilyn Kinslow did not have a record of criminal trespass.
25. *D.* Don Hudspeth's given alias was James H. Humphrey.
26. *D.* It was stressed early in the reading that if officers do not file a notice of infraction with the court within 48 hours, the court would dismiss the charges altogether. Since 72 hours had passed before Trooper Davis filed the notice, the violation would be dismissed without prejudice by the court.
27. *C.* It is mentioned at the start of the reading that anyone who willfully refuses to sign an issuance can be cited additionally for failure to sign. That misdemeanor by itself warrants arrest and can mean incarceration for the violator.
28. *D.* A defendant receiving a notice of infraction by this means officially has 14 days to respond in some way to the issuance or face prosecution for a misdemeanor, as described in the reading.
29. *B.* Quarterly, because there are four colors that identify the months of the year.

30. *C.*   Since the reading mentioned that fleet vehicles have to renew registration only once a year, in October, it can be categorized as an annual system.

31. *D.*   Since a Buick LeSabre is a passenger vehicle, red would correctly represent the month in question. The expiration tab year would correctly be identified as 1994. Selection C would have been correct had the vehicle been anything other than a passenger vehicle or truck (except a government-exempt or fleet-exempt vehicle).

32. *D.*   Mr. Turner is driving a government vehicle, which is exempt from tab and registration fees.

33. *D.*   Selection D would effectively concentrate patrol efforts in the area and at the time of day most needed. In all likelihood, there would be a corresponding decrease in residential burglaries at the Farmington Community Club.

34. *C.*   Selection C would effectively concentrate patrol efforts in the area and at the time of day most needed. In all likelihood, there would be a corresponding decrease in malicious mischief at the Carver Center Apartments.

35. *B.*   Selections B and C are essentially describing the same neighborhood and inherent crime problem. The only difference is that B incorrectly identifies the problem plaguing Meadowlark Estates. Vehicular prowling, not malicious mischief, is the concern here.

36. *B.*   This can seem like a confusing question, however, information common among witnesses is justifiable reason to believe that what is told to investigators is accurate. The general consensus is that the suspect is a Caucasian male who is 5'11" and weight between 175 and 180 pounds; he has light-colored hair and blue eyes. The witness who comes closest to describing the suspect in this manner is Mrs. Williams. Each detail she gave is verified by one or more other witnesses.

37. *C.*   Officer Pratt (Badge No. 152) is only scheduled to work on four days (i.e., 32 hours). All other personnel are either working full time or overtime.

38. *D.*   Despite the fact that Trooper Unger (Badge No. 314) drew a schedule that dictated overtime, four of the six work days did involve Tour A assignments. Troopers Brown (Badge No. 976) and Ryzek (Badge No. 612) were assigned Tour A on a couple days for the week, however, from a comparative standpoint, Trooper Unger fared substantially better.

39. *A.*   Trooper Tyson (Badge No. 718) was scheduled to work Tour C on Monday in Sector 9.

40. *B.*   If the given work schedule was implemented without revision, Officer Bateman (Badge No. 670) would be working a double shift on Mondays (i.e., Tours B and C/16 straight working hours). The fact that District 18 does not have a personnel shortage precludes the necessity of having any officers work that kind of overtime.

41. *B.*   This kind of question first requires a determination of which day of the week July 6 falls on. Since Independence Day (i.e., July 4) is said to be on a Saturday, then July 6 would be the following Monday. According to the duty roster, Officer Tyson (Badge No. 718) is assigned C shift in Sector 9.

42. *D.*   Because July 4 fell on Friday and July 18 is exactly two weeks following, it too is a Friday. Therefore, looking at the schedule for Friday, Officer Bateman (Badge No. 670) is shown to be assigned to A shift in Sector 14.

43. *C.*

S	M	T	W	T	F	S
		13	14	15	16	17
18	19	20	21	22		

By backtracking in calendar fashion as shown above, the day that July 13 falls on can easily be discerned. Since the 13th is a Tuesday, Tour C in Section 14 is normally assigned to Officer Klinger (Badge No. 131). However, that date coincides with his vacation leave. Therefore, Officer Locke (Badge No. 563) would serve as his relief. Trooper Hudson (Badge No. 410) could serve in a similar capacity but his name was not provided within the question for consideration.

44. *B.* SMITH: First five letters of last name

J: First letter of first name

D: First letter of middle name

100 − 56 = 44: Birth-year calculation

9: Check digit (could be any single number)

P: Month of birth

Z: Day of birth

45. *A.* HALVO: First five letters of last name

J: First letter of first name

L: First letter of middle name

100 − 75 = 25: Birth-year calculation

1: Check digit (could be any single number)

H: Month of birth

P: Day of birth

46. *D.* BARTE: First five letters of last name

V: First letter of first name

J: First letter of middle name

100 − 63 = 37: Birth-year calculation

8: Check digit (could be any single number)

L: Month of birth

4: Day of birth

47. *A.* Officer laxity, rather than a lack of knowledge of proper procedure, is the prime reason for unpredicted violence to occur. Complacency must be avoided at all times. Selection B is not practical in the line of duty for a police officer. Selection C cannot be deduced from this reading. Selection D may seem correct; however, it is virtually impossible to eliminate all aspects of danger associated with an incident regardless of how closely procedures are followed. Some incidents are impossible to predict.

48. B. In most cases, violators pull off onto the shoulder of the road. You can see by the illustration that the implementation of Selection B would not provide a safety corridor for the officer.

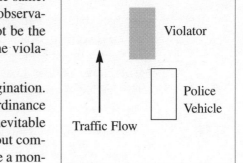

Parking offset to the left would protect the officer from any oncoming traffic. Selection C accomplishes the same. Selection A offers the patrolman a good field of observation of both the driver and vehicle. This would not be the case if the officer were to pull up any closer to the violator in question.

49. *B.* Selection B is not true by any stretch of the imagination. If you knew that by breaking a particular traffic ordinance you would, in fact, have to face a jury trial and inevitable incarceration, you would probably think twice about committing the infraction. However, if they simply face a monetary penalty for the same offense, most people will tend to push the limits of the law. Civil and criminal penalties do not evoke equal deterrence. In fact, A and C are quantitative benefits that result from streamlining the criminal justice system.

50. *D.* While negligent driving was neither defined nor implied in the reading as being a serious offense, it can be reasonably assumed that it can pose a danger to other lives, including that of the driver, as well as to property. Consequently, an arrest would remove the hazard posed by the violator from the public roadways. Separate transport of prisoners is standard procedure in most departments.

51. *D.* Due to a police officer's time limitations and the multitude of other duties he or she must perform, many minor violations, such as the one cited in the question, can be overlooked. Under the circumstances described in the question, stopping the vehicle in violation would create more of a hazard than the violation itself presented. Therefore, the minor violation observed by Officer Nichols would be best ignored. It should be noted, however, that officers should make every attempt to stop those who commit intentional or hazardous violations.

52. *C.* Armed men and busy intersections can cause a situation that places the public at significant risk. If an officer forces the issue, as dictated by A and D, an exchange of gunfire will be the likely result. The best thing to do initially would be to make a mental note of all physical descriptions, notify headquarters regarding the situation so that backup can be better coordinated, and then, as the primary officer on the scene, get statements from witnesses in the credit union and assess what happened.

53. *A.* Selections B, C, and D are all means of addressing crime symptomatically after the fact. Selection A can be an effective deterrent to crime before it occurs. Citizen block watches are examples of the kind of means that have been proven to reduce criminal activity in general.

54. *D.* Since the vehicle in question is wanted in connection with a felony, it is too dangerous for an individual officer to approach it. There would be no safe way to tell how many people are inside the van without the assistance of another one or two officers. Vans also present the special problem of having few windows to look through. Extreme caution should be exercised in this kind of situation.

55. *A.* Selection A best describes what happened in a fairly concise manner. Selections B and D are confusing in that they make it seem as if the victim herself had been struck by the suspect's vehicle. Instead, there needs to be clarification that it was the vehicle she was driving that was struck. Selection C could be better arranged by mentioning the damage last.

56. *C.* Selection C is a clear and concise description of the event. Selections A, B, and D are awkward or confusing statements detailing the incident.

57. **C.**   If 90 percent of the 380 drivers were arrested for drunk driving, that would mean the remaining cases involving drug impaired driving would constitute 10 percent of the total caseload (100% – 90% = 10%). Ten percent of 380 equates to 38 people caught driving while under the influence of drugs. Regardless of the potential for abuse, over-the-counter medication and prescription drugs are considered to be legal. Since it was given that approximately 5 percent of those affected utilized legal medication in some abusive capacity, that means 95 percent of the group used illegal drugs. Therefore, 95 percent of 38 people works out to 36 individuals affected.

58. **D.**   Without even figuring the mathematics, selection A and B can be discarded as viable choices. It was given within the question that the legislative intent was to toughen drunk driving laws. That would involve lowering, not raising, the legal blood-alcohol threshold for suspected drunk drivers.

.001 – .0008 = .0002 represents the difference involved by lowering the blood-alcohol threshold as specified. To figure what percentage change this different represents, we need to divide it by the original threshold limit (i.e., .001) and multiply by 100. Therefore,

$$\frac{.0002}{.001} \times 100 = 20\%$$

59. **A.**   Since it was stated in the question that you are working a direct proportion, the equation would be set up accordingly.

$$\frac{3\frac{1}{3} \ glasses}{130 \ pounds} = \frac{X \ glasses}{156 \ pounds} \ ; \ 130X = 519.95; \ X = 4.0$$

60. **C.**   When determining the class averages for a cadet, it is necessary to add all the given scores together and divide by the number of classes involved. Therefore, if we know what the four given class scores were, and the desired overall average, we can find the percent required in Criminal Justice studies by doing the following:

$$\frac{90\% + 70\% + 88\% + 94\% + X\%}{5} = 85\% \qquad \frac{3.42 + X\%}{5} = 8.5$$

$$3.42 + X\% = 4.25 \qquad X\% = .83 \qquad X = 83\%$$

61. **A.**   Since it is known that 129 traffic accident responses represent 86% of the total calls for the month (i.e., 100% – 14% = 86%), we can set up the following proportion to determine how many calls were received for the month altogether.

$$\frac{86}{100} = \frac{129}{X}$$
$$86X = 12,900$$
$$X = 150 \ calls$$

62. **D.**   Since we are dealing with two different units of measure (i.e., yards and inches), it is necessary to convert one to the other. This can be done one of two ways. The first way is to change inches to yards. Since there are 36 inches in a yard, 16 inches is equal to $^{16}/_{36}$ yard or, in reduced form, $^{4}/_{9}$ yard. Or we can change yards into inches; we simply multiply 2 $^{2}/_{3}$ or (or $^{8}/_{3}$) by 36:

$$\frac{8}{3} \times \frac{36 \ inches}{1 \ yard} = \frac{288}{3} = 96 \ inches$$

For simplicity sake, let's figure the ratio on the basis of inches.

$$2^{2}/_{3} \ yards : 16 \ inches = 96 \ inches : 16 \ inches = 6:1 \ when \ reduced$$

63. *B.* Always do multiplication or division before doing any addition or subtraction unless any part of the equation is in parentheses. In that case, work the parenthetical portion of the equation first, then do multiplication and division, and finally complete any addition or subtraction. Otherwise, you will end up with Choice A, which is incorrect.

$$\frac{9}{5} \times \frac{25}{1} = \frac{225}{5} = 45$$

45 + 32 = 77 degrees Fahrenheit

64. *D.* Rectangular square footage is determined by multiplying length by width. In this particular situation, 14.2 ft. × 37.5 ft. = 532.5 square feet

65. *C.* The faster an individual drives to get to a given destination, the shorter the period of time it will require to get there. Therefore, an inverse proportion is needed to solve the problem.

$$\frac{40 \; minutes}{X \; minutes} = \frac{45 \; MPH}{35 \; MPH}$$

$45X = 1400$ $\qquad$ $X = 31.1$ minutes

If you selected B, you failed to recognize the need for an inverse proportion and utilized a direct proportion instead.

66. *C.* Reckless driving and vehicular theft are indexed at 20% and 5% respectively. 20% of the total traffic infractions accounted for (i.e., 560) equates to 112 cases of reckless driving; 5% of 560 equates to 28 cases involving vehicular theft.

67. *B.* First it is necessary to figure how many seconds there are in one hour. Since there are 60 seconds per minute and 60 minutes per hour, there are 3600 seconds per hour. Then just divide the time factor given for each crime into 3600 to arrive at the answer. Therefore:

3600 ÷ by 30 = 120 murders
3600 ÷ by 15 = 240 robberies
3600 ÷ by 12 = 300 aggravated assaults

68. *A.* Examine the intersection of CY-15 and CY-40 as two legs of a right triangle. By employing the Pythagorean Theorem, A^2 and B^2 can be represented as (59.5 meters)^2 and (62.5 meters)^2, respectively. The distance between points A and C is the unknown, which is represented by C^2. Therefore:

$(59.5)^2 + (62.5)^2 = C^2$
$3,540.25 + 3,906.25 = C^2$
$7,446.5 = C^2$
$C = 86.3$ meters

69. *B.* From the most recent figures (1998), men committed 2,712 burglaries, while women committed 1,204, which when divided (i.e., 2,712 divided by 1,204) reflects a 2.25:1 relationship.

70. *C.* There were 18,241 crimes committed by female juveniles in 1998. 3,687 of those cases constituted shoplifting. To determine the annual caseload percentage for this particular crime, simply divide 3,687 by 18,241 and then multiply the quotient by 100. The answer is 20%.

71. *C.*   Vandalism

Murder   121 – 105 = 16 additional cases

$$\frac{16 \; additional \; cases}{105 \; reference \; case \; load} \times 100 = 15.23\% \; increase$$

Arson   475 – 432 = 43 additional cases

$$\frac{43 \; additional \; cases}{432 \; reference \; case \; load} \times 100 = 9.95\% \; increase$$

Vandalism   4,639 – 4,008 = 631 additional cases

$$\frac{631 \; additional \; cases}{4008 \; reference \; case \; load} \times 100 = 15.74\% \; increase$$

Forcible rape   215 – 173 = 42 additional cases

$$\frac{42 \; additional \; cases}{173 \; reference \; case \; load} \times 100 = 24.27\% \; increase$$

72. *C.*   Juvenile Males

Adult Males   1,444 – 1,230 = 214 fewer cases

$$\frac{214 \; fewer \; cases}{1,444 \; reference \; case \; load} \times 100 = 14.82\% \; decrease/robberies$$

Adult Females   506 – 213 = 293 fewer cases

$$\frac{293 \; fewer \; cases}{506 \; reference \; case \; load} \times 100 = 57.9\% \; decrease/robberies$$

Juvenile Males   480 – 322 = 158 fewer cases

$$\frac{158 \; fewer \; cases}{480 \; reference \; case \; load} \times 100 = 32.91\% \; decrease/robberies$$

Juvenile Females   157 – 120 = 37 fewer cases

$$\frac{37 \; fewer \; cases}{157 \; reference \; case \; load} \times 100 = 23.57\% \; decrease/robberies$$

73. *D.*   Since the area of a circular search pattern needs to be determined, use the geometric formula $(3.1416)R^2$. The given radius of the area in question is 12 feet. Therefore,

$(3.1416)(12 \; ft)^2 = X$ area in square feet
$(3.1416)(144) = X$
$X = 452.39$

74. *A.*   Responsible
75. *C.*   Persistent
76. *D.*   Juvenile
77. *C.*   Relevant
78. *B.*   Transferred
79. *A.*   Perspiration
80. *B.*   Barricade
81. *D.*   Misdemeanor

82. *C.* Psychology

83. *A.* Prudence

84. *D.* Mitigated

85. *C.* Disguised and appease

86. *A.* Idiosyncrasies

87. *B.* Disregarding and clear

88. *C.* Shocked and excessive

89. *C.* Reserved

90. *A.* Acquiescence and permeative

91. *D.* Inconspicuous

92. *B.* Excludes and excessive

93. *C.* Unselfish

94. *A.* Indisputable

95. *D.* This statement is grammatically correct in every way.

96. *B.* The words *judgement* and *competant* are both misspelled. The correct spellings are *judgment* and *competent*.

97. *B.* Labratory should be spelled *laboratory*.

98. *C.* An apostrophe needs to be placed before the *s* in *attorney* in both instances to indicate possession (*attorney's*).

99. *A.* *They're* is an improperly used contraction meaning "they are." *Their* is also wrong since it is plural where singular is needed. Replacing *they're* with his or her would render the statement grammatically correct.

100. *B.* The word *to* that follows the word *spread* should be spelled *too*, which is an adverb indicating "in addition." *Percieved* is misspelled as well; it should be *perceived*. Remember the basic rule: *i* before *e* except after *c*.

101. *A.* A singluar verb should be used after phrases beginning with *one of* (*has been* instead of *have been*).

102. *A.* This statement is confusing due to a misplaced modifier. The statement would be better structured by placing *for* prior to *their parents*.

103. *B.* Affect is a verb that means "to act upon." *Effect* is a noun that means "something produced by an agency or cause."

104. *D.* This statement is grammatically correct in every way.

105. *B.* *Elude* means "to escape or avoid." *Allude* means to "refer to indirectly."

106. *C.* This statement lacks parallel structure. The phrase *can be detained for fourteen to sixty days* does not describe a condition for involuntary commitment.

107. *B.* Billy White should be charged with second-degree malicious mischief, a Class C felony, because the damage estimate of $850 falls within the limits for that crime.

108. *D.* Relying on only the information contained in the reading, Mr. Blakemore would have to be charged with first-degree malicious mischief, a Class B felony. Selection A would seem more appropriate for the crime committed; however, neither A nor B was addressed in the reading. Therefore, they cannot be considered viable answers to this question.

109. *C.* If damage estimates had been in excess of $300, B would have been the correct answer. However, the damage estimate came in right at $300, thus justifying C. Selections A and D could have been initially eliminated purely on the basis that they are one and the same.

110. *B.* The injuries sustained by the victim are not severe enough to constitute first-degree assault. Second-degree assault better defines these circumstances.

111. *B.* Even though third-degree assault specifically mentions the involvement of a law enforcement authority, police officers are also people. Since Officer Beaumont's injury was substantial, the offense committed by Ms. Williams should be upgraded to the more serious charge of second-degree assault.

112. *A.* The fact that the syringe tested negative for the virus is irrelevant. AIDS is a life-threatening illness, and Mr. Briggs used the threat against Mr. Evans in an attempt to escape. Therefore, Mr. Briggs should be charged with first-degree assault as well as shoplifting.

113. *B.* The word *any* is a key word; it may entail lethal force. After a warrant for arrest is served and the suspect flees, this may hold true. However, this case was not specifically addressed in the reading. Choices A, C, and D would be considered valid points of view.

114. *D.* As established in *Steagold v. U.S.* (1981), Mr. Livermore's presence in a third party's residence would require a search warrant in addition to an arrest warrant to effect an arrest.

115. *B.* You can figure out from the reading that if the porch of a person's home is considered to be a public domain (*Watson v. U.S.* 1976), then a driveway would reasonably be considered a public domain as well. Therefore, an arrest warrant would not be required. In fact, Officer Anderson did save himself time and paperwork by arresting the suspect in the manner described. Selection D is proper; however, it fails to define the legality of the situation.

116. *C.* Subject A has a fuller face and thinner lips.

Subject B has different ears.

Subject D has different eyes and a wider nose.

117. *C.* Subject A has a narrower jawline.

Subject B has a different nose.

Subject D has fewer facial lines.

118. *A.* Subject B has a wider mouth and thinner lips.

Subject C has a narrower lower face.

Subject D has different ears.

119. *A.* Subject B has a fuller face and different eyes.

Subject C has different head shape.

Subject D has a different nose and cleft chin.

120. *B.* Subject A has a higher cheekbone structure.

Subject C has a smaller mouth and fuller lips.

Subject D has different ears.

121. *C.* Southwest

122. *B.* Selection A is incorrect because the officer would be driving the wrong direction on a one-way street at two points: south on Charolette and south on Constance. Selection C is incorrect because turning left on 37th Avenue from Charolette runs counter to established traffic flow. Selection D, if followed accordingly, would place the officer at a point that is completely off the map.

123. *D.* Selection A is incorrect with respect to turning right on 14th Avenue from Wyoming; even-numbered streets were given to be one-way streets heading east, not west. Selection B is incorrect because 40th Avenue is a one-way street heading east; going from Wyoming to Gregory by way of 40th Avenue would run counter to traffic flow. Selection C would actually place the officer within the boundaries of Sorenson Park; a left turn instead of a right turn onto Southworth from 23rd Avenue is required to reach the scene of the accident given.

124. *D.* Selection A is wrong because Sorenson Park interrupts an easterly heading on 29th Avenue. Selection B is incorrect because turning left from Dekalb onto 44th Avenue would be a westward heading; maintaining this course for approximately nine blocks would place Officer Kimbell at a point off the map. Both choices C and D are viable routes of getting to the place of concern. However, selection D stands out as being the shortest or quickest means of responding.

125. *D.* Selection A is wrong for two reasons: A right turn onto 48th Avenue from Beech Street would have Officer Blakemore going the wrong direction on a one-way street, in addition to the fact that at 1330 hours (i.e., 1:30 P.M.) the intersection of Lovell and 48th Avenue is closed due to a gas line repair. So, even if 48th Avenue was a two-way street, the utility repair would deny any such approach. Selection B is wrong for two reasons as well: An easterly heading on 47th Avenue would come to an abrupt halt at the Stenman intersection because of the ongoing repaving project specified earlier. Additionally, were it even possible to get through that, a northern heading on Wayne Street would run counter to one-way traffic flow. Selection C is incorrect because the four square block perimeter set up around the chemical spill that had taken place precludes vehicular transit on Adele Street between Dekalb and Southworth. Had it been any later than 1:45 P.M., this would not have been a factor to consider and the route given would have, indeed, served as a viable means of approach.

TEST RATINGS ARE AS FOLLOWS:

120–125 correct — Excellent
113–119 correct — Very good
106–112 correct — Good
100–105 correct — Fair
99 or fewer correct — Unsatisfactory

Go back to each question you missed and determine if the question was just misinterpreted for one reason or another, or if your response reflects a weakness in subject matter. If it is a matter of misinterpretation, try reading the question more slowly while paying particular attention to key words such as *not, least, except,* or *without.* If, on the other hand, you determine a weakness in a certain area, do not despair, because that is what this study guide is for: to identify any area of weakness before you take the actual exam. Reread the material on the area of concern in this study guide. If you still feel a need for supplemental material, your local library is an excellent source.

Chapter 9

Practice Exam 2

The time allowed for the entire examination is two and a half hours. Each question has four answers, letters A, B, C, and D. Choose the best answer and then, on the answer sheet provided on pages 275–276 (which you can remove from the study guide), find the corresponding question number and darken the circle corresponding to the answer you have selected.

Study the sketch provided on the following page for only five minutes. When your time is up, turn to the next page to answer questions 1–15 relating to the scene studied. *You may not look back at the sketch for further reference; notes are prohibited.*

1. The incident portrayed in the sketch took place where?

    A. Highway 28, mile post marker 24

    B. Highway 66, mile post marker 24

    C. Highway 24, mile post marker 85

    D. A locational reference was not provided within the sketch.

2. From the combined effects of the collision and the consequent hazardous material spill, how many victims were apparent in the sketch?

    A. 2

    B. 3

    C. 4

    D. 6

3. The vehicle that apparently collided into the side of the train is which of the following:

    A. Service fuel truck

    B. Tanker transport truck carrying milk

    C. Liquid petroleum tanker

    D. Four-door sedan

4. What was the license-plate number of the vehicle referred to in the previous question?

    A. Idaho 78126-CT

    B. Washington 18752-TC

    C. Iowa 17832-BT

    D. Wisconsin 14871-AF

5. Where in the sketch was a discarded broken liquor bottle?

    A. Close beside a mile post marker

    B. At the base of the posted speed limit sign

    C. In the middle of the highway

    D. No such article was apparent within the sketch

6. According to a road sign in the sketch, which of the following towns was only twenty miles away from the scene of the accident?

    A. Charlottville

    B. Devonsville

    C. Greenville

    D. None of the above

7. What was the four-digit identification number shown on the diamond-shaped placard prominently displayed on the rail tanker car?

   A. 3282

   B. 6628

   C. 8561

   D. 1782

8. What was the ten-digit Dept. of Transportation specification number stenciled to the bottom right side of the same tanker transport referred to in the previous question?

   A. 1872578126

   B. 1581213890

   C. 1582131200

   D. 3285416744

9. The posted speed-limit sign for this particular location was apparently altered in what respect?

   A. 35 MPH was made to look like 85 MPH

   B. 25 MPH was made to look like 75 MPH

   C. 45 MPH was made to look like 95 MPH

   D. The sign was broken off at the base of the post

10. The officer shown in the vapor protective suit surveying the accident scene is a hazardous materials specialist from which of the following departments?

    A. Virginia State Department of Ecology

    B. Idaho Department of Emergency Management

    C. Washington State Fire Department

    D. Washington State Patrol

11. The state trooper that apparently was the first to respond to the incident but was overcome by exposure to the toxic material released is identified in the picture as unit number:

    A. 28

    B. 32

    C. 42

    D. 82

12. The Department of Transportation number stenciled to the front of the livestock transport rail car is which of the following?

    A. G 4743600

    B. J 4473006

    C. J 4743600

    D. 15847150

13. What kind of livestock was evidently being transported via rail?

    A. Cattle

    B. Horses

    C. Swine

    D. Chickens

14. Judging by the position of the vehicle that collided with the train, what direction was the driver originally heading?

    A. North

    B. South

    C. East

    D. West

15. The victim's positioning in the sketch would tend to indicate that toxic gases being vented by the ruptured tanker rail car are being blown in what general direction?

    A. North

    B. South

    C. East

    D. West

Study the following narrative for five minutes. Do not exceed the time allowance. When your time is up, turn to questions 16–25 without making further reference to this reading.

> At 1845 hours on February 11, 1997, State Patrol officers Denise Williams, badge number 1419, and Curt Hansen, badge number 8725, pulled up behind a disabled 1993 Ford Aerostar van parked on the shoulder of Brice Canyon Freeway. When Officer Williams approached the driver to inquire about the problem and offer roadside assistance, if needed, Officer Hansen ran a standard computer check on the van's license plate number AVL-653 for any existing wants and warrants. The driver of the van, Rick Porter, told Officer Williams that they had simply run out of gas. He also insisted that their assistance was not necessary because another friend was already en route to a nearby filling station to get some gas. When the records search came up that the van was, in fact, reported to be stolen, both the driver and lone passenger in the front seat of the van, Sarah Conners, were placed under arrest for being in possession of a stolen vehicle. At the same time the suspects were being placed in the back seat of the patrol vehicle, a 1989 Ford Mustang GT, license number BOK-151, pulled up behind them. Assuming this was the friend the driver of the van made reference to, Officer Hansen approached the driver and requested to see his license and registration. While inspecting the documents, he asked the driver, Martin Brooks, if he was aware that the van belonging to his friend was stolen. He responded rather flippantly that it was news to him, but anyone who would even contemplate stealing an Aerostar deserved to go to jail anyway! There was a five-gallon gas can in plain view on the back seat as well as a small, black nylon duffle bag on the front passenger seat. As a backup unit arrived to assist, Officer Hansen asked the driver to step out of the vehicle to allow for a pat-down search. Nothing of significance was found on his person. However, the duffle bag contained incriminating drug paraphernalia as well as five unwrapped bricks of marijuana. Brooks was placed under arrest for possession of controlled substances. Backup State Patrol Officer Vernon Fuller, badge number 1458, took custodial responsibility of the suspect.

Despite the van's driver denying officers permission to search the van without a warrant, it did not preclude a search of the area within proximate reach of either the driver or passenger. The subsequent search turned up a brown leather fanny pack beneath the front passenger seat containing $3,750.00 in cash and close to half a pound of suspected methamphetamines. Additionally, a cache of weapons were discovered beneath the driver's seat which included a Colt Python 357 Magnum revolver, Smith and Wesson Model 19 .38 special revolver, and a Series 80 Colt Mark IV .45 pistol with two spare seven-round clips. The driver did not have a concealed weapons permit so, in addition to narcotics trafficking and auto theft, he was also charged with illegal possession of concealed firearms. Both vehicles were impounded for state's evidence and the three suspects were transported to Evans County Adult Detention for intake and booking. The incident was assigned arrest report number 6781 and filed with Lieutenant Howard Pope, badge number 1580 (acting desk officer for District 3 of the State Patrol) at 2115 hours.

16. The rank of the acting desk officer referred to in the narrative is which of the following?

    A. Captain
    B. Sergeant
    C. Lieutenant
    D. Chief

17. The name of the patrol officer who took custodial responsibility of Martin Brooks was given to be:

    A. Sarah Conners
    B. Vernon Fuller
    C. Rick Porter
    D. Curt Hansen

18. Referring to the previous question, what was the officer's badge number?

    A. 1458
    B. 1518
    C. 1419
    D. 8752

19. What was the year, make/model, and license-plate number of the car driven by Martin Brooks?

    A. 1993 Ford Taurus GL, AVL-635
    B. 1989 Ford Thunderbird LX, BKU-997
    C. 1993 Chevrolet Lumina, AVL-653
    D. 1989 Ford Mustang GT, BOK-151

20. According to the narrative, which of the following items was not found beneath the driver's seat in the van?

    A. Series 80 Colt Mark IV .45 revolver
    B. Two spare seven-round clips
    C. Colt Python 357 Magnum revolver
    D. Smith and Wesson Model 19 .38 special revolver

21. When and where did the described incident initially take place?

    A. 2115 hours, February 11, 1997 – Black Canyon Highway

    B. 1845 hours, February 11, 1996 – Brice Canyon Freeway

    C. 1845 hours, February 11, 1997 – Brice Canyon Freeway

    D. 1930 hours, February 1, 1996 – Canyon Falls Highway

22. What was the year, make/model, and license-plate number of the vehicle found stranded on the roadside because of running out of gas?

    A. 1989 Ford Aerostar van, AVL-635

    B. 1993 Ford Aerostar van, AVL-653

    C. 1989 Ford Mustang GT, BKO 151

    D. 1991 Ford Probe GT, ALK-791

23. What was the badge number of the patrol officer who ran a standard computer check on the vehicle described in the previous question?

    A. 6871

    B. 8725

    C. 1419

    D. It was not given in the reading.

24. What was seen by Officer Hansen in the back seat of Mr. Brooks' vehicle?

    A. A black nylon duffle bag

    B. A brown leather fanny pack

    C. Illegal contraband

    D. A five-gallon gas can

25. Rick Porter was charged with all of the following crimes except?

    A. Narcotics trafficking

    B. Illegal possession of concealed firearms

    C. Attempted felony elude of a police officer

    D. Auto theft

Answer questions 26 and 27 on the basis of the reading provided below.

Conventional guidelines for high-speed pursuits are somewhat varied between law enforcement agencies. However, the overall consensus of policy is that such pursuits are justifiable on the grounds that immediate apprehension appears to outweigh the degree of danger posed to the community from the pursuit itself. Termination of pursuits are mandated when officers have reasonable assurance as to the identity of those responsible, thereby allowing probable apprehension at a later time, or if the pursuit itself presents adverse risk to the public or the officers involved. Officers who fail to comply with these guidelines can face serious reprimand or sanctions imposed by the department as well as potential civil liability suits filed on behalf of those harmed as a consequence of such pursuits.

26. At 1:00 A.M. Trooper David Pavlacek pulled over a 1991 Chevy Corvette Roadster for speeding 20 MPH over the posted highway speed limit. But even before receiving information back from the department's communication center regarding a routine records check, let alone having a chance to talk to the driver, the vehicle in question took off. Pursuit speeds reached up to 120 MPH before the assistance of two other patrol units convinced the driver to give up. Under such circumstances, Trooper Pavlacek's actions were:

    A. Within pursuit guidelines because in the end he managed to effect an arrest without anyone getting hurt.

    B. Violated pursuit guidelines because vehicle speeds reached 120 MPH.

    C. Within pursuit guidelines because termination mandates did not apply to the situation given.

    D. Violated pursuit guidelines because he should have radioed for immediate backup after pulling over the violator in question.

27. State Patrol Officer Sarah Clemons had Dwayne Stevens pulled over for driving a vehicle with a badly cracked windshield. When she was in the process of issuing a written warning, she inadvertently detected the smell of liquor on his breath. Subsequent to being ordered by Officer Clemons to step out of the vehicle to conduct a preliminary field sobriety test, Stevens started up his vehicle and sped off. Officer Clemons managed to stay within five to ten car lengths distance from the suspect, maintaining speeds 20 to 30 MPH above the posted highway speed limit. Stevens, however, came to realize he was not eluding the officer, so he abruptly exited onto a parallel frontage road traversing through a residential area with complete disregard for any and all traffic signs. Trooper Clemons fervently kept pace with the suspect and left her emergency lights and siren on continuous mode to forewarn anyone of the imminent danger posted by Stevens. She also provided control dispatch with up-to-date locational headings that enabled two other units to establish an effective roadblock. The combined efforts paid off with Stevens' arrest. No bystanders were injured and damage was restricted to one patrol cruiser sustaining minor sideswipe scrapes to the driver's side door. Under the circumstances, Trooper Clemons' actions were:

    A. Demonstrative of an officer using exceptional insight; had she not continued to use her emergency lights and siren to warn people of Stevens' approach, someone, in all likelihood, would have been killed or injured.

    B. Meritorious because the violator was apprehended expeditiously with a minimum of property damage.

    C. Questionable, at best, because she should have attempted to cut off his highway egress, thus circumventing the prospect of Stevens' driving endangering the public in a residential setting.

    D. A flagrant violation of standing pursuit guidelines and wholly deserving of sanctions imposed by District Command.

28. State Patrol Public Safety Officer Patricia Stewart was the featured guest speaker on residential theft protection at a public forum. Towards the conclusion of the meeting she was asked for specific recommendations regarding private security firms that offer such services. Her best approach to the matter would be to do which of the following?

    A. Offer a condensed list of reputable businesses in the immediate area.

    B. Avoid making any particular recommendation because it may be perceived as an official endorsement by the State Patrol.

    C. Explain that such expense is unwarranted considering the fact that police protection services via various law enforcement agencies should be sufficient to discourage residential burglary.

    D. Suggest searching the yellow pages in the local telephone directory for security firms that are in good standing with the Better Business Bureau.

29. Every police department has a bulletin board in the squad room or elsewhere in the station house that posts information about wanted criminals, problems, law changes, crime analysis reports, etc. What is the most likely reason for a posted bulletin, supervisory order, or policy change to be rescinded?

    A. The posting date is old.

    B. It conflicts with a notice issued later.

    C. It is not readily accepted by most rank and file officers.

    D. It undermines the effectiveness of the department as a whole and is, therefore, ignored by most officers.

30. While working his patrol assignment, Officer Dunkin observes a small group of youths inside the lobby of a public transit building that should have been locked for the evening. Without seeing any evidence of breaking and entering, he orders the youths to leave and radios dispatch to alert the proper authorities to secure the building. All but one of the youths comply with the officer's demands. At this point, he places the noncompliant individual under arrest for first-degree criminal trespass—a gross misdemeanor. On the way to the parked patrol vehicle, the arrestee calls on his friends for assistance. If the arrestee's cohorts approach the officer in a manner that seems threatening, what would his best reaction to the situation be?

    A. Call for backup and wait out the incident.

    B. Pull out his revolver and threaten to shoot the first person who moves any closer.

    C. Release the prisoner.

    D. Tell them they are making the biggest mistake of their lives.

31. En route to a felony in progress, Trooper Billings receives a radio call from his immediate supervisor concerning several updated advisories. However, due to partial inattentiveness, Officer Billings did not fully hear or comprehend the given directives. Under the circumstances, what should Trooper Billings do?

    A. Operate on the presumption that what was said was insignificant and maintain the present course of action.

    B. Act on his own judgment because after completion of state police academy training he has the necessary skills to effectively discern what should be given priority in all situations encountered.

    C. Request that his supervisor repeat the advisories.

    D. Circumvent the embarrassment of having to ask that instructions be repeated by assuming what his supervisor would do under the given circumstances.

32. Troopers Blaine Underwood and Kyle Hennings, both fifteen-year veterans with the department and longtime friends, decide to have lunch together one afternoon. During the course of conversation, Hennings takes issue with equal employment opportunity guidelines and expresses absolute contempt for female subordinates. Given the situation, Officer Underwood's best action at this point would be to do which of the following?

    A. Since they are on lunch break, the remarks should be overlooked.

    B. Ignore the partner's diatribes because, in all likelihood, it will not amount to anything.

    C. Contact the District Commander and file an official EEO complaint against his friend.

    D. Despite the prospect of upsetting the friendship, it should be explained to Hennings in no uncertain terms that such behavior is intolerable.

33. Sergeant Boyle, acting desk officer for Post 9, receives a call from a citizen voicing a complaint against a coworker that he does not particularly like. Officer Boyle's best means to handle such a problem would be to do which of the following?

    A. Establish a radio relay between the complainant and the officer of concern and let them settle the matter on their own.

    B. Hear the complainant out and then discuss the incident with the officer involved. If deemed necessary, make suggestions as to how the incident could have been better handled.

    C. Tell the complainant that he/she must be wrong because the degree of professionalism exhibited by this officer over the years is second to none.

    D. Immediately suggest that he/she file a formal complaint with a departmental supervisor.

34. Trooper Christine Whitley happens to observe a fellow officer transferring company oil, antifreeze, and flares from his troop car to his own personal vehicle. Having witnessed such an event, what would be the best approach to handle the matter?

    A. Confront the coworker directly and enquire as to the reason behind it.

    B. Assume it is inconsequential and ignore the situation altogether.

    C. Immediately notify the post commander of the imminent theft.

    D. Share her concerns with other coworkers.

35. State Patrol Officer Larsen felt that fellow officer Claymore failed in several aspects to serve as adequate backup during a felony pursuit that occurred earlier. The best means for Officer Larsen to address such concerns would be which of the following?

    A. Wait until the time comes that Officer Claymore needs backup and, in retaliation, refuse to provide it.

    B. Confront Officer Claymore directly and discuss the problem.

    C. Report to an immediate supervisor Claymore's inability to perform his duty.

    D. File a written requisition for a more competent partner.

36. Officer Wentworth is in close pursuit of a driver wanted on two counts of felony elude of a police officer. As the suspect gets near the crest of a steep hill above a busy intersection he abandons the vehicle and sets off running towards some nearby woods. In his haste to flee the immediate area, he neglected to put the vehicle in park or set the emergency brake. The vehicle subsequently begins rolling backwards downhill. What should Officer Wentworth do at this point?

    A. Continue his pursuit of the suspect on foot.

    B. Use his cruiser as an effective backstop by allowing the vehicle to crash into it.

    C. Place his car in reverse to run in tandem with the runaway vehicle and then utilize his brakes to bring both vehicles to a safe stop.

    D. Radio dispatch with an out-of-service call and take that long-awaited coffee break.

37. While on patrol, Trooper Smith receives a call to investigate an indecent exposure incident at a nearby residence. Upon his arrival, he notices a middle-aged man in an overcoat standing in the driveway. What would be the best course of action to take at this point?

    A. Draw his weapon and shoot the individual because he is a sexual psychopath who is a threat to the public.

    B. Ascertain from the complainant if the individual standing in the drive is the person who committed indecent exposure.

    C. Immediately place the man in the overcoat under arrest.

    D. Explain to the complainant that people who commit indecent exposure are harmless and will usually leave if they are ignored.

38. What is the single most important reason that a State Police officer wears a badge?

    A. It represents an effort to maintain a professional appearance.

    B. It serves as a means of identification.

    C. It is meant to convey authority.

    D. It serves to intimidate people with whom State Police have a run-in.

39. Officer Hansen, a five-year veteran with the State Patrol, receives a new directive from a high-level administrator that is to be implemented immediately. However, Officer Hansen is absolutely certain that such a policy would be difficult to enforce given his present patrol assignment. His best means to handle such a situation would be to do which of the following?

    A. Share his misgivings with other officers working similar assignments.

    B. Circumvent the new directive because through past experience he knows what is and is not practical in the field.

    C. Adamantly oppose the mandate until needed changes are made.

    D. Act as directed without reservation, but convey his concerns to an immediate supervisor.

40. Trooper Shelley White pulls over a late-model station wagon for conducting an improper lane change. As she approaches the driver to ask for a driver's license and vehicle registration, she notices the barrels of two high-powered rifles protruding from beneath a blanket on the back seat. Neither the male driver nor his male companion in the front seat remotely resemble hunters. Both individuals appear to be somewhat edgy as well. Under the circumstances, Officer White should initially do what?

    A. Keep the license and registration of the driver and return to the troop car and radio for immediate assistance.

    B. While issuing a notice of infraction, inquire about the arms on the back seat.

    C. Ask the pair to exit the vehicle and place their hands on the hood of the car to allow for a stop and frisk.

    D. Go back to the cruiser and check for existing wants or warrants for both suspects.

41. Trooper Gary Porter pulls over an individual for doing 15 miles per hour over the given speed limit. During the course of inspecting the driver's license and registration, the individual in question launches into a tirade about receiving an unjustified speeding ticket the day before given out by another State Patrol officer working in the same area. Officer Porter would best handle the situation by doing which of the following?

    A. Let the individual off with a verbal warning instead of another notice of infraction.

    B. Do his level best to defend the other trooper referred to.

    C. Listen attentively to what is said, however, address only the issue at hand by writing a citation befitting the violation observed.

    D. Remark that the individual's week is off to a bad start.

42. Sergeant Vicky Morrison had been summoned to appear in court as a prosecution witness for a DUI case that she was a part of four months earlier. During the trial, Sergeant Morrison, under oath, stated that four containers of unopened beer and one opened container of hard liquor were observed on the floor of the defendant's vehicle during an enforcement stop. Cross examination by the defense, however, counters that her recollection of the facts is not true according to the reports filed earlier. Officer Morrison would best be advised to respond how?

    A. State that she may be unsure considering the time that has passed since the incident occurred, but the reports filed are an accurate accounting.

    B. Recant her testimony and allow the defendant to be cleared of all charges.

    C. Claim another kind of infraction that was observed but not documented within the reports.

    D. State that it must have then been one open container of beer and four unopened containers of hard liquor.

43. Trooper Ben Holmes is traveling approximately 25 miles per hour on a two-lane highway laden with hard-packed snow and ice. The posted speed limit is 65 miles per hour but, since his cruiser had only snow tires with studs, he felt his current speed was warranted for safety reasons. Four other motorists were on his immediate tail when a fifth vehicle, which happened to be a 4x4 sports utility vehicle with chains on, initiated a pass of his patrol vehicle. What should Officer Holms do at this point?

   A. Pull over to the shoulder to allow the vehicles to his rear to pass and then continue in the same way without impeding traffic flow.

   B. Pull over the 4x4 vehicle and cite the driver for driving unsafe under adverse weather conditions.

   C. Speed up to stay apace with the 4x4.

   D. Give all drivers to his rear citations for tailgating.

44. State Police Detective Dan Schultz is involved in conducting an investigation into a multiple-car pile-up that resulted in two fatalities. As he was rechecking the complete reports in his office, he notices that, through an apparent oversight, a particular measurement was not accounted for. Under the given circumstances Officer Schultz should do which of the following?

   A. Contact his immediate supervisor and ask if such information needs to be incorporated into the report.

   B. Personally return to the scene of the accident to get the measurement.

   C. Supply an approximated measurement that is basically in line with other assessments.

   D. Assign another trooper to look into the matter.

45. Officer Dicks was headed toward a lighted intersection displaying a green light when another motorist crossed directly in front of her, almost causing an accident. When Officer Dicks pulled over the driver, she was calmly told that he had the right of way because the light was green upon entering the intersection. If Officer Dicks is aware of the fact that a Department of Transportation road crew had recently worked on the traffic signal equipment for this area not more than a day ago, how should she handle this particular incident?

   A. Only issue a warning to the driver because of the circumstances given.

   B. Give the motorist a written notice of infraction because his or her actions almost resulted in an accident.

   C. If the driver's claim is verified, he or she should be summarily released. A follow-up report should then be forwarded to DOT to immediately rectify the problem.

   D. If the traffic signal equipment is indeed malfunctioning, ticketing the driver in question is completely unwarranted. Officer Dicks should immediately radio DOT to inform them of the problem and remain at the intersection to direct traffic until the situation is resolved.

46. Trooper Dale Overton was patrolling a small strip plaza when he noticed two individuals in the parking lot exchanging drugs for money. Almost immediately after the transaction had taken place both suspects became aware of his presence and took off running in opposite directions. What would be Officer Overton's best course of action at this point?

   A. Give chase to the suspect who has the drugs.

   B. Give chase to the suspect who has the money.

   C. Fire a warning shot and order the pair to halt.

   D. Write down a complete physical description of both suspects and issue warrants for their arrest.

47. Toward the end of his evening shift, Trooper Buckner radar checks a vehicle doing 35 miles per hour over the posted highway speed limit. Pursuant to an enforcement stop, the driver of the vehicle hurriedly explains that his wife lying on the back seat is in labor and experiencing severe medical complications. Considering the fact that their present location was at least 25 miles from the nearest emergency medical facility, what would be the best course of action for Officer Buckner to take?

    A. Transport the woman directly to the nearest hospital.

    B. Radio for an emergency medic unit.

    C. Quickly issue a speeding citation to the driver and then provide an escort to the nearest hospital.

    D. Since it was getting close to the end of his shift, verbally warn the driver to observe the legal speed limit despite the circumstances concerning his wife.

Below are hypothetical codes established by a statute law committee to address various infractions. Each code has three parts: a title, a chapter, and a section, in that order. Review each of these before proceeding with questions 48–58.

    RCX 38.12.012 concerns the operation of a nonhighway vehicle under the influence of a controlled substance or alcohol.

    RCX 38.47.071 concerns certificates of registration and ownership.

    RCX 38.49.008 concerns the operation of nonhighway vehicles.

    RCX 38.32.047 concerns the operation of a motor vehicle with a revoked or suspended license.

    RCX 38.23.047 concerns driving with a revoked or suspended license.

    RCX 38.32.074 concerns driving without a valid driver's license.

    RCX 38.23.074 concerns unauthorized persons allowed to drive a motor vehicle.

    RCX 43.67.132 concerns the striking of an unattended car or other property.

    RCX 43.76.312 concerns the injury or death of a person as a result of striking an unattended vehicle or property.

    RCX 43.74.132 concerns driving while under the influence of drugs or alcohol.

    RCX 43.10.509 concerns assisting another to start a vehicle equipped with an ignition interlock device.

    RCX 43.21.075 concerns failure to stop and give identification to an officer.

    RCX 43.12.057 concerns disobedience to directions given by firefighters, flaggers, or police officers.

    RCX 43.21.057 concerns refusal to give information or cooperation to a police officer.

    RCX 48.12.018 concerns reckless driving.

    RCX 48.12.081 concerns the attempt to elude pursuing police vehicles.

    RCX 48.21.018 concerns homicide by a motor vehicle.

    RCX 48.21.075 concerns persons under the influence of a controlled substance or alcohol.

    RCX 48.10.509 concerns a nonappearance in court after signing a written promise to show up.

    RCX 48.01.72 concerns racing vehicles on a public street or highway.

    RCX 48.15.017 concerns vehicular assault.

    RCX 48.51.071 concerns leaving children in an unattended vehicle while the engine is running.

48. Officer Pettibone was driving behind a 1985 Thunderbird when he noticed that its rear taillight was out. Before attempting to stop the vehicle, he made a routine check of the vehicle's license number. According to dispatch, the vehicle in question had a license that had been revoked three months earlier. Officer Pettibone immediately turned on his emergency lights and attempted to pull

the suspect over. However, the suspect went through two stoplights and struck an unattended parked vehicle before Officer Pettibone could effect an arrest. A breathalyzer test administered to the driver at the scene registered above the legal limit of 0.1%. On the basis of this situation, which of the alternatives provided below would most comprehensively address the infractions committed by the driver?

A. RCX 38.32.047, RCX 38.12.012, RCX 43.67.132, RCX 48.12.018, RCX 48.12.081, and RCX 43.21.075

B. RCX 48.12.081, RCX 48.12.018, RCX 43.74.132, RCX 43.21.075, RCX 43.67.132, and RCX 38.32.047

C. RCX 48.12.081, RCX 43.74.132, RCX 48.12.018, RCX 43.67.132, RCX 38.32.047

D. RCX 48.21.075, RCX 38.32.047, RCX 43.67.132, RCX 43.21.075, RCX 48.12.081, and RCX 48.12.018

49. A mechanic who was caught bypassing ignition interlock systems for people willing to pay $250 would be appropriately charged and prosecuted under which code.

A. Title 10, Chapter 509, Section 43

B. Title 43, Chapter 1, Section 509

C. Title 431, Chapter 05, Section 9

D. Title 43, Chapter 10, Section 509

50. Bill Heston, a local farmer, was driving his tractor south on State Highway 60 to get to one of his alfalfa fields. State Trooper Don Weiss had seen the traffic back up, and when he got to the front of the line he immediately pulled Mr. Heston over to the shoulder of the road. In attempting to comply with Officer Weiss, Mr. Heston inadvertently ran over a milepost before coming to a complete stop. Mr. Heston was put through a field sobriety test. The results neither confirmed nor denied that Mr. Heston was intoxicated. However, a breathalyzer reading indicated that Mr. Heston's blood alcohol level was below the legal limit. Under the circumstances, which of the alternatives provided below would comprehensively account for the infractions committed by Mr. Heston?

A. RCX 38.12.012 and RCX 43.67.132

B. RCX 38.49.008 and RCX 43.67.132

C. RCX 43.21.075, RCX 43.67.132, and RCX 38.49.008

D. RCX 43.67.132, RCX 38.32.074 and RCX 38.49.008

51. Kate Jennings was accompanied by her older sister, Kathy (ages 15 and 18, respectively) when Kate drove to the local grocery store. On the way back home, Kate encountered a small patch of black ice that caused her to lose control of the vehicle and sideswipe an unattended parked vehicle. A neighbor witnessed the incident and immediately called 911. A police officer was quick to respond. Kate did not have a learner's permit. Under the circumstances, Kathy should be charged with which of the following?

A. RCX 38.23.074

B. RCX 38.32.074

C. RCX 38.23.047

D. RCX 38.47.071

52. On the basis of the previous question, Kate should be charged with which of the following?

    A. RCX 38.23.074

    B. RCX 38.32.074

    C. RCX 38.23.047

    D. RCX 38.47.071

53. In a fit of jealousy, Mark Kilpatrick attempted to run over his ex-girlfriend with his Honda Civic before crashing into a light standard. Fortunately, the victim suffered only minor bruises to her left leg and a small laceration to her right elbow. The suspect was also believed to have been on amphetamines at the time of the incident. Pursuant to arrest, Mr. Kilpatrick could be comprehensively charged with which of the following?

    A. RCX 43.67.132, RCX 48.21.018, RCX 43.74.132, and RCX 48.12.018

    B. RCX 48.12.018, RCX 43.74.132, RCX 43.76.312, and RCX 48.15.017

    C. RCX 48.15.017, RCX 43.67.132, RCX 48.12.018, and RCX 43.74.132

    D. RCX 48.12.018, RCX 48.21.075, RCX 48.15.017, and RCX 43.67.132

54. Chris Marshall double-parked in front of a convenience store so she could run in for a quick cup of coffee. The car's engine was left running so Mrs. Marshall's two kids, ages 1 and 3, would not get cold. The children were strapped in rear-seat restraints. When Officer Daniels saw Mrs. Marshall return to the vehicle, he ran the plate number through dispatch and then pulled her over one and a half blocks later. The car's plates were valid; however, her driver's license had expired two months earlier. When Officer Daniels asked whether the home address on her expired license was still current, Mrs. Marshall refused to answer. She felt that her ex-husband would somehow become involved. Under the circumstances, which of the alternatives provided below would comprehensively cover the infractions committed by Mrs. Marshall?

    A. RCX 38.32.074, RCX 48.15.017, and RCX 43.21.057

    B. RCX 48.51.071, RCX 43.21.057, and RCX 38.23.047

    C. RCX 43.21.075, RCX 38.32.074, and RCX 48.51.071

    D. RCX 43.21.057, RCX 38.32.074, and RCX 48.51.071

55. Joe Evans was in a hurry to meet a friend at the Four Corners Tavern. Unfortunately, the shortest route there went through a temporary detour due to a residential fire. Because he was late, Mr. Evans had no intention of driving any further than he had to. Against the direction of a volunteer firefighter, Mr. Evans drove through the congestion of emergency vehicles and over two charged hoses without the benefit of ramps. Motorcycle Patrolman Carl Best witnessed the infraction and promptly pulled Mr. Evans over. When Officer Best called dispatch to run Mr. Evans' license to determine if there were any wants or warrants, he discovered that Mr. Evans did, in fact, have a warrant out for his arrest. Apparently Mr. Evans had not shown up for an earlier hearing in municipal court to explain mitigating circumstances involved in an unrelated incident. Officer Best asked Mr. Evans several questions pertaining to the incident at hand; however, no reply was offered. Pursuant to the defendant's arrest, he could be comprehensively charged with which of the following alternatives?

A. RCX 48.10.509, RCX 43.21.057, and RCX 43.12.057

B. RCX 43.12.057, RCX 43.12.075, and RCX 48.10.509

C. RCX 43.21.057, RCX 38.47.071, RCX 43.12.057, and RCX 48.10.509

D. RCX 38.23.074, RCX 48.10.509, RCX 43.21.057, and RCX 43.12.057

56. Mrs. Hartford had just purchased a new Audi 5000. After she left the dealership with the new vehicle, Mrs. Hartford was pulled over by a State Patrolman conducting a random license and vehicle inspection test. Her license checked out fine; however, she could not produce an owner's registration. Mrs. Hartford did not have any outstanding wants or warrants. Under the circumstances, Mrs. Hartford was given a written warning instead of a notice of infraction. Had it been an NOI rather than a warning, Mrs. Hartford could have been charged with which of the following?

A. RCX 38.32.007

B. RCX 38.23.509

C. RCX 38.47.071

D. RCX 38.02.071

57. Tom and Richard McCann were racing their convertibles down Second Avenue when Tom lost control of his vehicle. It jumped a curb and struck and killed two pedestrians waiting to cross in the crosswalk. When officers arrived at the scene, they learned that Tom's driver's license had been suspended thirty days earlier for reckless driving. Drugs or alcohol were not believed to have been factors contributing to the accident. Under the circumstances, Richard McCann should be charged with which of the following?

A. RCX 38.32.047, RCX 48.12.018, and RCX 48.01.72

B. RCX 38.23.047, RCX 48.01.72, RCX 48.12.018, and RCX 48.15.017

C. RCX 48.01.72, RCX 48.12.018, RCX 38.23.047, and RCX 43.74.132

D. None of the above alternatives are completely correct.

58. On the basis of the previous question, Tom McCann should be charged with which of the following?

A. RCX 48.12.018, RCX 48.01.72, and RCX 38.23.047

B. RCX 48.01.72, RCX 48.12.018, and RCX 38.23.047

C. RCX 38.23.047, RCX 48.01.72, and RCX 48.12.018

D. None of the above alternatives are completely correct.

59. Trooper Collins wrote an incident report regarding a burglary of a private residence. The following five sentences were taken out of the text of that report in no particular order:

1. Value of property recovered: $345.

2. Value of property reported stolen: $345.

3. Doug Clavering is presently in the Fuller County jail in lieu of $50,000 bail.

4. He apparently accessed the dwelling via an unlocked kitchen window.

5. Doug Clavering was arrested and charged with second-degree burglary.

Which of the following alternatives represents the correct logical order of events?

A. 4 2 1 5 3
B. 4 1 2 5 3
C. 3 5 2 1 4
D. 4 1 5 2 3

60. State Patrol Officer Becker wrote an incident report regarding a shoplifting that had taken place in a hardware store. The following five sentences were taken out of the text of that report in no particular order.

1. He had asked the woman, Susan Daly, whether she intended to pay for the article underneath her coat.
2. I received the call to investigate a woman being held on suspicion of shoplifting at 8:30 P.M.
3. The store detective, Sid Lowry, had noticed a woman place a curling iron beneath her coat.
4. Susan Daly was placed under arrest for petty larceny.
5. She told Sid that she had a good lawyer and would definitely sue the establishment for false arrest.

Which of the following alternatives represents the correct chronological order of events?

A. 2 5 3 1 4
B. 3 1 5 2 4
C. 5 3 2 4 1
D. 3 2 1 5 4

61. The following sentences are notes taken from an officer's activity log detailing an attempted suicide. The sentences are not arranged in any particular order. Select the alternative that represents the facts as they would appear chronologically in the officer's activity log.

1. Mr. Crawford was placed in protective custody at 1950 hours.
2. I attempted to talk Mr. Crawford out of what he was attempting to do.
3. I was walking my beat when a passerby by the name of Ms. Dora Sanders pointed out someone threatening to jump from a third-story window.
4. I radioed for immediate backup to cordon off the area as well as the Fire Department for their assistance.
5. The person identified himself and explained the motive for his actions.

A. 3 4 5 2 1
B. 3 5 4 2 1
C. 3 2 5 4 1
D. 3 2 4 5 1

Questions 62–66 involve composite sketch cross comparisons. Look at the original sketch of the subject and then try to discern which of the four other sketches provided is the same individual attempting to disguise his or her appearance. Unless otherwise stated, assume the individual in question has not undergone any surgery.

62.

A.    B.    C.    D.

63.

A.    B.    C.    D.

64.

A.

B.

C.

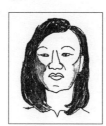

D.

65.

A.

B.

C.

D.

66.

A.   B.   C.   D.

Questions 67–76 relate to grammar, punctuation, and spelling. Each question will provide a written statement that may or may not contain specific errors. From the choices provided, select the answer that represents an accurate assessment of the statement in question and then mark your answer sheet accordingly.

67. Forgery is commited by an individual who, with intent to defraud, knowingly makes or utters a false writing that apparently imposes a legal liability on another or affects his legal right or liability to his prejudice.

The above statement, in terms of English usage,

    A. Is structurally incorrect.

    B. Contains one or more misspellings.

    C. Lacks necessary punctuation and/or capitalization.

    D. Is grammatically correct.

68. When police officers take their lunch hour with Lieutenant Branstad, you usually end up talking about procedural policies.

The above statement, in terms of English usage,

    A. Is structurally incorrect.

    B. Contains one or more misspellings.

    C. Lacks necessary punctuation and/or capitalization.

    D. Is grammatically correct.

69. To judges and juries, few kinds of evidence are as persuasive as fingerprints; however, investigating officers often miss fingerprints that might help insure convictions.

The above statement, in terms of English usage,

    A. Is structurally incorrect.

    B. Contains one or more misspellings.

    C. Lacks necessary punctuation and/or capitalization.

    D. Is grammatically correct.

70. Containing a glove pouch, handcuff case, mace holder, and pen holder, a police officer wears a belt that stores much more than a gun.

    The above statement, in terms of English usage,

    A. Is structurally incorrect.

    B. Contains one or more misspellings.

    C. Lacks necessary punctuation and/or capitalization.

    D. Is grammatically correct.

71. The FBI, in the uniform crime reports, predicts that a total of 4,500,000 robbery offenses will be committed in the United States in 1993.

    The above statement, in terms of English usage,

    A. Is structurally incorrect.

    B. Contains one or more misspellings.

    C. Lacks necessary punctuation and/or capitalization.

    D. Is grammatically correct.

72. Because Pete Mitchell was too young he was immediately disqualified from further consideration for employment.

    The above statement, in terms of English usage,

    A. Is structurally incorrect.

    B. Contains one or more misspellings.

    C. Lacks necessary punctuation and/or capitalization.

    D. Is grammatically correct.

73. An incident report should be typewritten if possible; if not, it should be neatly and legibly written by pen in black or blue ink. Erasures and whiteout should be avoided; there should be no more than two to a page, and they should be neatly made and present no difficulty in reading and no possibility of misinterpretation.

    The above statement, in terms of English usage,

    A. Is structurally incorrect.

    B. Contains one or more misspellings.

    C. Lacks necessary punctuation and/or capitalization.

    D. Is grammatically correct.

74. A person who desires to be a firefighter for example may set fire to a structure and endeavor to achieve a spectacular rescue in order to gain notoriety.

    The above statement, in terms of English usage,

    A. Is structurally incorrect.

    B. Contains one or more misspellings.

    C. Lacks necessary punctuation and/or capitalization.

    D. Is grammatically correct.

75. The appropriate examination and correct evaluation of real evidence is a responsibility of the technician or expert, whom by reason of his training and experience is qualified in the specialty involved.

The above statement, in terms of English usage,

A. Is structurally incorrect.

B. Contains one or more misspellings.

C. Lacks necessary punctuation and/or capitalization.

D. Is grammatically correct.

76. The importance of the proceedure becomes apparent when consideration is given to the fact that the police officer may be called to the witness stand several months after an investigation has been completed.

The above statement, in terms of English usage,

A. Is structurally incorrect.

B. Contains one or more misspellings.

C. Lacks necessary punctuation and/or capitalization.

D. Is grammatically correct.

Questions 77–81 pertain to spelling. Each question has four numerically identified columns, each comprising various word sets. One of the word sets given will contain an intentionally misspelled word. Select the column number that represents the misspelled word and mark your answer sheet accordingly.

77.

I	II	III	IV
pursue	prosecutor	perimeter	gymnasium
search	grazed	extradite	eliminate
original	borderline	consistent	coordinate
beaton	purpose	educational	suffocate

A. I

B. II

C. III

D. IV

78.

I	II	III	IV
escape	judge	policies	combative
retribution	aggressive	maximum	frequently
instinct	excellant	institutional	history
accurate	gambling	disabled	lawyer

A. I
B. II
C. III
D. IV

79.

I	II	III	IV
inhaled	detached	schizophrenic	public
organized	deterrent	react	diabetic
prisoner	superior	request	promotional
exclude	manipulate	confusian	threaten

A. I
B. II
C. III
D. IV

80.

I	II	III	IV
sodomy	administrative	leisure	proceded
occurred	relevant	prosecute	reckless
expression	profane	recurrence	hostage
belligerent	mischief	malicious	captain

A. I
B. II
C. III
D. IV

81.

I	II	III	IV
telephone	interrogate	premises	evidence
resistance	sanitary	illegel	tamper
notify	trespassing	religious	vehicle
liaison	victim	immediately	tattoo

A. I

B. II

C. III

D. IV

Questions 82–86 pertain to vocabulary proficiency. Each question will pose a statement that will have a particular word(s) in italics. You must determine from the four choices given which one correctly defines the word(s) in question and then mark your answer sheet accordingly.

82. It is not uncommon for State Police applicants to experience some degree of *trepidation* going into an oral interview. *Trepidation* most nearly means:

    A. Sobriety

    B. Fear

    C. Clarity

    D. Contempt

83. Commander Breston's remarks at the awards banquet were *succinct* and pointed. *Succinct* most nearly means:

    A. Terse

    B. Outrageous

    C. Acidic

    D. Coarse

84. Mayor Richmond *lauded* the *heightened* efforts of the State Patrol to crack down on DUI's statewide. *Lauded* and *heightened* respectively mean:

    A. Lamented and concentrated

    B. Criticized and abated

    C. Applauded and provisional

    D. Praised and intensive

85. Despite the *gravity* of the situation, the driver seemed somewhat *bemused*. *Gravity* and *bemused* respectively mean:

    A. Importance and ebullient

    B. Difficulty and preoccupied

    C. Seriousness and inattentive

    D. Heaviness and excited

86. The expression is popular among law enforcement officers as a *euphemism* for various mental disorders. *Euphemism* most nearly means:

   A. Enunciation

   B. Equivocation

   C. Clear definition

   D. Categorical

Answer questions 87–91 on the basis of the reading below.

A JUDICIAL SUMMARY OF A CRIMINAL CASE IN SUPERIOR COURT

Basically, each municipality has its own police department, which responds to calls within its jurisdiction. Unincorporated areas are usually served by some other agency or multijurisdictional law enforcement task force. Criminal cases begin when the police are called to respond to an incident. Typically, an officer travels to the crime scene and fills out an incident report that describes the circumstances involved and lists the names and addresses of prospective witnesses. This incident report is then filed with the department and subsequently forwarded to the appropriate detective division responsible for investigating that type of crime. Detectives formalize the process by taking written statements from any witnesses, obtaining evidence, and writing a report detailing the known facts of the case. This information is then given to the prosecuting attorney. A filing unit clerk logs the case in and assigns a case number to it. At this point, a senior deputy prosecuting attorney will either approve the filing of formal charges or move to dismiss. If the senior deputy feels that sufficient evidence exists to prosecute the crime successfully, he or she pursues the case. Court clerks type the formal documentation required for the senior deputy's final approval. After approval, the documentation is given to a legal desk clerk who assigns a superior court case number as a permanent record. After it has been signed by an appropriate magistrate, the compiled paperwork is then processed by the Information and Records Department.

A defendant must be identified before charges are formally filed. Custody is not at issue here. The defendant may have already been arrested and placed in custody for the crime, or he or she may remain at large; identification is the important issue.

Once the person in question is arrested and subsequently taken to jail, he or she has the right to appear before a judge within twenty-four hours to seek a release. If a judge is reasonably assured that the defendant will honor a promise to return for the hearing, he or she is released without bail or, in other words, on personal recognizance. If, on the other hand, a defendant has a dangerous criminal history, he or she may be asked to post significant bail. In either case, the presiding magistrate must render a decision concerning the defendant's disposition by 2:00 P.M.

The Administrative Recognizance Release Program (ARRP) is a fairly recent innovation that attempts to streamline this process. If a suspect is determined to be nonviolent and has demonstrated past reliability, he or she may be released on personal recognizance prior to the hearing. If the bond set by the magistrate cannot be met by the defendant, he or she has the right to petition the court for a reduction of bail.

Once charges have been formally filed, the defendant is summoned to appear for arraignment. The arraignment is basically a formal hearing of the charges levied against the defendant. At the arraignment, it is explained that an attorney is needed (if one has not already been retained) and if the defendant cannot afford one, a court-appointed defense attorney is made available at state expense.

Within two weeks of this hearing, the defendant has to appear for another hearing called an *omnibus*. It is at this point that a plea is entered and a trial date is formally set. During the course of this hearing, both the defense attorney and the prosecuting attorney must exchange information pertinent to the case. In legal parlance, this is referred to as *discovery*; it allows all parties concerned equal access to information for formal case preparation.

A defendant who wishes to plead guilty in exchange for a lesser charge or dismissal of certain counts (plea bargaining) must do so prior to or during the omnibus hearing. If the judge accepts the plea, the defendant waives the right to trial and is convicted of the lesser charges set by the prosecution. If plea bargaining is not utilized and the defendant pleads not guilty and is in custody, a trial date must be set within sixty days of arraignment. If the defendant has been released pending trial, the trial date must be established within ninety days. These time limits preserve the defendant's right to a speedy trial. While waiting for the trial, the deputy prosecutor assigned to the case issues subpoenas for any witnesses. These subpoenas state specifically when and where witnesses must appear.

Pretrial hearings may also be required to determine whether certain incriminating evidence, offered voluntarily by the defendant after being duly informed of his or her constitutional rights, can be used by the prosecution. Court Rule 3.5 establishes that a hearing ("3.5 hearing") must be held to determine the admissibility of such evidence.

Another form of pretrial hearing occurs when a defendant attempts to prove that the evidence against him or her was seized illegally and is thus inadmissible in court. If the constitutional rights of the defendant were violated, the suppression hearing rules in favor of the defendant.

Prior to the actual trial date, either the defense or the prosecution may ask to have the trial delayed (or *continued*) for various reasons. If either party wishes to avoid a deferment, a presiding judge determines if it is warranted. If there are sufficient grounds to justify it, everyone who has been subpoenaed is informed of the new place and time of the trial. Otherwise, the case is heard as scheduled.

The court may have to hear several cases in a day; however, criminal cases usually take precedence over civil cases and are assigned accordingly. Once the trial actually begins, the defendant must choose whether to have a jury hear the case or to waive that right. If the defendant prefers the jury trial, the attorneys conduct jury selection, referred to as *voir dire*. Prospective jurors are interviewed by both counsels and accepted or eliminated depending on the attitudes they exhibit toward the defendant. At the close of the jury selection, the trial begins. Attorneys make opening statements and call witnesses to testify under oath about what they know of the defendant and their connection to the crime involved. Witnesses are allowed to be cross-examined by opposing counsel.

When this phase of the trial has ended, the defendant may elect to take the stand to further defend him or herself. The state has the right to call rebuttal witnesses at the completion of such testimony. The jury is then instructed by the judge and both attorneys about what the law requires and what their duty involves. Final statements are rendered first by the prosecutor, then by the defense before deliberations begin.

A unanimous decision by jurors is required to convict the defendant. A jury that fails to agree is referred to as a *hung jury*. Depending on state discretion, the case will either be dismissed or retried at a later date. Hung juries are usually the consequence of insufficient evidence. The state must prove its charge beyond a reasonable doubt to effect a conviction. If a conviction is handed down in Superior Court, a judge issues a sentence approximately four to six weeks later. State sentencing guidelines normally dictate that the punishment be appropriate for the crime. This can come either in the form of serving time in a state prison or as probation.

87. What kind of crimes were specifically addressed within the context of the reading?

    A. Felonies

    B. Misdemeanors

    C. Traffic citations

    D. None of the above

88. All of the following statements from the reading are true except:

    A. The state must prove its charges beyond a reasonable doubt before a person can be convicted in Superior Court.

    B. Magistrate precedence normally dictates the punishment appropriate for the crime.

    C. Another term for a delayed trial is *continued*.

    D. Final statements for a trial are rendered first by the prosecuting attorney.

89. What kind of hearing was said to be held in the event that there is some question about the legality of evidence seizure and possible infringement of a defendant's constitutional rights?

    A. Omnibus hearing

    B. Preliminary hearing

    C. Deferment hearing

    D. Suppression hearing

90. What was mentioned within the narrative to be of primary importance prior to charges being formally filed?

    A. Investigators furnishing complete details of the crime involved.

    B. Defendant identification.

    C. An appropriate magistrate signature.

    D. The assignment of a court case number for information and records.

91. If a defendant was well aware of his or her constitutional rights and offered authorities a confession (incriminating evidence) and then later decided that the confession should not be used, which of the following hearings determines admissibility of such evidence in superior court?

    A. Omnibus hearing

    B. Plea bargaining hearing

    C. 3.5 hearing

    D. Arraignment hearing

Answer questions 92–95 on the basis of the reading provided below:

Extortion is defined as the obtaining of property or services from another by wrongful use or actual or threatened force, violence, or fear.

First-degree extortion involves the direct or indirect threat to cause future bodily injury or physical damage to the property of another or to subject the person threatened to restraint or confinement. First-degree extortion is a Class B felony punishable by up to ten years in prison.

Second-degree extortion involves the direct or indirect threat to expose a secret, whether true or not, that instills contempt or hatred toward another; to withhold crucial testimony or disseminate false testimony that affects another person's legal defense or claim; to perpetuate a strike or boycott to obtain property unrelated to the event itself; or to act in a way harmful to another person's safety, health, business, or personal relationships. Second-degree extortion is a Class C felony punishable by up to seven years in prison.

Bribery is defined as the offering, giving, receiving, or soliciting of anything of value to influence action as an official or in the discharge of legal or public duty. Any person whose official conduct is connected with the administration of government is subject to this legal provision. Bribery is a Class A felony punishable by up to fifteen years in prison.

92. Ann Compton threatened a neighbor who was currently standing trial for first-degree theft that she would make a materially false statement against her defense in court if she did not receive $500. Under these circumstances and according to the preceding narrative, which of the following could Ms. Compton be charged with?

    A. Class A felony

    B. Perjury

    C. Class C felony

    D. The narrative is not applicable to this situation.

93. Harold Russell, a recently furloughed convict, telephones one of the witnesses who had testified against him in court ten years earlier. He explains that the streets are unsafe these days, and that the witness or his wife may have an unfortunate "accident" if they are not careful. At this point, Mr. Russell hangs up. Accordingly, Mr. Russell could be prosecuted under which of the following statutes if the witness in question was the Mayor?

    A. Bribery

    B. First-degree extortion

    C. Second-degree extortion

    D. None of the above

94. Barb Waterhouse threatened to expose a local congressman's extramarital affair if he failed to enact legislation that would render harsher sentences for repeat sex offenders. If the congressman made local authorities aware of the threat, Ms. Waterhouse could be prosecuted under which of the following statutes?

   A. Bribery

   B. First-degree extortion

   C. Second-degree extortion

   D. None of the above

95. Dan Evans, a person twice convicted for the collection of unlawful debt, calls Charlie McKay and explains in no uncertain terms that if he does not pay the $1800 owed as interest from an earlier gambling activity, Mr. Evans and some "friends" would break both of Charlie's legs later in the week. On the presumption that Mr. Evans is arrested and prosecuted for the offense, how much prison time could Mr. Evans potentially face?

   A. 7 years

   B. 10 years

   C. 15 years

   D. None of the above

Answer questions 96–98 on the basis of the reading provided below.

Homicide is defined in *Black's Law Dictionary* as "the act of a human being taking the life of another human being either through felonious, excusable, or justifiable means."

First-degree murder involves causing the death of another with premeditated intent or, through indifference to life, causing circumstances that create a grave risk and actually result in the death of another; or causing the death of another, whether the victim or a third party, in the commission or attempt to commit rape, robbery, arson, burglary, or kidnapping, or in flight therefrom. First-degree murder is considered a Class A felony.

Second-degree murder involves intentionally causing the death of another without premeditation, or during the commission or attempt to commit offenses not specically mentioned under first degree murder or flight therefrom. Second-degree murder is considered a Class A felony.

First-degree manslaughter involves a person recklessly causing the death of another, or the intentional and unlawful killing of a fetus by causing injury to the mother. First-degree manslaughter is considered a Class B felony.

Second-degree manslaughter involves criminal negligence that results in the death of another. Second-degree manslaughter is considered a Class C felony.

Homicide by abuse involves causing the death of either a child under the age of fifteen or a dependent adult suffering from severe developmental disabilities through a pattern of extreme indifference to life. Homicide by abuse is considered a Class A felony.

96. Elaine Stevens and Joyce Patterson had gotten into a heated argument over the use of some food stamps. When Ms. Patterson realized that Mrs. Stevens had neither the means nor the desire to reimburse her for the alleged loss, she pushed Mrs. Stevens to the floor and kicked her in the stomach. Consequently, Mrs. Stevens, who was in her third trimester of pregnancy, suffered severe abdominal pain. After she summoned help on the telephone, firefighter paramedics transported her to County General Emergency. Despite the efforts of the hospital personnel, she miscarried two hours later. According to the reading, under the circumstances, Ms. Patterson should be charged with which of the following crimes?

A. Class A felony

B. First-degree murder

C. Homicide by abuse

D. Class B felony

97. Ricky Matthews was driving his 1991 Ford Taurus west on Interstate 80 when he made an improper lane change that forced another vehicle off the road. The driver of that vehicle, Tracy Cummings, was killed instantly when her car collided with an oak tree. Mr. Matthews' blood-alcohol level registered far above what was legally tolerated by the state. In this instance, according to the reading, Mr. Matthews should be charged with which offense?

A. Class A felony

B. Class C felony

C. First-degree manslaughter

D. He should not be charged with anything besides driving while under the influence (DUI).

98. Mr. and Mrs. Bradford's marriage had been on shaky ground for several months. One evening during dinner, an argument ensued concerning the family's finances. It was all that Mrs. Bradford could take, and she spontaneously grabbed a knife lying on a kitchen counter and stabbed Mr. Bradford several times in the neck and back. Mr. Bradford died three hours later in the critical care unit at Mercy Hospital. According to the reading, which offense should Mrs. Bradford be charged with?

A. Murder in the first degree

B. Manslaughter in the first degree

C. Murder in the second degree

D. Manslaughter in the second degree

Answer questions 99–101 on the basis of the following passage.

Evidence is essentially a means of proof or the establishment of facts in a trial. Evidence may be manifested in trial in one of several forms. According to *Black's Law Dictionary*:

- *Direct evidence* is a form of testimony from a witness who actually saw, heard, or touched the subject of interrogation.

- *Opinion evidence* is a form of testimony from a witness describing what he or she thinks, believes, or infers in regard to facts in dispute, as distinguished from his or her personal knowledge of the facts themselves.

■   *Circumstantial evidence* is a form of testimony not based on actual personal knowledge or observation of the facts in controversy, but of other facts from which deductions are drawn showing indirectly the thoughts sought to be proved.

■   *Real evidence* are objects or items furnished for view or inspection, as distinguished from a description furnished by a witness.

99. During a murder trial, a State Patrol firearms identification expert testified that the ballistics of the .44-caliber revolver recovered from the defendant at the time of arrest matched the bullet recovered from the victim's body. Additionally, the medical examiner testified that this same bullet was the cause of the victim's death. What form of evidence would both of these testimonies be considered?

   A. Direct evidence

   B. Opinion evidence

   C. Circumstantial evidence

   D. Real evidence

100. The .44-caliber bullet recovered from the body of the victim described in the previous question would be considered what form of evidence?

   A. Direct evidence

   B. Opinion evidence

   C. Circumstantial evidence

   D. Real evidence

101. A second witness testified that she did not hear any gunshots per se but she did corroborate with the first witness that the defendant was seen running down Main Street from the murder scene shortly after 10:00 P.M. According to the reading, this form of testimony would be considered as:

   A. Direct evidence

   B. Opinion evidence

   C. Circumstantial evidence

   D. Real evidence

102. If a State Patrol officer was driving northeast on a county road and in getting to a particular destination made two right turns followed by two left turns, and then another right turn, what direction would he or she then be headed? (Assume all turns were right angle 90-degree change of direction.)

   A. North

   B. Southeast

   C. Northeast

   D. Southwest

Key (applies to questions 103–106)

→   indicates one-way streets

◄   parked vehicle

▷   moving vehicle

●   pedestrians in a stationary location

O→   pedestrians walking; arrow indicates direction

----------   line of travel

▬   buildings (commercial or residential)

103. The following information is a statement from a witness that was used in compiling a State Patrol report detailing the circumstances of a vehicular accident. After you read it, determine which of the four sketches provided accurately portrays the incident described.

Jane Christenson was waiting for a friend at the northeast corner of Fourth Street and First Avenue. At about 1:00 P.M. she noticed an elderly woman jaywalk south across Fourth Street directly in the path of a westbound vehicle. The driver narrowly averted striking her by swerving left and collided with a car parked on the south side of Fourth Street.

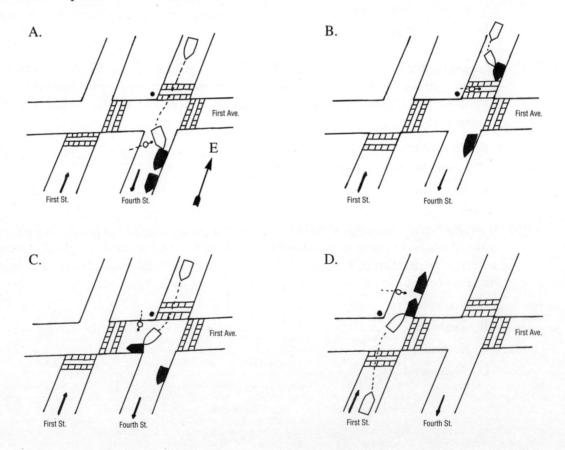

104. The following information is a statement from a witness that was used in compiling a State Patrol report detailing the circumstances surrounding a robbery of a gasoline station. After you have read it, determine which of the four sketches provided accurately depicts the incident described.

Carl Estevez was waiting for a metro bus at the southeast corner of the Ninth Street and Seventh Avenue intersection when he heard two shots from inside the gas station kitty-corner from where he was standing. Moments later, two Caucasian male juveniles exited the station, both of whom were brandishing handguns, and fled on foot two blocks south before turning east and disappearing from view.

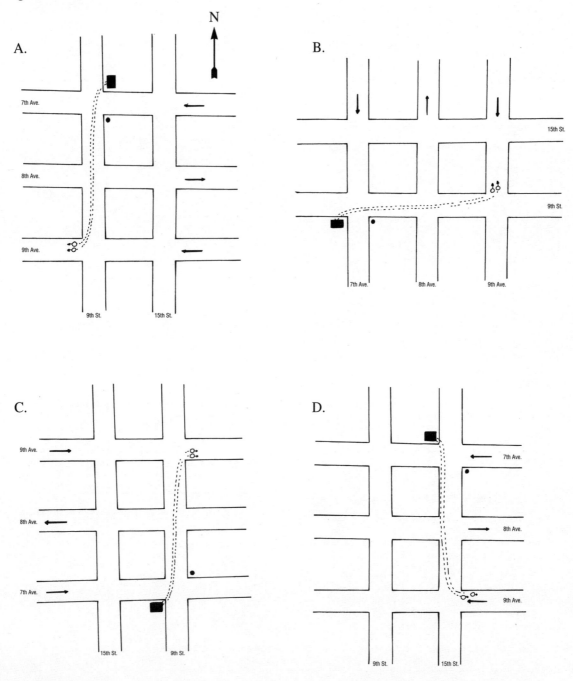

105. Debra Sorenson and Jim Fellows were jogging east across the Lakemont overpass when they both witnessed a westbound vehicle on Lakemont mistakenly make a left turn onto the exit ramp dedicated for northbound traffic from Highway 40. Without realizing the error, the driver in question was half way down the ramp before coming upon another vehicle that had just exited Highway 40. Both of the vehicles slammed on their brakes and attempted to swerve out of the other's way. Unfortunately, both of them swerved the same direction and the result was a head-on collision. If these statements were to be incorporated into a State Patrol report, which of the four sketches below would serve as an accurate representation?

A.

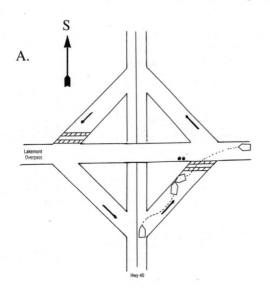

B.

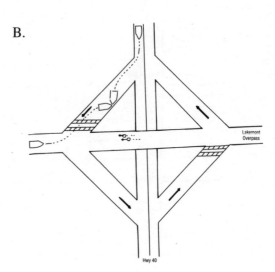

C.

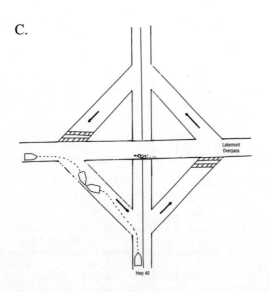

D.

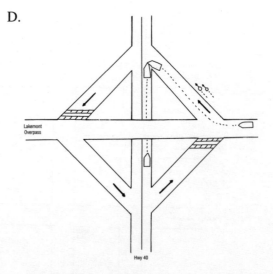

106. Ben Hollins was jogging southeast through Evergreen Park when he noticed the driver of a Cadillac Seville traveling north on 33rd Street failed to notice the car in front was stopped waiting for a light to change. At the last second, the driver in question braked hard and swerved right in an attempt to avoid a serious rear end collision. Consequently, the vehicle jumped the curb, crossed over the sidewalk and plowed into the southwest corner of a coffee shop. The turn of events involved in the incident was corroborated by another witness standing on the southwest corner of 33rd Street and 33rd Ave. Which of the following sketches accurately depicts the circumstances just described?

A.

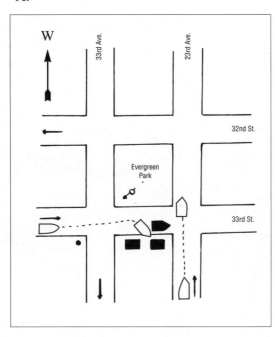

B.

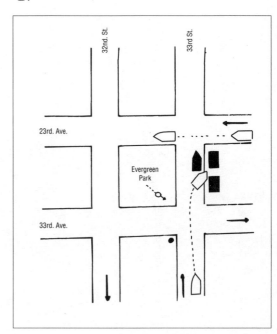

C.

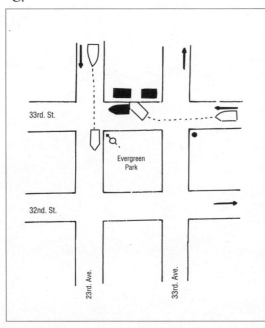

D.

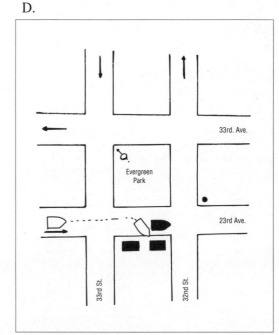

Answer questions 107–110 on the basis of the following map.

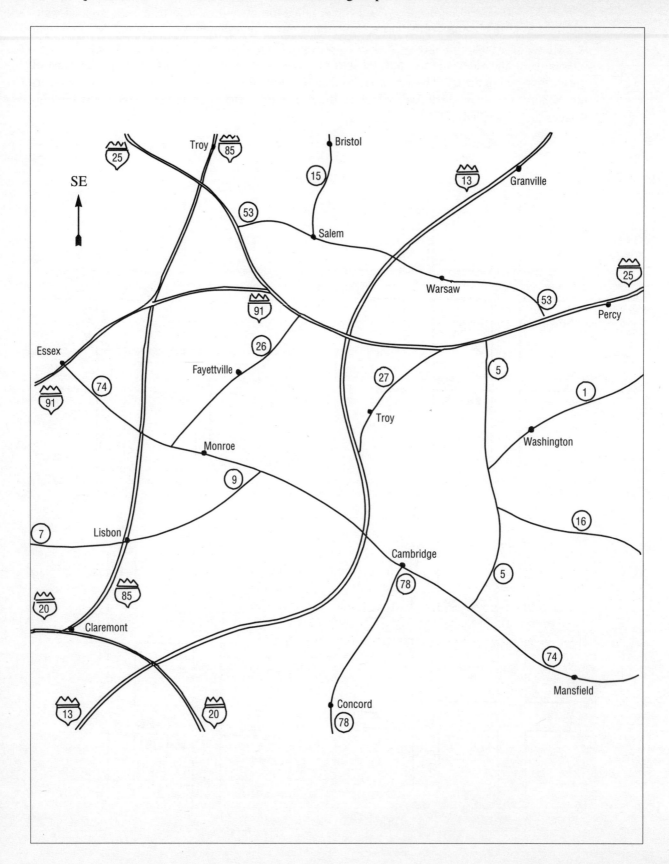

107. A vehicle traveling from Fayetteville to Troy utilizing Interstate 25 as part of the route would initially have to travel in which direction?

    A. East

    B. Southeast

    C. North

    D. South

108. Where is the town of Lisbon in relation to Cambridge?

    A. Southwest

    B. Northwest

    C. Southeast

    D. Northeast

109. State Patrol Officer Alice Brown was assisting in a commercial vehicle inspection at a checkpoint located just southwest of Salem when she was dispatched to investigate a cell phone report of a suspected DUI driver heading south from Troy. The most expeditious means for Officer Brown to intercept the driver in question would involve which of the following routes? (*Note:* For the purpose of this question, state highway route and interstate speed limits are equivalent.)

    A. Head northeast on State Route 53 to Interstate 25, turn left, and then catch up with the suspect once he or she has merged onto Interstate 25 from State Route 27.

    B. Head northeast on State Route 53 to Interstate 25, turn left, and proceed to Interstate 13, turn right, and then catch up with the suspect once he or she has merged onto Interstate 13 from State Route 27.

    C. Head southwest on State Route 53 to Interstate 25, turn right, and proceed towards State Route 27.

    D. Head southwest on State Route 53 to Interstate 13, turn right, and proceed to Interstate 25, turn right again, and head towards the last reported position of the suspect vehicle.

110. State Police Officer William Henricks was traveling west on State Route 74 just outside of Cambridge when he received a call to investigate a situation involving road debris obstructing traffic. In getting to that particular destination, it requires Officer Henricks to take the first two available left turns followed by the first right turn possible, and then proceed to a point a couple miles prior to reaching the community shown on the map. Which direction would Officer Henricks' point of origin be with respect to this given destination?

    A. Northwest

    B. Southeast

    C. Northeast

    D. Southwest

111. According to one state's Department of Motor Vehicles, there were 2,506,040 fee-paid vehicle registrations in 1997. If the most recent census has the same state's population as being 3,490,500, what would be the person-to-vehicle ratio for this particular state?

    A. 1.4:1

    B. 1:1.4

    C. 3.4:1

    D. 3.4:2.5

112. If a Crown Victoria troop cruiser can be driven 224 highway miles on seven gallons of premium unleaded fuel, how many miles could it be driven under the same conditions with a full tank of gas? (*Note:* Consider this particular vehicle as having a 25-gallon capacity gas tank.)

    A. 625 miles

    B. 700 miles

    C. 800 miles

    D. 825 miles

113. Suppose a state correctional facility has enough emergency provisions on hand to sustain 180 prisoners (i.e., capacity) for twelve days. If the current inmate population was at 125% of the prison's capacity, how long would the same provisions last?

    A. 15 days

    B. 9.6 days

    C. 8.3 days

    D. 8 days

114. If a State Patrol service revolver's gun barrel has a bore (i.e., interior diameter) of nine millimeters and the barrel wall's thickness is given to be 2.15 millimeters, what is the exterior diameter of the gun barrel in question?

    A. 9.15 millimeters

    B. 11.15 millimeters

    C. 12.45 millimeters

    D. 13.3 millimeters

Answer questions 115–117 on the basis of the statistics provided.

1996	Reported Cases of DUIs	Reported cases of individuals driving with a revoked or suspended license	Reported cases of motor vehicle theft
District 5	16	1	1
District 19	137	14	14
District 13	252	32	25
1997			
District 5	27	3	2
District 19	149	18	7
District 13	213	47	12

115. District 13 is shown to have had fewer reported cases of DUIs in 1997 than in 1996. This reflects what percentage decrease?

    A. 14.8%

    B. 15.5%

    C. 16.2%

    D. 18.0%

116. Which patrol district experienced the largest percentage increase in reported cases of individuals driving with a revoked or suspended license from 1996 to 1997?

    A. District 19

    B. District 13

    C. District 5

    D. This determination cannot be made on the basis of the data provided.

117. If Patrol District 19 experienced a 350% increase in reported cases of motor vehicle theft from 1998 to 1996, how many cases of motor vehicle theft were reported in 1998?

    A. 54

    B. 60

    C. 63

    D. 74

Answer question 118 on the basis of the following chart.

STATEWIDE DISTRIBUTION OF LICENSE REGISTRATION FEES

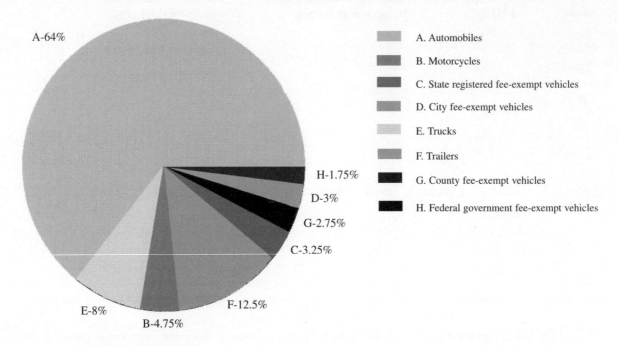

118. If the state Department of Motor Vehicles in this particular instance collected 13.92 million dollars in total license registration fees, how much of that amount came from truck and trailer registrations, respectively?

    A. $1,113,600 and $1,740,000

    B. $1,311,300 and $1,470,600

    C. $1,740,000 and $1,113,600

    D. $1,470,600 and $1,311,300

119. Suppose a mechanic who worked for the State Patrol had to winterize all of the patrol vehicles' coolant systems. All vehicles in question had 12-quart cooling system capacities and currently contain 40% antifreeze solution. If guidelines specify that a 70% solution of antifreeze is required for adequate protection against colder weather, how many quarts of the original solution would have to be drained out of each vehicle and replaced with pure antifreeze to comply?

    A. 4.75 quarts

    B. 5.25 quarts

    C. 5.9 quarts

    D. 6 quarts

Read the narrative that follows and then use the blank report form provided on the next page to answer questions 120–125.

On May 18, 1998, State Patrol Officer Tina Mendoza, badge number 1568, was working Tour III patrol duty in the northeast sector of Precinct 5. At 1:37 A.M., she received a call from central communications to investigate a silent alarm that had been activated at Bickford Furniture and Appliance located on Eastgate Road and Highway 101. The business was actually located in Precinct 9, but because of her close proximity and the fact that other units were unable to immediately respond, Officer Mendoza was dispatched to look into the matter. During the eighteen minutes it took to get there, central communications relayed a suspicious activities report concerning the same location phoned in by a Mr. James Darrington. He lives at 16705 Westmont Court, Auburn, WA 98555, which is a small cul-de-sac residential area located directly behind the store. According to him, he could see out his back kitchen window, and a tall, Caucasian male with long, blonde hair tied into a ponytail was hurriedly loading some kind of large-size crated merchandise into the back of a light-colored Chevrolet pickup truck. The security lighting at the back of the store was too dim to discern the truck's license-plate number, but it was apparent the lone suspect had the larger of the two freight doors open and was utilizing a pallet jack to expedite the transfer. Mr. Darrington also mentioned that if he needed to be reached his home phone number is 769-5431. State Patrol Officer Tim Beckman, badge number 3471, had just radioed in that he was clear from assisting in a DUI arrest in Precinct 12 and that he could be there in approximately ten minutes to serve as backup for Officer Mendoza. Between the two officers, it was decided that Mendoza would approach from the back side of the store and Beckman would watch the front. However, just as Officer Mendoza was turning into the alley that leads to the back of the store on a silent approach, she noticed the suspect vehicle starting to leave the loading dock. Officer Mendoza pulled directly in front of the truck's path, forcing the vehicle to come to a stop and then ordered the suspect out of the vehicle. Pursuant to a pat-down search of the suspect, an Oregon state driver's license contained in his wallet identified him as John E. Connors, residing at 7612 Pennsylvania Drive NE, Portland, Oregon 98440. His birth date was given to be 11-25-59, in addition to a physical description of being 6'2" tall, weighing 205 pounds and having brown eyes. A record check of the pickup truck's Oregon state license-plate number BNG-549 matched that of a vehicle reported stolen two days earlier in Portland. When Mr. Connors could neither produce registration for the truck he was driving nor a receipt for the Toshiba Stereo Projection TV/Entertainment Center loaded in the back of the vehicle, Mr. Connors was placed under arrest for auto theft and burglary. Officer Beckman took custodial responsibility of transporting the suspect to Monroe County Adult Detention for booking and intake. Patrol Officer Mendoza filed a completed arrest report on the incident with Post Command Desk Officer Lt. Chris Johnson, badge number 9870. The case was forwarded to the Monroe County Deputy Prosecutor's office and assigned file number 89-45696.

① File #								② Case #		
GENERAL REPORT			(All entries must be typed or printed)							
③ Incident	④ Arrest	⑦ Precinct of Report	⑧ Report Name/Offense/Charge					⑨ Type		
⑤ Vehicle	⑥ Property									
⑩ Date Occurred	⑪ Time	⑫ Date Discovered	⑬ Time	⑭ Date Reported	⑮ Time	⑯ ☐ In Person ☐ Written ☐ By Phone ☐ Radioed In			⑰ Day of Week	
⑳ Residence		⑲ Business		⑱ Auto		㉑ Will victim prose-cute? Yes / No		㉒ Occupants at home at the time of offense? Yes / No		㉓ Is prop-erty in-sured? Yes / No
㉔ Entry Point?		㉕ Entry Method?		㉖ Was Force Used?		Yes / No	㉗ Name: Insurance Co./Agent			

VICTIM

㉘ Name: (Business) Last	First	Middle	㉞ Race	㉟ Sex	㊱ Age
㉙ Address: Street City	State	Zip	㉛ Home Phone	㊲ Date of Birth	
㉚ Occupation	㉝ Place of Employment Street City State Zip			㉜ Business Phone	

㊳ Victim	㊷ Name: Last First Middle (Maiden)	Race	Sex	㊾ Age
㊴ Witness				
㊵ Suspect	㊸ Address: Street City State Zip	㊹ Home Phone	Date of Birth	
㊶ Arrested				
Business Name Street City State ZIP	㊺ Business Phone (Reportee)	㊻ Occupation (Reportee)		

Physical Ident.	Outstanding Mark/Scar	㊼ Height	㊽ Weight	㊾ Build	㊿ Complexion	51 Hair	How Worn	52 Eyes	53 Glasses ☐ Yes ☐ No

Description of Clothing

54 Reportee	58 Name: Last First Middle (Maiden)	Race	Sex	Age
55 Witness				
56 Suspect	59 Address: Street City State Zip	60 Home Phone	Date of Birth	
57 Arrested				
Physical Ident.	Outstanding Mark/Scar 61 Height 62 Weight 63 Build 64 Complexion 65 Hair How Worn 66 Eyes 67 Glasses ☐ Yes ☐ No			

88 Description of Clothing

VEHICLES

69 Stolen	73 License No.	74 State	75 Year	76 Type	Loc. Stolen / Loc. Recov.	A	83 Stolen	What is it?	Serial Number
70 Recovered									
71 Wanted	77 Vehicle Identification Number (VIN)				Loc. Stolen / Rec. Outside	B	84 Lost	Brand Name/Make	Model/Caliber
Suspect							Found		
Victim	78 Year	79 Make	80 Model		Stolen Out / Loc. Recov.	C		Action	Barrel Length
Impnd. - Hold							Damgd.		
Impound	81 Body Style	82 Color		Tow Truck Oper. No.			85 $ Theft	86 Type & Wheel Size	87 Frame Color
72 Inv/Cond									
Imp. Hold: Requested By			Tow Truck Business Name				$ Damage	88 Fender Color	89 Seat Color
Tow From:							90 Total $	Unique Features	

TIME

91 Dispatched	92 Arrived	93 In Service	94 Signature of Reporting Officer/Person		95 Badge/Identification Number	96 Approved By
Evidence Seized Yes ☐ No ☐	**DIST**	Board	Detective Div.	Patrol Div.	Court	Prosecutor City Atty.	TOTAL
		Traffic	Armed Forces Pol.	Coroner	JUV	Other	

120. Assuming that box 54 is checked, which of the following numbers would be appropriate for box 60?

    A. 16705

    B. 769-5431

    C. 754-6931

    D. BNG-549

121. What information should be entered in box 29?

    A. 7612 Pennsylvania Drive NE, Portland, OR 98440

    B. 16705 Westmont Court, Auburn, WA 98555

    C. Eastgate Road and Highway 101, Auburn, WA 98555

    D. None of the above

122. In which box would the number BNG-549 appropriately be inserted?

    A. Box 77

    B. Box 76

    C. Box 18

    D. Box 73

123. The respective times appropriately inserted beneath numbers 91 and 92 in the report would be which of the following?

    A. 1:37 A.M. and 1:55 A.M.

    B. 1:37 A.M. and 1:47 A.M.

    C. 1:45 A.M. and 1:55 A.M.

    D. The information requested was not revealed within the context of the narrative.

124. Which of the following numbers would be appropriately inserted in box 7?

    A. 5

    B. 9

    C. 12

    D. 15

125. Which of the following names would be correctly entered in box 94?

    A. Connors

    B. Johnson

    C. Mendoza

    D. Beckman

ANSWER SHEET TO PRACTICE EXAM 2

1. Ⓐ Ⓑ Ⓒ Ⓓ	31. Ⓐ Ⓑ Ⓒ Ⓓ	61. Ⓐ Ⓑ Ⓒ Ⓓ
2. Ⓐ Ⓑ Ⓒ Ⓓ	32. Ⓐ Ⓑ Ⓒ Ⓓ	62. Ⓐ Ⓑ Ⓒ Ⓓ
3. Ⓐ Ⓑ Ⓒ Ⓓ	33. Ⓐ Ⓑ Ⓒ Ⓓ	63. Ⓐ Ⓑ Ⓒ Ⓓ
4. Ⓐ Ⓑ Ⓒ Ⓓ	34. Ⓐ Ⓑ Ⓒ Ⓓ	64. Ⓐ Ⓑ Ⓒ Ⓓ
5. Ⓐ Ⓑ Ⓒ Ⓓ	35. Ⓐ Ⓑ Ⓒ Ⓓ	65. Ⓐ Ⓑ Ⓒ Ⓓ
6. Ⓐ Ⓑ Ⓒ Ⓓ	36. Ⓐ Ⓑ Ⓒ Ⓓ	66. Ⓐ Ⓑ Ⓒ Ⓓ
7. Ⓐ Ⓑ Ⓒ Ⓓ	37. Ⓐ Ⓑ Ⓒ Ⓓ	67. Ⓐ Ⓑ Ⓒ Ⓓ
8. Ⓐ Ⓑ Ⓒ Ⓓ	38. Ⓐ Ⓑ Ⓒ Ⓓ	68. Ⓐ Ⓑ Ⓒ Ⓓ
9. Ⓐ Ⓑ Ⓒ Ⓓ	39. Ⓐ Ⓑ Ⓒ Ⓓ	69. Ⓐ Ⓑ Ⓒ Ⓓ
10. Ⓐ Ⓑ Ⓒ Ⓓ	40. Ⓐ Ⓑ Ⓒ Ⓓ	70. Ⓐ Ⓑ Ⓒ Ⓓ
11. Ⓐ Ⓑ Ⓒ Ⓓ	41. Ⓐ Ⓑ Ⓒ Ⓓ	71. Ⓐ Ⓑ Ⓒ Ⓓ
12. Ⓐ Ⓑ Ⓒ Ⓓ	42. Ⓐ Ⓑ Ⓒ Ⓓ	72. Ⓐ Ⓑ Ⓒ Ⓓ
13. Ⓐ Ⓑ Ⓒ Ⓓ	43. Ⓐ Ⓑ Ⓒ Ⓓ	73. Ⓐ Ⓑ Ⓒ Ⓓ
14. Ⓐ Ⓑ Ⓒ Ⓓ	44. Ⓐ Ⓑ Ⓒ Ⓓ	74. Ⓐ Ⓑ Ⓒ Ⓓ
15. Ⓐ Ⓑ Ⓒ Ⓓ	45. Ⓐ Ⓑ Ⓒ Ⓓ	75. Ⓐ Ⓑ Ⓒ Ⓓ
16. Ⓐ Ⓑ Ⓒ Ⓓ	46. Ⓐ Ⓑ Ⓒ Ⓓ	76. Ⓐ Ⓑ Ⓒ Ⓓ
17. Ⓐ Ⓑ Ⓒ Ⓓ	47. Ⓐ Ⓑ Ⓒ Ⓓ	77. Ⓐ Ⓑ Ⓒ Ⓓ
18. Ⓐ Ⓑ Ⓒ Ⓓ	48. Ⓐ Ⓑ Ⓒ Ⓓ	78. Ⓐ Ⓑ Ⓒ Ⓓ
19. Ⓐ Ⓑ Ⓒ Ⓓ	49. Ⓐ Ⓑ Ⓒ Ⓓ	79. Ⓐ Ⓑ Ⓒ Ⓓ
20. Ⓐ Ⓑ Ⓒ Ⓓ	50. Ⓐ Ⓑ Ⓒ Ⓓ	80. Ⓐ Ⓑ Ⓒ Ⓓ
21. Ⓐ Ⓑ Ⓒ Ⓓ	51. Ⓐ Ⓑ Ⓒ Ⓓ	81. Ⓐ Ⓑ Ⓒ Ⓓ
22. Ⓐ Ⓑ Ⓒ Ⓓ	52. Ⓐ Ⓑ Ⓒ Ⓓ	82. Ⓐ Ⓑ Ⓒ Ⓓ
23. Ⓐ Ⓑ Ⓒ Ⓓ	53. Ⓐ Ⓑ Ⓒ Ⓓ	83. Ⓐ Ⓑ Ⓒ Ⓓ
24. Ⓐ Ⓑ Ⓒ Ⓓ	54. Ⓐ Ⓑ Ⓒ Ⓓ	84. Ⓐ Ⓑ Ⓒ Ⓓ
25. Ⓐ Ⓑ Ⓒ Ⓓ	55. Ⓐ Ⓑ Ⓒ Ⓓ	85. Ⓐ Ⓑ Ⓒ Ⓓ
26. Ⓐ Ⓑ Ⓒ Ⓓ	56. Ⓐ Ⓑ Ⓒ Ⓓ	86. Ⓐ Ⓑ Ⓒ Ⓓ
27. Ⓐ Ⓑ Ⓒ Ⓓ	57. Ⓐ Ⓑ Ⓒ Ⓓ	87. Ⓐ Ⓑ Ⓒ Ⓓ
28. Ⓐ Ⓑ Ⓒ Ⓓ	58. Ⓐ Ⓑ Ⓒ Ⓓ	88. Ⓐ Ⓑ Ⓒ Ⓓ
29. Ⓐ Ⓑ Ⓒ Ⓓ	59. Ⓐ Ⓑ Ⓒ Ⓓ	89. Ⓐ Ⓑ Ⓒ Ⓓ
30. Ⓐ Ⓑ Ⓒ Ⓓ	60. Ⓐ Ⓑ Ⓒ Ⓓ	90. Ⓐ Ⓑ Ⓒ Ⓓ

91. Ⓐ Ⓑ Ⓒ Ⓓ
92. Ⓐ Ⓑ Ⓒ Ⓓ
93. Ⓐ Ⓑ Ⓒ Ⓓ
94. Ⓐ Ⓑ Ⓒ Ⓓ
95. Ⓐ Ⓑ Ⓒ Ⓓ
96. Ⓐ Ⓑ Ⓒ Ⓓ
97. Ⓐ Ⓑ Ⓒ Ⓓ
98. Ⓐ Ⓑ Ⓒ Ⓓ
99. Ⓐ Ⓑ Ⓒ Ⓓ
100. Ⓐ Ⓑ Ⓒ Ⓓ
101. Ⓐ Ⓑ Ⓒ Ⓓ
102. Ⓐ Ⓑ Ⓒ Ⓓ

103. Ⓐ Ⓑ Ⓒ Ⓓ
104. Ⓐ Ⓑ Ⓒ Ⓓ
105. Ⓐ Ⓑ Ⓒ Ⓓ
106. Ⓐ Ⓑ Ⓒ Ⓓ
107. Ⓐ Ⓑ Ⓒ Ⓓ
108. Ⓐ Ⓑ Ⓒ Ⓓ
109. Ⓐ Ⓑ Ⓒ Ⓓ
110. Ⓐ Ⓑ Ⓒ Ⓓ
111. Ⓐ Ⓑ Ⓒ Ⓓ
112. Ⓐ Ⓑ Ⓒ Ⓓ
113. Ⓐ Ⓑ Ⓒ Ⓓ
114. Ⓐ Ⓑ Ⓒ Ⓓ

115. Ⓐ Ⓑ Ⓒ Ⓓ
116. Ⓐ Ⓑ Ⓒ Ⓓ
117. Ⓐ Ⓑ Ⓒ Ⓓ
118. Ⓐ Ⓑ Ⓒ Ⓓ
119. Ⓐ Ⓑ Ⓒ Ⓓ
120. Ⓐ Ⓑ Ⓒ Ⓓ
121. Ⓐ Ⓑ Ⓒ Ⓓ
122. Ⓐ Ⓑ Ⓒ Ⓓ
123. Ⓐ Ⓑ Ⓒ Ⓓ
124. Ⓐ Ⓑ Ⓒ Ⓓ
125. Ⓐ Ⓑ Ⓒ Ⓓ

ANSWERS TO PRACTICE EXAM 2

Refer to the sketch for any clarification on questions 1–15

    1.   *B.*   Highway 66, mile post marker 24

    2.   *C.*   Four people: State Patrol officer, kid on bicycle, driver of milk transport truck, and an apparent passenger in the freight rail car.

    3.   *B.*   Tanker transport truck carrying milk

    4.   *A.*   Idaho 78126-CT

    5.   *B.*   At the base of the posted speed limit sign

    6.   *D.*   None of the above; Greenville was given to be two miles away — not twenty

    7.   *D.*   1782

    8.   *C.*   1582131200

    9.   *A.*   35 MPH was made to look like 85 MPH

    10.   *D.*   Washington State Patrol

    11.   *A.*   Unit number 28

    12.   *C.*   J4743600

    13.   *C.*   Swine

    14.   *B.*   South

    15.   *C.*   East

Refer to the narrative for any clarification on questions 16–25.

    16.   *C.*   Lieutenant

    17.   *B.*   Vernon Fuller

    18.   *A.*   1458

    19.   *D.*   1989 Ford Mustang GT BOK-151

    20.   *A.*   Series 80 Colt Mark IV .45 revolver

    21.   *C.*   1845 hours (i.e., 6:45 P.M.) February 11, 1997 – Brice Canyon Freeway

    22.   *B.*   1993 Ford Aerostar van, AVL-653

    23.   *B.*   Officer Hansen, badge number 8725, ran the standard computer check on the van in question.

    24.   *D.*   Five-gallon gas can

    25.   *C.*   Attempted felony elude of a police officer

    26.   *C.*   It can be reasonably assumed that highway traffic at one o'clock in the morning is relatively light. Consequently, the risk posed by such a pursuit to the public would be substantially minimized. That is not to say that high-speed pursuit is not without risk, but, under the given circumstances, Officer Pavlacek's actions were within established guidelines.

    27.   *D.*   Trooper Clemons' actions were in stark contrast to standing guidelines for high-speed pursuits. Her immediate chase of Stevens within the confines of highway driving was within acceptable risk considering that speeds only reached twenty to thirty miles per hour over the given speed limit. However, as soon as Stevens egressed into a residential area and demonstrated a blatant disregard for public safety, Clemons should have broken off the pursuit and radioed in the location of where the suspect was last seen heading. Her continued pursuit was the impetus behind Stevens' evasive actions. The driver's identity having already been established would have allowed authorities to apprehend him at a later time under safer conditions.

28. *B.*   Impartiality towards any such service precludes the perception of favoritism by the department. With that said, selection D would be the next best suggestion to make. Selection C is ludicrous because they wouldn't have a meeting of this nature if residential burglary was held in check by the current level of police protective service. Obviously this was an ongoing concern for most of those in attendance despite existing law enforcement efforts.

29. *B.*   Only B gives sufficient foundation to rescind an earlier order. The remaining reasons given do not justify such action. Selections A, C, and D may appear controversial to the department as a whole, but not contradictory as B would have it.

30. *C.*   Discretion is the better part of valor; the best choice here would be to release the prisoner. Since the crime is only a misdemeanor, it would not warrant the use of deadly force as prescribed in selection B unless the officer's life is directly threatened. In the case at hand, the suspect can be picked up at a later time under better circumstances. Selection D could potentially make the situation worse, and selection A may not be available in time to assist the officer. Trooper Dunkin should consider his own safety first.

31. *C.*   Problems that occur in coordinating police activities can almost always be traced to poor communication between officers. If a directive is not fully comprehended or clearly heard, it is better to have it repeated than to undertake action on one's own initiative. Effective teamwork is imperative for any kind of operation to be conducted efficiently. The other choices offered in the question run counter to this concept.

32. *D.*   An attitude of this nature, albeit an expressed opinion between two longstanding friends, is unbecoming of a professional. An official reprimand, as suggested in choice C, is out of line considering the circumstances. However, Officer Underwood would be doing a terrific disservice not only to his friend but to the department as a whole if he does not address the problem directly as suggested in selection D. Henning's prevailing attitude, if left unchecked, may manifest itself into a sexual discrimination lawsuit and concurrent dismissal from the department.

33. *B.*   Despite Officer Boyle's dislike for the officer involved, handling the matter as prescribed in selection B would be the correct choice. Selections A and C would only serve to inflame the given situation. Tempting as it may be for Officer Boyle to initially do what is suggested in choice D, selection B should remain the primary option. However, if choice B serves to no avail and the unspecified problem becomes recurrent, selection D would then be a suitable follow up.

34. *A.*   Choice A is the best approach because what may be perceived as an obvious theft may, in fact, be an authorized action. The coworker in question may have been given permission to take the items for reasons unbeknown to Officer Whitley. Jumping to any such conclusions, without learning the facts first, could lead to an embarrassing end.

35. *B.*   Selection B would be the most appropriate approach to handle an incident of this nature. If the question had implied that this was a recurrent problem, then selection C would have been an appropriate response. Retaliation or "getting even" is an attitude unbecoming of a professional officer. Inadequate backup can result in an officer being seriously injured or killed. Selection D is of the same order as selection C. It should be considered only after the officer has been addressed directly and the problem continues to persist.

36. *B.*   The out-of-control vehicle heading downhill towards a busy intersection takes immediate precedence over continued pursuit of the suspect. Selection B is the best action taken because the downhill momentum should be fairly minimal considering Officer Wentworth's close proximity. His cruiser should suffice as an effective backstop. Choice C would be a difficult, if not precarious, maneuver to undertake. Not only would he be dealing with

increased downhill momentum, but complete reliance of his own brakes to slow both vehicles to a stop prior to re-entering the intersection may be marginal at best. Successful implementation of such an action would also depend on the runaway vehicle maintaining straight downhill inertia (i.e., no swerving) and the road being clear of other traffic. Selection D is an excellent choice for Officer Wentworth if he had aspirations for a different career.

37. *B.*   Before taking any action, an officer needs to collect as much information as he or she can. Only after that has occurred, can he or she take appropriate steps to alleviate the problem. Both Selections A and C automatically assume that the man standing in the driveway is the suspect in question. It could turn out that this individual was just a curious neighbor or an innocent bystander. Choice B would confirm or deny the identity of the man. Choice D is obviously wrong because indecent exposure is a crime and should be treated as such by law enforcement officers.

38. *B.*   Selection A is true to some extent; however, the badge more importantly serves as a means to identify the police officer. Both selections C and D are false on their own merit.

39. *D.*   All directives from higher-level personnel should be followed regardless of potential inconvenience or perceptions regarding their effectiveness. Constructive feedback in the form of suggestions to an immediate supervisor would be an appropriate means of expressing relevant concerns. However, to do what is suggested by either choice B or C is tantamount to insubordination, meriting the prospect of reprimand or dismissal.

40. *C.*   At issue in this question is the immediate need for Officer White to separate the suspects from any and all weapons. Selection C accomplishes this need with minimal risk to the officer. As long as the suspects have accessibility to the weapons seen, not to mention other weapons unseen, the distraction of filling out citation paperwork is all that is needed for a routine traffic stop to turn deadly. This is particularly true during the brief moment the officer has his back turned to the suspects while returning to the cruiser. Troopers should always be observant and maintain their guard during any vehicular stop.

41. *C.*   It is important that State Police attentively listen to those whom they come into contact with. However, the issue taken by the motorist in this case has no relevance to the present situation. Trooper Porter should maintain professional courtesy and an impartiality while addressing the violation observed. Selections B and D do not obviously accomplish that end. Choice A is a possible option, but that is based on the presumption that the individual involved is not being deceptive and playing on the sympathies of Officer Porter. A routine records check, which was not implied as having been done prior to the enforcement stop, precludes such a discretionary measure; never assume anything.

42. *A.*   The reports applicable to the case should have been reviewed prior to the start of the trial. Without that, details pertinent to the incident can understandably be misconstrued with the passage of time; that is why written reports are imperative. Selection A would be an honest assessment on behalf of Sergeant Morrison. The other choices would evoke questions regarding the officer's credibility as a witness.

43. *A.*   Officer Holms' safe driving constraints for the prevailing road conditions cannot be universally applied to all drivers. Such situations are handled better by some vehicles as opposed to others. Selection A would be the appropriate action to take.

44. *B.*   Accident reconstruction investigations are particularly thorough when fatalities are involved. Experts in this field would not compromise an investigation into what actually happened by allowing certain facts to be omitted. The smallest of details can be pivotal in establishing accident cause. The assignment of another officer into such a situation who either lacks ongoing case familiarity or the required expertise would most likely be counterproductive to the investigation.

45. *D.*   If the traffic light malfunction claim checks out to be true, the driver's close call with Officer Dicks was caused through no fault of his or her own. Circumstances of this nature would not warrant a written citation for the driver in question. However, selection D would be an appropriate follow up because the intersection remains a public safety hazard until the necessary repairs are made.

46. *A.*   Since the possession of money by itself does not constitute a crime, the best approach would be to apprehend the suspect who has the illegal drugs. The other individual can be implicated at a later time. Issuing warrants for the arrest of both suspects is all well and good, but the officer's best chance of apprehending the suspects would be to give immediate chase. Firing a warning shot is not condoned because it could put the public at risk.

47. *A.*   Any unnecessary delay in a medical emergency can further endanger the person requiring immediate medical attention. Waiting for an ambulance to respond to such a distant location or issuing a written citation for speeding, as suggested in selections B and C, effectively delay needed medical assistance. Selection A would be the best approach taken by Officer Buckner.

48. *B.*   Selection A should include RCX 43.74.132 instead of RCX 38.12.012 because the Thunderbird can operate on a public highway. Selection C fails to account for failure to stop, which is RCX 43.21.075. Selection D lists the code RCX 48.21.075 that applies only to people in general; in this case, however, it is the driver who is intoxicated. Therefore, RCX 43.74.132 would be applicable.

49. *D.*   Decimals are used to separate the three components of a code. Selection D is the appropriate breakdown of the code in question.

50. *B.*   Selection A is wrong for the reason that Mr. Heston was not intoxicated at the time of the incident. RCX 38.49.009 would better define this situation. Selection C is wrong because Mr. Heston did pull over immediately for Officer Weiss. RCX 43.21.075 would be an inappropriate citation. Selection D is wrong because we can assume Mr. Heston did have a valid driver's license since the reading did not mention otherwise. Therefore, RCX 38.32.074 would not apply.

51. *A.*   Kathy can be charged with allowing an unauthorized person to drive a motor vehicle (i.e., RCX 38.23.074). It can be assumed that she had a valid driver's license, but that really was not the issue since she was not driving the vehicle. Therefore, B cannot be considered. Selections C and D are inapplicable as well.

52. *B.*   Since Kate was doing the driving, B would be the appropriate charge. The remainder of the selections are inapplicable.

53. *C.*   Selection A should include RCX 48.14.017 instead of RCX48.21.018 because the victim sustained only minor injuries. Selection B incorrectly substitutes RCX 43.76.312 for RCX 43.67.132. It was the actual vehicular assault (RCX 48.15.017) that caused the victim to suffer injuries. Selection D incorrectly substitutes RCX 48.21.075 for RCX 43.74.132. The driver was under the influence of an illegal substance.

54. *D.*   Selection A is incorrect because RCX 48.15.017 (vehicular assault) did not occur. Instead, RCX 48.51.071 (leaving children unattended in a running vehicle) needs to be accounted for. These two codes can be easily mistaken if numbers are transposed. Selection B indicates Ms. Marshall as driving with a revoked or suspended license (RCX 38.23.047). The truth of the matter is that she was driving with an expired driver's license, which is covered by RCX 38.32.074. Selection C wrongly implies that Ms. Marshall did not stop for Officer Daniels to answer any questions (RCX 43.21.075). In fact, she did stop her vehicle but refused to answer Officer Daniels' question. Code RCX 43.21.057 would be applicable. Here again, care must be exercised not to accidentally transpose numbers, as that will result in two entirely different codes.

55. *A.* Selection B is incorrect in citing RCX 43.12.075 (failure to stop and provide identification to a police officer). Instead, RCX 43.21.057 should be applied since the defendant refused to answer Officer Best's questions. Selection C is incorrect in citing RCX 38.47.071 because the certificate of ownership and registration were of no consequence. Selection D is wrong because RCX 38.23.074 (unauthorized persons driving a motor vehicle) was not an issue.

(Note: Reckless driving could probably be thrown in as well; however, since it was not offered in any of the choices presented, this prospect must be overlooked.)

56. *C* Only C (certificate of registration) is correct. The other choices were not included in the list of codes provided.

57. *A* Selection B is wrong because Richard McCann did not commit vehicular assault (RCX 48.15.017). Selection C is wrong because RCX 43.74.132 (driving under the influence) would not apply.

(Note 1: RCX 38.32.047 and RCX 38.23.047 mean basically the same thing. Either one would be considered correct.)

(Note 2: Racing is considered to be reckless driving even if an accident does not result.)

58. *D.* All three selections (A, B, and C) correctly apply; however, they all fail to address RCX 48.21.018, vehicular homicide. Notice that A, B, and C are the same; only their order has been changed.

59. *A.* It was fairly evident that Sentence 4 and Sentence 3 took place first and last, respectively. Selection C is therefore eliminated on that basis alone. By looking at the second, third, and fourth numbers given in each of the remaining alternatives, Selections B and D can be eliminated. Property has to be identified and reported as stolen prior to its recovery. Both Selections B and D have this expected order reversed.

60. *B.* The first event of this report would be Detective Lowry initially witnessing the shoplifting incident that culminated in Ms. Daly's arrest for petty larceny. Therefore, A and C can be eliminated on that basis alone. By looking at the second and third numbers in D, it can be safely surmised that Officer Becker would not receive the call to investigate a suspected shoplifter prior to Mr. Lowry's confronting the suspect in the first place. The process of elimination leaves B as being the correct answer.

61. *A.* In this question, the knowledge that Sentence 3 and Sentence 1 happened first and last does not help in narrowing the options. However, it should be evident that the officer involved would notify headquarters of the situation and request backup to gain better control of the situation and crowd. This leaves only A as correct.

62. *A.* Subject B has different lips and eyes.

Subject C has higher cheekbones and cleft chin.

Subject D has smaller ears and different nose.

63. *A.* Subject B has smaller lips and smaller ears.

Subject C has a different nose.

Subject D has larger ears and fewer facial lines.

64. *B.* Subject A has a different nose.

Subject C has a different chin.

Subject D has a fuller face.

65. *B.* Subject A has lower cheekbones and different eyes.

Subject C has different eyes and nose.

Subject D does not have a cleft chin.

66. D.   Subject A has more facial lines.

Subject B has a thinner mouth.

Subject C has smaller ears and a different chin.

67. B.   *Commited* is misspelled. It should be spelled *committed*.

68. A.   The antecedent, *police officers*, fails to agree with the pronoun *you*. It would be correctly written by using *they* in place of *you*.

69. B.   The word *insure* is an inappropriate homonym which means "to guarantee against loss or harm." *Ensure* means "to secure or guarantee." This is a subtle kind of misspelling that many people tend to overlook.

70. A.   The sentence contains a misplaced participial phrase. A better way to say the same thing is, "Containing a glove pouch, handcuff case, mace holder, and pen holder, a police officer's belt stores much more than a gun."

71. C.   *Uniform Crime Reports* is a proper adjective requiring capitalization.

72. C.   The independent clause *he was immediately disqualified* should have been preceded by a comma.

73. D.   This statement is grammatically correct.

74. C.   The words *for example* are nonrestrictive modifiers that should be preceded and followed by commas.

75. A.   When the relative or interrogative pronoun is the subject of the verb, the nominative form *who* is used, not *whom*, even when the subject is separated from its verb by other words.

76. B.   *Proceedure* is misspelled. It should be spelled *procedure*.

77. A.   Beaten

78. B.   Excellent

79. C.   Confusion

80. D.   Proceeded

81. C.   Illegal

82. B.   Fear

83. A.   Terse

84. D.   Praised and intensive

85. C.   Seriousness and inattentive

86. B.   Equivocation

87. D.   The reading discusses how serious criminal charges—namely, felonies—are handled in Superior Court. However, there were no direct references within the narrative.

88. B.   State sentencing guidelines, not the judge, were mentioned near the end of the narrative as being the determining factor.

89. D.   A pretrial suppression hearing would determine evidence admissibility in this case.

90. B.   The reading emphasized that a defendant, whether in custody or not, must be identified prior to charges being formally filed.

91. C.   Court rule 3.5 establishes the admissibility of such evidence.

92. C.   Ms. Comptom has committed second-degree extortion, a Class C felony.

93. D.   Even though Mr. Russell had implied the threat of physical harm to either the witness or his

wife, it cannot be classified as either bribery or extortion because he did not ask to receive anything in the way of property or services. This is more along the lines of malicious harassment, which was not discussed in the narrative.

94. *A.*   Since Ms. Waterhouse stood to gain a favor from a public servant because of the threat, she could be prosecuted for bribery.

95. *B.*   Under the circumstances, Mr. Evans can be prosecuted for first-degree extortion, which carries a maximum sentence of ten years in prison.

96. *D.*   Specifically, Ms. Patterson should be charged with first-degree manslaughter, a Class B felony.

97. *C.*   Mr. Matthews' actions would be considered reckless, especially with alcohol involved. Ms. Cummings' death should be treated as first-degree manslaughter. Selection D is incorrect because no act committed by anyone in a state of intoxication is deemed less criminal as a result of his or her condition.

98. *C.*   The key word in this story is *spontaneous*. Mrs. Bradford lacked premeditation in killing her husband. Consequently, it would be considered second-degree murder instead of first-degree murder.

99. *B.*   Both the medical examiner and State Patrol firearms identification expert are considered to be expert witnesses who gave an opinion on matters they were qualified to testify about by virtue of their knowledge, special skill, or other abilities.

100. *D.*   Both the revolver and the bullet can be considered real or physical evidence.

101. *C.*   Since the witness in question was not aware of the murder and simply corroborated the fact that the defendant was seen fleeing the scene of the crime, the evidence can be considered circumstantial in that it indirectly ties the defendant to the murder. Selection A would be more in line if the witness involved actually saw the murder take place.

102. *B*   Southeast

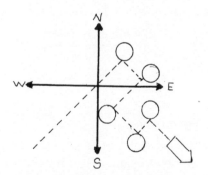

103. *A.*   Selection B is incorrect because it illustrates the pedestrian as using a crosswalk instead of jaywalking. Selection C is incorrect with respect to pedestrian placement and accident location. Selection D is wrong for the same reasons as selection C in addition to incorrectly depicting where the witness was at the time of the accident.

104. *C.*   Selection A is incorrect because witness placement is on the wrong corner. Selection B is inaccurate because the store location is incorrect in addition to the perpetrators heading east on Ninth Avenue instead of west. Selection D is incorrect in virtually every regard.

105. *B.*   Selection A is incorrect because the accident is portrayed on the exit ramp for southbound traffic (instead of northbound traffic) from Highway 40. Additionally, the two witnesses are depicted as being stationary as opposed to jogging east across the Lakemont overpass.

Selection C incorrectly illustrates a vehicle traveling in the wrong lane of Highway 40 before exiting on the wrong ramp and causing a head-on collision with a vehicle attempting to merge with northbound traffic on Highway 40. Selection D demonstrates wrong witness placement as well as incorrect accident location.

106. *B.* Selection A is wrong because the stationary witness is improperly located. Selection C has the jogger running in the wrong direction. Selection D demonstrates the accident as occurring on a different street as well as incorrect placement of the stationary witness.

107. *D.* Traveling from Fayetteville to Troy would necessitate initially taking State Highway 26 to Interstate 25, which is a southerly heading.

108. *D.* Northeast

109. *C.* Both selections A and C are viable options of pursuing the suspect. However, considering the last reported direction of where the suspect vehicle was heading, choice C would be a prudent approach taken by Officer Brown. An expeditious intercept would take precedence over a protracted interstate pursuit. Selection B is incorrect in the assumption of the suspect vehicle heading towards Interstate 13. Selection D is wrong for the sake of making a right turn onto Interstate 25; that would place the officer in a direction opposite to where the suspect vehicle was heading.

110. *A.* Officer Henricks is described as turning left off of State Route 74 onto State Route 5, proceeding to Interstate 25, turning left on Interstate 25 and proceeding to Interstate 13, turning right onto Interstate 13 and proceeding to a point a couple miles prior to reaching the town of Granville. Officer Henricks' point of origin is northwest of this destination.

111. *A.* 3,490,600 people : 2,506,040 automobiles

or

1.392 or 1.4 : 1 when properly reduced.

112. *C.* This question is essentially a direct proportion.

$$\frac{7 \text{ gallons}}{25 \text{ gallons}} = \frac{224 \text{ highway miles}}{X \text{ highway miles}}$$

Therefore,

$7X = 5600$
$X = 800$ highway miles

113. *B.* This is basically a two-part question involving an inverse proportion. First it must be determined how many inmates are in the overcrowded facility. 1.25 (i.e., 125%) x 180 (facility capacity) = 225 inmates. The second step involves setting up an inverse proportion to determine the answer. *Note:* It is an inverse proportion as opposed to a direct proportion because the more inmates incarcerated, the shorter the time that emergency provisions will last. Therefore,

$$\frac{225 \text{ inmates}}{180 \text{ inmates}} = \frac{12 \text{ days}}{X \text{ days}}$$

$225X = 2160$
$X = 9.6$ days

If you selected A as the answer, you used the wrong kind of proportion.

114. *D.* To figure the barrel's external diameter, the wall thickness must be counted twice to accurately represent a true cross section. See illustration.

Therefore, $2.15 + 2.15 + 9 = 13.3$ mm outside diameter.

115. *B.* District 13 had 39 fewer cases of reported DUIs in 1997 than in 1996. To calculate what percentage this difference corresponds to, 39 needs to be divided by 252 and then multiplied by 100. Therefore,

$$\frac{39}{252} = 0.15476$$

$0.15476 \times 100 = 15.476\%$ or 15.5% when rounded off.

116. *C.* Patrol District 5. Patrol District 19 had four more reported cases of individuals driving with a revoked or suspended license in 1997 than in 1996.

$$\frac{4}{14} \times 100 = 28.57\% \text{ increase}$$

Patrol District 13 had fifteen more reported cases of individuals driving with a revoked or suspended license in 1997 than in 1996.

$$\frac{15}{32} \times 100 = 46.87\% \text{ increase}$$

Patrol District 5 had two more reported cases of individuals driving with a revoked or suspended license in 1997 than in 1996.

$$\frac{2}{1} \times 100 = 200\% \text{ increase}$$

117. *C.* Sixty-three cases of motor vehicle theft were reported in 1998 according to the information provided.

$$\frac{X-\text{reported cases of motor vehicle theft for 1996}}{\text{reported cases of motor vehicle theft for 1996}} = 3.5 \ (i.e., 350\%)$$

Therefore,

$$\frac{X-14}{14} = 3.5$$

$X - 14 = 49; X = 49 + 14 = 63$ cases

118. *A.* Trucks accounted for 8% of all license registration fees.

$$13.92 \times .08 = \$1,113.600.00$$

Trailers accounted for 12.5% of all license registration fees.

$$13.92 \times .125 = \$1,740,000.00$$

119. *D.* The best way to work this kind of problem is as follows: amount of 100% antifreeze ($1.00X$) + amount of 40% antifreeze solution ($.40[12-X]$) = amount of pure antifreeze in 70% solution ($.70 \times 12$).

$$1X + 4.8 - .40X = 8.4$$
$$1X - .40X + 4.8 = 8.4$$
$$.60X = 3.6$$
$$X = 6 \text{ quarts of } 100\% \text{ antifreeze}$$

To verify that this is indeed the appropriate amount, insert 6 into the equation designed for this problem and see if it holds true:

$$1.0 \times 6.0 + .40 (12 - 6.0) = 8.4$$
$$6.0 + 2.4 = 8.4$$
$$8.4 = 8.4$$

120. *B.* Mr. James Darrington would be considered the reporter in this particular instance.

121. *C.* Eastgate Road and Highway 101 was the given address for Bickford Furniture and Appliance. A city location and applicable zip code were not directly referenced. However, such references were made for the neighbor (James Darrington) that lived directly behind the store. It would be a reasonable assumption that both are one and the same.

122. *D.* BNG-549 is the license number of the stolen pickup truck that should be entered in box 73.

123. *A.* It was given that Officer Mendoza received the call to investigate a silent alarm trip at 1:37 A.M and it took her 18 minutes to get to Eastgate Road and Highway 101. 1:37 A.M plus 18 minutes = 1:55 A.M.

124. *B.* It was stipulated within the narrative that Officer Mendoza was originally assigned to the northeast sector of Precinct 5. However, due to lack of manpower availability, she was called to respond to an incident in Precinct 9.

125. *C.* Patrol Officer Tina Mendoza's signature would be required in box 94.

TEST RATINGS ARE AS FOLLOWS:

120–125 correct — Excellent
113–119 correct — Very good
106–112 correct — Good
100–105 correct — Fair
99 or fewer correct — Unsatisfactory

Chapter 10

Physical Fitness

With the physical demands that law enforcement may entail, it is not hard to understand why State Police departments require employees to be in top physical shape. In-station tasks require little exertion; however, when police officers are called to active duty, the switch from a sedentary pace to substantial physical exertion is stressful. This is particularly true for someone who is out of shape. The job may demand running, climbing, jumping, twisting, pulling, and lifting. The difficulty is also compounded by the fact that work may be performed under extreme temperatures and/or in poor quality air. A State Patrol officer must be physically able to respond to these conditions while always being careful of his or her own safety. This is the primary reason State Police departments place an emphasis on physical fitness exams.

As mentioned in the introduction, physical fitness exams can be quite varied. What one department considers suitable may be considered inadequate by another. The point of the matter is that all physical ability tests are designed specifically to measure strength, stamina, and flexibility. How these capabilities are determined lies solely with the department you have applied to, as there is no nationally recognized standard. Try to ascertain in advance what will be expected by the department you are interested in. Then, practice these events in trial runs as best you can prior to the actual exam. It is better to learn of potential weaknesses beforehand, rather than fall short during a timed event and perform poorly or, worse, fail the test altogether. There should be no reason to let this job opportunity slip away simply because of physical unpreparedness. Approach this part of the screening process in the same manner as you did the written exam. By practicing the workout schedule suggested below, not only will you get in better shape, but you will be able to approach the physical fitness exam with the same degree of confidence and sense of ease as you did the written exam.

Before charging into any fitness workout, however, it is suggested that you visit your family doctor and get a complete medical evaluation. This will be a precondition to your employment in order to determine if any disease or physical condition may impair your ability to perform. (For further reference, see the section on Medical Evaluation at the beginning of this guide.) If, in fact, you do have a condition that potentially warrants rejection from employment consideration, consult your doctor. He or she may be able to prescribe treatment through a change of diet, specialized workout, medication, or surgery to correct the problem.

Inform your physician of your intentions concerning any kind of physical workout. No two people are the same; workout schedules vary. The guidelines provided in this book are just that — guidelines. Your doctor is better able to tailor a training program that will benefit you. Keep your doctor's advice in mind while you prepare for the exam.

Prior to actually taking the physical abilities test, you will be asked either to sign a liability waiver or to fill out some form of medical questionnaire. The latter involves a wide range of questions relating to your present state of health. This kind of information will allow examiners to make an educated decision as to whether such an exam poses a health risk to a test candidate. Be truthful in filling out such a questionnaire because this is one more element that is cross-checked in a routine background investigation. Falsifying any information is grounds enough to disqualify an applicant.

Despite the variation seen in physical fitness exams, it can be generally assumed that three kinds of physical attributes are being scrutinized during these exams: flexibility, cardiovascular fitness, and muscular strength and endurance. Each of these areas uses different groups of muscles, and the exercises suggested below for each will improve them. However, it is important to realize that prior to any exercise there are preliminaries that can help to prevent injury.

RELAXATION AND WARM-UP ROUTINE

The first thing to do before starting any rigorous exercise is a relaxation and warm-up routine, which involves the head roll, paced breathing, and shoulder shrugs.

For the head roll, you can either stand, sit, or kneel. Allow your head to go limp and roll it around your neck two or three times in one direction and then two or three times in the other direction. It helps to close your eyes during this exercise to prevent any dizziness or loss of balance. Try to conduct this exercise slowly and smoothly.

Paced breathing involves lying on your back and placing your hands on your stomach. Concentrate on your breathing by paying close attention to how far your chest rises during each inhalation. Breathe evenly and slowly, and relax for about one minute during this exercise.

The third relaxation exercise is shoulder shrugs. Again, lie on your back. Simply pull your shoulders upward and maintain that position for a few seconds before allowing your shoulders to return slowly to their original position. Try to coordinate your breathing so that you inhale while pulling your shoulders up and exhale when your shoulders drop. Perform this exercise for approximately one minute.

FLEXIBILITY EXERCISES

Stretching exercises are important, too, because they prepare tendons and ligaments for further stretching and increase the flow of fluid around various joints. The whole concept is based on smooth, even, and slow motion. This kind of exercise is not intended to be conducted in fast or jerky movements.

The back stretch or swivel is the first flexibility exercise to do. Stand and, with your arms at your sides, try to lean as far forward as possible. Then lean as far backward as you can. Repeat these exercises at least four times in both directions. Now, to limber up your back for bending sideways, remain standing, turn your head to the right, and slide your right hand down the length of your right leg as far as possible. Do this exercise at least four times on the right side, then four times on the left side.

To stretch the quadriceps (thigh muscles), stand and lean against a wall using your left hand as support. Reach behind with your right hand and lift your right leg up so that you can grasp your toes. Slowly pull your heel closer to your buttocks until the thigh feels stretched. Maintain this position for approximately five seconds. Repeat this exercise four times with the right leg before doing the same with the left leg.

To stretch the calf muscles in your leg, remain standing within arm's length of the wall. While facing the wall, keep your feet flat on the ground (do not allow your heels to lift), and allow yourself to lean forward for a few seconds. Push off against the wall to return to the starting position. Repeat this exercise three or four times.

Now, while sitting on the floor with your legs spread apart and the back of your legs flat on the floor (your knees should not lift), slide both hands as far down one leg as possible. Hold this position for a few seconds before sitting erect again. Repeat this exercise three to four times, and then do the same for the other leg. This exercise stretches both back and hamstring muscles.

Remain in the sitting position and cross your legs, putting the soles of your feet together. Now, lean forward as far as possible and hold this position for a few seconds before sitting erect again. Repeat this exercise three or four times. This exercise stretches the groin muscles.

To stretch the hips, remain in the sitting position with your legs straight. Now, take your right leg and cross it over the left leg. Take the knee of the right leg and slowly bring it up to your chest. Hold that position for three to four seconds, and then repeat this exercise twice more. Do the same with the left leg.

The final exercise involves stretching chest, shoulder, and back muscles. While kneeling, place your palms on the floor, then slowly slide both hands forward until your elbows touch the floor. Keep your head and back straight during this exercise. Return to your starting position and repeat this exercise three or four times.

Remember, the whole point of these exercises is to stretch various muscles. If you force a muscle to extend too far, pulling or tearing can occur, defeating the purpose of stretching and possibly incurring injury. Stretch various muscles only to the point of mild sensation, hold for a few seconds, then relax. This procedure has the effect of increasing flexibility and loosening muscles for other exercises.

The last preliminary needed before any exercise is a cardiorespiratory warm-up. This simply involves conducting an exercise that is not too stressful, such as brisk walking or slow jogging for a few minutes. This allows the heart rate to increase gradually and prepares the heart for vigorous exercise. To prevent potential injury, a warm-up routine should always be done before any stressful exercise.

CARDIOVASCULAR FITNESS

Cardiovascular fitness has to do with your heart and lung capacity. As both of these organs become more fit, your body's ability to transport oxygen to its cells improves. Another beneficial result is that the heart beats less quickly but pumps with greater strength—or, in other words, works more efficiently. There is also a corresponding increase in the peripheral circulatory system, thereby making it easier for various cells to absorb oxygen.

The best way to achieve cardiovascular endurance is to employ what physiologists call aerobic exercise. This may come in one of four forms: running, swimming, bicycling, or walking. When any of these forms of exercise is conducted fairly rigorously for approximately twenty-five minutes three times a week, cardiovascular endurance will improve. The key point here is to exercise at a moderate intensity, nonstop for the full twenty-five minutes. Less time makes the exercise much less useful. That is why sports such as baseball, tennis, or basketball do not suffice. These sports require tremendous energy output some of the time; however, there are breaks in between. To be effective, the exercise has to be conducted for twenty-five *consecutive* minutes, stopping only to check your pulse.

To calibrate your progress using aerobics, physiologists have come up with a pulse-rated system. Your pulse measures the number of times your heart beats per minute. As your cardiovascular endurance improves, your heart beats less quickly when subjected to stress. To measure your pulse, simply apply one or two of your fingers (not your thumb) to the front of your neck next to the larynx and feel for the carotid artery. The pulse should be fairly obvious there. Be careful not to press too hard on this artery because unconsciousness may result, particularly after exercise. Count the number of times your heart beats within ten seconds, and then multiply that number by six. This will provide you with an accurate assessment of your pulse. When performing a rigorous exercise for twenty-five minutes, stop after the first ten minutes to take a brief pulse (ten seconds), and immediately resume the exercise.

Intermix the four events of running, swimming, bicycling, and walking in your training. This helps to alleviate boredom and perpetuates the desire to continue training. When your twenty-five minutes of exercise is completed, it is necessary to follow it with a cool-down period. Walk or jog slowly for five to ten minutes. The general idea is to permit your body to return to its normal condition gradually. This cool-down can be followed by a few stretching exercises as well.

MUSCULAR STRENGTH AND ENDURANCE

Strength development can be accomplished by weight training and calisthenics. Both improve muscular endurance through repetitive movement but do so in different ways. Calisthenics essentially uses exercises that employ your own body weight to serve as resistance. On the other hand, weight training involves lifting progressively heavier weights or resistances in the form of barbells or variable-resistance weight-training equipment.

CALISTHENICS

Calisthenics, like cardiovascular endurance exercises, need to be proceeded by relaxation, stretching, and warm-up exercises. A daily routine of push-ups, sit-ups, pull-ups, leg lifts, and squats should be conducted over a period of fifteen to twenty-five minutes. Start out doing fifteen repetitions of each exercise, and then work your way up to thirty. Don't expect this to occur overnight. Regularity is the key. Your persistence will reward you with greater strength within three to four weeks. Descriptions of each exercise are given below.

Push-ups

Lie on your abdomen on the floor and place your hands, palms down, beneath your chest. As you extend your arms and push off from the floor, be sure to keep your back and knees straight. Once your arms are fully extended, lower yourself to the floor slowly and repeat the exercise.

Sit-ups

Lie on your back on the floor and either place your feet beneath a sofa or other heavy object, or have someone restrain your feet from lifting. Your knees should be straight and flat. With your hands locked behind your head, sit up and attempt to touch your knees with your elbows without lifting your knees. Do not try to force yourself to extend beyond what is comfortable. Stretch as far as possible, then return to the starting position to repeat.

Pull-ups

Use a chinning bar that is just a few inches higher than your highest reach when you are standing up and your arms are extended overhead. Using an overhand grip on the bar, raise yourself to the point where you bring your chin level with the bar. Try not to kick or swing while raising yourself. Lower yourself slowly to the starting position and repeat.

Leg Lifts

Lie on the floor on your right side with your legs kept straight and in line with one another. Use your left arm to gain support from the floor to prevent rolling over. Lift your left leg as far as possible before returning to the starting position. Repeat this exercise a minimum of fifteen times before changing sides and doing the same exercise with the other leg.

Squats

In the standing position, extend your arms forward and then squat until your thighs are parallel to the ground. Return to the standing position and repeat the exercise.

WEIGHT TRAINING

Weight training, when done correctly, significantly increases muscular strength and endurance. However, three things should always be kept in mind before starting any kind of weight-training routine. Supervision by either a professional weight-training assistant or someone to act as a safety person during your lifts is essential. This is particularly true while bench-pressing barbells. The second consideration is always to begin light and progressively increase the weight you lift as you become stronger. Starting heavy is an open invitation to injuring muscle tissue instead of building it. The third consideration is to conduct a weight-training routine only three times per week at the maximum. Keep the number of repetitions to only three sets of ten. Doing more will tend to increase bulk rather than strength. If the repetitions seem fairly easy initially, increase the weight load by five or ten pounds at a time. Continue this progressive addition of weight as your strength improves. Below are exercises that concentrate on developing muscles needed most for state police fitness exams: chest, shoulder, arm, and back.

Bench Press

For safety reasons, it is better to use bench press equipment rather than free weights. Whichever is available, lie on your back and grip the bar with both hands at shoulder width. Begin with light weights, as mentioned earlier, and lift or press the bar in a direction directly perpendicular to the chest by extending your arms. Try not to lock your elbows when fully extended. Slowly lower the bar to your chest and repeat the exercise.

Arm Curls

While standing, preferably with your back to a wall, allow your arms to be fully extended downward. Grasp the barbell with an underhand grip, with hands spaced shoulder width. Raise the barbell to your chest without allowing your elbows to move from your side. Lower the barbell to the starting position and repeat.

Half Squats

This is similar to squat calisthenics. The difference is that a barbell rests on the back of your neck while it is supported by both hands at shoulder width. As the weight is steadied on your shoulders, conduct squat repetitions as described under calisthenics.

Bent-over Rows

Begin in the standing position with the weight bar on the floor directly in front of you. While keeping your legs straight, lean over the barbell in such a way that your back becomes parallel to the floor. With an overhand grip, grasp the weight bar with both hands spaced shoulder width and lift the weight to your chest. Try to keep your back straight (i.e., parallel to the floor) and your head up while attempting the lift. Return the weight to the floor and repeat the exercise.

Chapter 11

The Oral Board

Once you have reached this point in the selection process, there are a few things to bear in mind in preparing for the oral board. You will be notified by mail of the time and place of the interview. Pay particular attention to the date and become familiar in advance with the location of the interview. One sure way to disqualify yourself from serious consideration is to show up late for the interview. There really are no excuses for this.

Appearance is also important. Most people are told not to judge others by outward appearance; however, interviewers gain a distinct impression from the manner in which a candidate dresses. If an applicant is not well groomed (e.g., unshaven, hair uncombed), interviewers perceive that candidate, before so much as asking one question, as uncaring and somewhat sloppy. Even though the candidate may be the hardest-working and most concerned person among those being interviewed, he or she will, in all likelihood, be passed over for another with a better appearance. First impressions are just as important as how you respond to questions asked by the interviewers. Therefore, be well groomed for the occasion and dress neatly. For men, this would entail a nice shirt (tie is optional), slacks, and a pair of dress shoes. For women, an attractive blouse, dress pants (or suit, or skirt, or a conservative dress) and dress shoes would be appropriate.

Also avoid smoking or chewing gum prior to or during an oral board. Habits like these can create a poor appearance. The whole idea is to put your best foot forward to indicate you are the most enthusiastic and best-qualified candidate for the job. Contrary to what some applicants may think, outward appearance is very important. For the limited amount of time an interview board spends with a test applicant, all things become relevant, including the smallest details.

The interview itself is normally conducted by a board of three to five people. Most interview panels consist of State Police Department officials or Civil Service personnel. Occasionally, people outside the State Police Department and Civil Service are brought in to avoid potential bias on the board.

Ideally, those conducting the interview and the applicant being interviewed are complete strangers to one another. This way, a candidate who is not hired cannot discredit the selection process on the basis of bias or favoritism. Board members are also made aware that race, sex, color, creed, and political background have no bearing on these proceedings. Each interviewer has a rating sheet listing specific qualifications. The series of questions provides the interviewers with enough insight to accurately gauge the applicant's potential capabilities. Usually the beginning of the interview will focus attention on your job application form. Such things as your educational background, past employment history, and references are examined. It would behoove you to review everything you listed on your application form and have supportive reasoning for any career changes. If you can somehow demonstrate that the direction you took was based on the underlying aspiration to work in criminal justice, so much the better. However, do not deceive the panel regarding past choices. Chances are that if you do, you may contradict yourself at one point or another, and this will become immediately evident to the interviewers. The best policy here is to answer all questions honestly, even if some past decisions were not necessarily the best ones. If you feel that you have made a questionable career move or have had a falling out with one or more past employers, explain why. If you can also show that something was learned or gained from the experience, point that out as well. Interviewers will appreciate your honesty and sincerity. A history of switching jobs or changing careers all too frequently without just cause is usually reason enough not to be hired.

While you are being interviewed in these areas of concern, interviewers will be assessing your communications skills and how well you respond to the questioning. It is well understood that oral boards are stressful to applicants. However, if an applicant appears excessively fidgety or worried or perspires profusely, and such nervousness encumbers the applicant's ability to answer questions, it can detract from what otherwise would have been a good interview. Advance preparation for the interview should help in this regard. Knowing (in general) the kinds of questions interviewers most likely will ask enhances your confidence. Besides further expounding on information given on the application form, questions such as the following are equally important:

- Why do you want to become a police officer?

- Why should you be hired over other similarly qualified applicants?

- Now that we know your strong points, what are your weaknesses?

- If you had to do everything over, what would you do differently?

- Do you have any regrets for anything in the past?

- What, if anything, do you feel are major accomplishments or achievements in your life?

- How do you feel you can help the community by working in the police department?

These and a myriad of other questions are thought-provoking. If you are prepared for such questioning, you will be better able to answer these questions in a satisfactory manner, rather than pausing at length to think of something. Simply answering "yes" or "no" is not sufficient. Supportive reasoning, even if it is brief, is what interviewers want to hear.

The interview will also focus on what your interests or hobbies are, as well as attitudes toward particular job requirements. For instance,

- Why do you like to hunt, swim, bike, camp, etc.?

- Couldn't you have used your leisure time to better purpose?

- Do you do any extracurricular reading and, if so, what?

- Do you keep current with local events by reading the paper?

- How do you feel about working irregular hours?

- Do you respond to criticism in a positive manner?

- Have you ever displayed a temper with coworkers at past jobs?

- What do you think of drugs and alcohol, both in the work place and at home?

- Are you afraid of anything such as dying, heights, or speaking in front of large groups of people?

- How do you feel about using lethal force against another person when necessary?

Having prepared answerers to these questions and others of a similar nature will definitely give you an edge over those who aren't prepared. Try to think of as many questions about your life as possible and prepare some reasoning to support your answers. You may be caught off guard by a few questions, but overall your preparation will pay off.

One other form the interview may take may concern your reaction to hypothetical circumstances or emergencies. It is not expected that you will have advanced knowledge of any specialized law enforcement training. However, this kind of question can give interviewers insight into how well you can quickly reason and solve a problem. You may be given certain conditions to work within, and then be expected to show how you would bring the situation under control.

These kinds of questions are obviously more difficult to prepare for, but two things are important to keep in mind. First, the safety of both police personnel and the victim or member of the public involved is a primary consideration. Second, nearly everything police personnel do should be part of a team effort. Consider these two things during any questioning. Interviewers will describe some situation and may very well throw in some constraints that may make the situation worse. Whatever is given, think the question through as best you can, and decide how you would handle the circumstances. Immediate answers to questions of this nature without much forethought are bound to be incomplete and show poor judgment. Interviewers will observe how well you can assimilate information and identify specific problem areas. Your initiative and leadership beyond what is minimally necessary are other factors assessed.

If your interview is more in line with this kind of questioning, answer to the best of your ability and see the exercise through to the end. Whatever you do, don't become exasperated with the situation given and give up. Remember, the interviewers know that they are placing you in a very stressful position. Reacting in an appropriate and confident manner bodes well for your employment consideration.

When the interview is coming to a close, one of the panel members will ask you if you have any questions or concerns regarding the police department. If you feel that you have other positive qualities that were not discussed during the interview, now is the time to mention them briefly. If you have some specific concerns regarding the department, this is the appropriate time to ask. Since there are other candidates to be interviewed, do not protract your own interview beyond a few minutes after the interviewers ask you for any further comments. Rambling on about something longer than necessary is viewed with disdain. Be brief with your questions if you have any, then thank each interviewer for his or her time and consideration. Don't loiter after the interview to see how well you did. It will be another week or two before all things are considered and decisions are made with regard to hiring.

If you later learn you did not fare as well as expected in the interview, don't become upset and write the experience off as though the examiners made the mistake. Rather, find out where your weaknesses were and learn from the experience. That way, on a follow-up interview to another exam, you will not make the same mistakes. It can also be said that a candidate who goes through the testing and selection process more than once is very determined. That attribute is looked upon favorably by any department because it shows that the applicant is truly dedicated to becoming a State Police officer. More often than not, these are candidates that departments seek to hire. There may be a few disappointments along the way to being hired; however, hard work and persistence are two key virtues that are prerequisites to a fulfilling career in law enforcement.

REFUND POLICY

In the unlikely event that you use this book but score less than 80 percent on the State Trooper/Highway Patrol examination, your money will be refunded. This guarantee specifically applies to the written exam, not the physical fitness, psychological, or medical exams or the oral board. If a test applicant scores above 80 percent on the written test, but fails any of the other requirements, he or she will not be eligible for a refund.

The following conditions must be met before any refund will be made. All exercises in this guide must be completed to demonstrate that the applicant did make a real attempt to practice and prepare to score 80 percent or better. Any refund must be claimed within 90 days of the date of purchase shown on your sales receipt. Anything submitted beyond this ninety-day period will be subject to the publisher's discretion. Refunds are only available for copies of the book purchased through retail bookstores. The refund amount is limited to the purchase price and may not exceed the cover price of the book.

If you mail this study guide back for a refund, please include your sales receipt, validated test results,* and a self-addressed, stamped envelope. Requests for refunds should be addressed to Adams Media Corporation, State Trooper/Highway Patrol Exam Officer Division, 260 Center Street, Holbrook, MA 02343. Please allow approximately four weeks for processing.

---

* On occasion, exam results are not mailed to the test applicant. Test scores may be posted at either the administrative offices of the department or at the place of examination. If this is the case for you, procure a copy of your test score and be sure that your name and address are indicated; Social Security numbers without identification are insufficient to claim a refund.

This policy also recognizes that a select number of jurisdictions utilize a multistage testing format that prohibits applicants from learning their scores on individual written exams. Written test scores along with other various assessments (i.e., oral interview ratings, background verifications, psychological assessments, etc.) are combined to determine an applicant's eligibility. If these circumstances apply in your situation, three requirements must be met to receive a refund from the publisher: You must complete all exercises in this book, give the time and location of where you took the exam, and include some written explanation as to why you feel this study guide failed to live up to its guarantee.